HALO®

ESCALATION

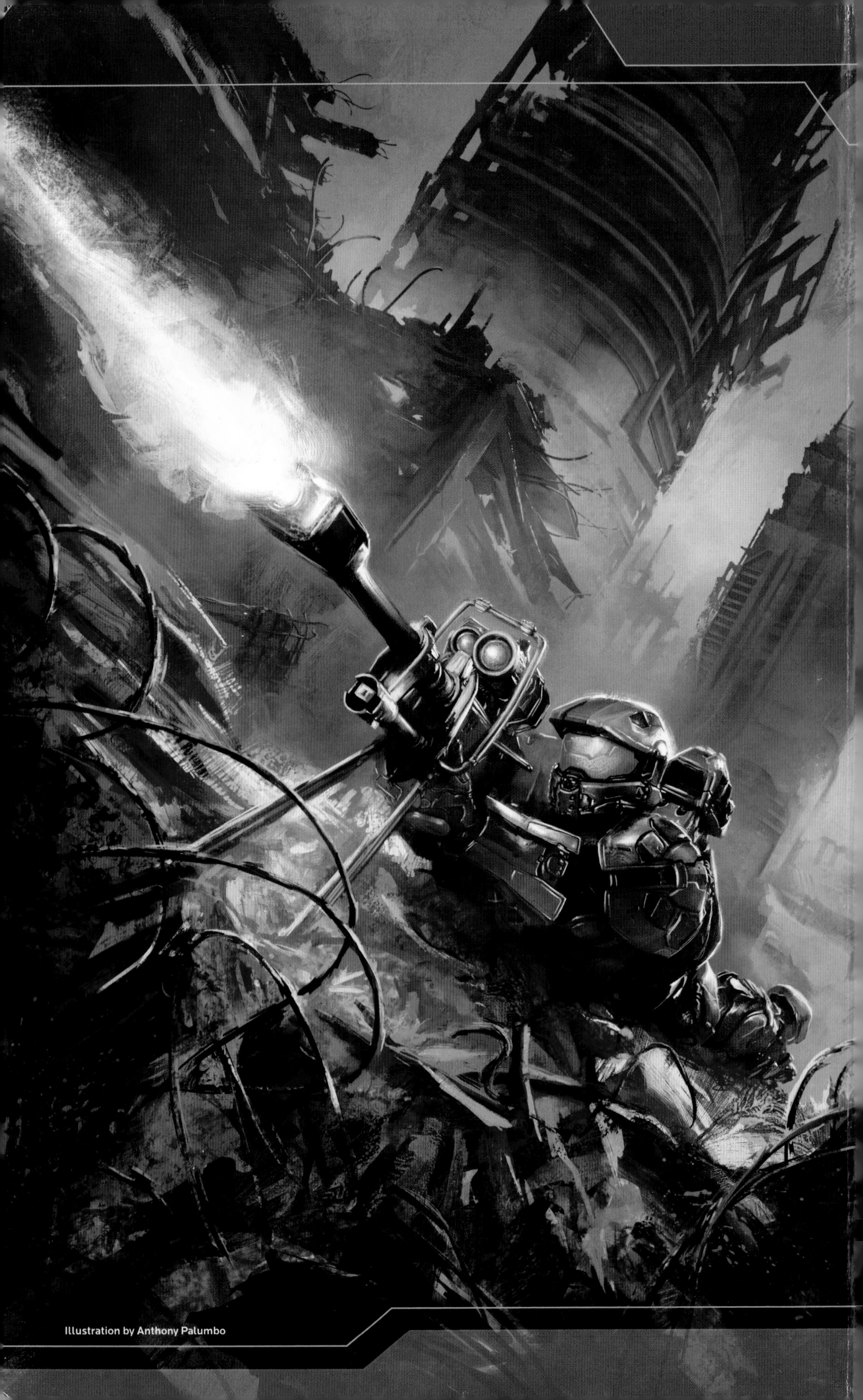

Illustration by Anthony Palumbo

ESCALATION

VOLUME 2

SCRIPTS
BRIAN REED
DUFFY BOUDREAU

PENCILS
SERGIO ARIÑO
RICARDO SÁNCHEZ
DOUGLAS FRANCHIN

INKS
JUAN CASTRO
ROB LEAN
DENIS FREITAS
CARLOS EDUARDO

COLORS
MICHAEL ATIYEH

LETTERING
MICHAEL HEISLER

COVER ART
ANTHONY PALUMBO

DARK HORSE BOOKS

PUBLISHER
MIKE RICHARDSON

COLLECTION DESIGNER
SANDY TANAKA

ASSISTANT EDITORS
ROXY POLK
AARON WALKER

EDITOR
DAVE MARSHALL

HALO: ESCALATION Volume 2

This volume collects issues #7–#12 of the Dark Horse comic-book series *Halo: Escalation*.

Special thanks to Christine Finch, Nicholas Gallagher, Mike Gonzales, Kevin Grace, Tyler Jeffers, Carlos Naranjo, Tiffany O'Brien, Frank O'Connor, Jeremy Patenaude, Kenneth Peters, Sparth, and Kiki Wolfkill at Microsoft.

Published by
Dark Horse Books
A division of Dark Horse Comics, Inc.
10956 SE Main Street
Milwaukie, OR 97222

DarkHorse.com
HaloWaypoint.com

First edition: April 2015
ISBN 978-1-61655-628-0

1 3 5 7 9 10 8 6 4 2
Printed in China

Mike Richardson, President and Publisher **Neil Hankerson**, Executive Vice President **Tom Weddle**, Chief Financial Officer **Randy Stradley**, Vice President of Publishing **Michael Martens**, Vice President of Book Trade Sales **Scott Allie**, Editor in Chief **Matt Parkinson**, Vice President of Marketing **David Scroggy**, Vice President of Product Development **Dale LaFountain**, Vice President of Information Technology **Darlene Vogel**, Senior Director of Print, Design, and Production **Ken Lizzi**, General Counsel **Davey Estrada**, Editorial Director **Chris Warner,** Senior Books Editor **Diana Schutz**, Executive Editor **Cary Grazzini**, Director of Print and Development **Lia Ribacchi**, Art Director **Cara Niece**, Director of Scheduling **Mark Bernardi**, Director of Digital Publishing

Illustration by Sparth

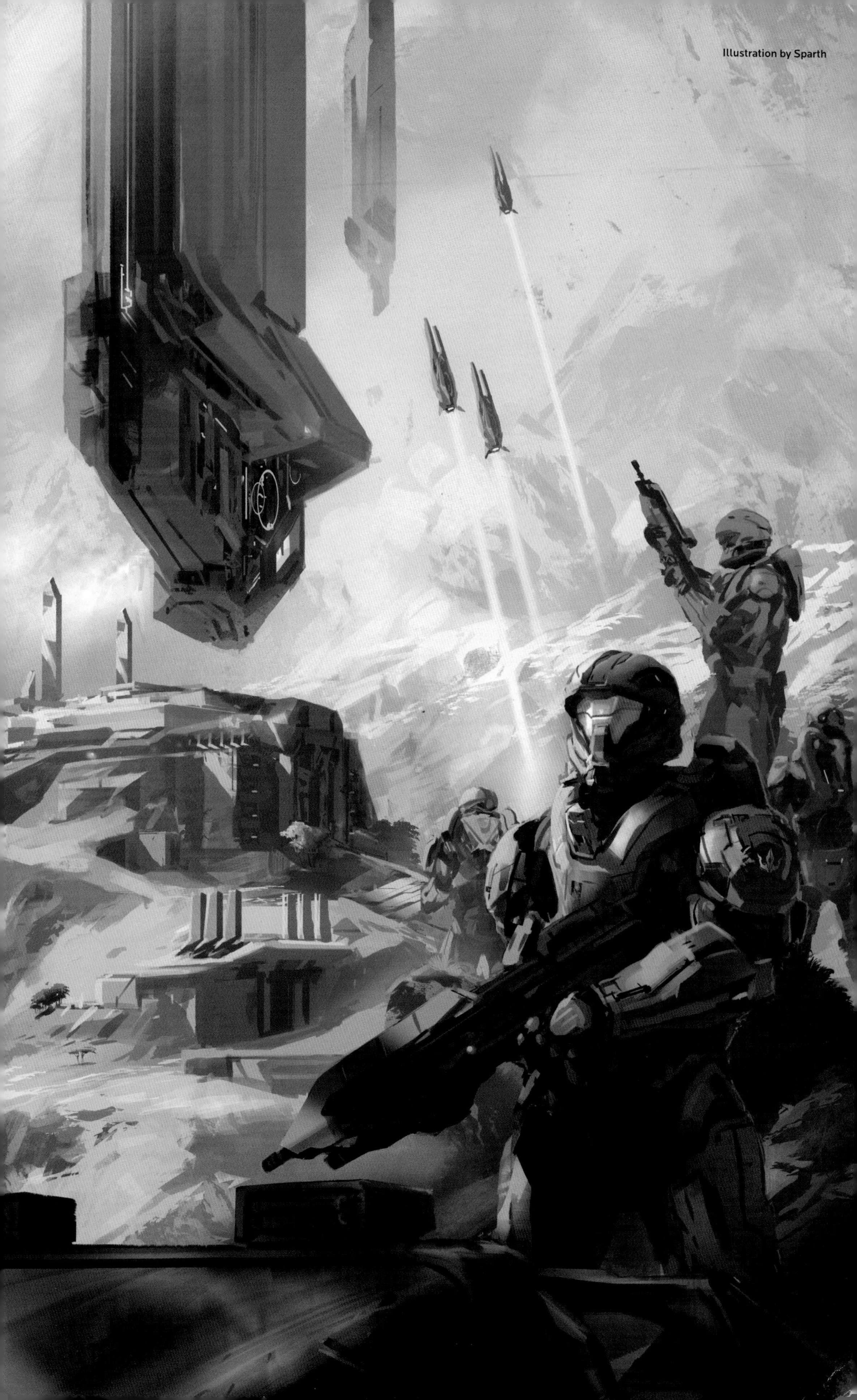

After an encounter with a madman bent on revenge, the UNSC *Infinity* is damaged and has spent the last several weeks in spacedock, undergoing extensive repairs.

Eight months ago, Earth was attacked by the Forerunner known as Didact. His weapon of choice, the Composer, digitized the citizens of New Phoenix in a flash of light, killing millions while leaving the city standing.

Among those composed were the family of Spartan Gabriel Thorne . . .

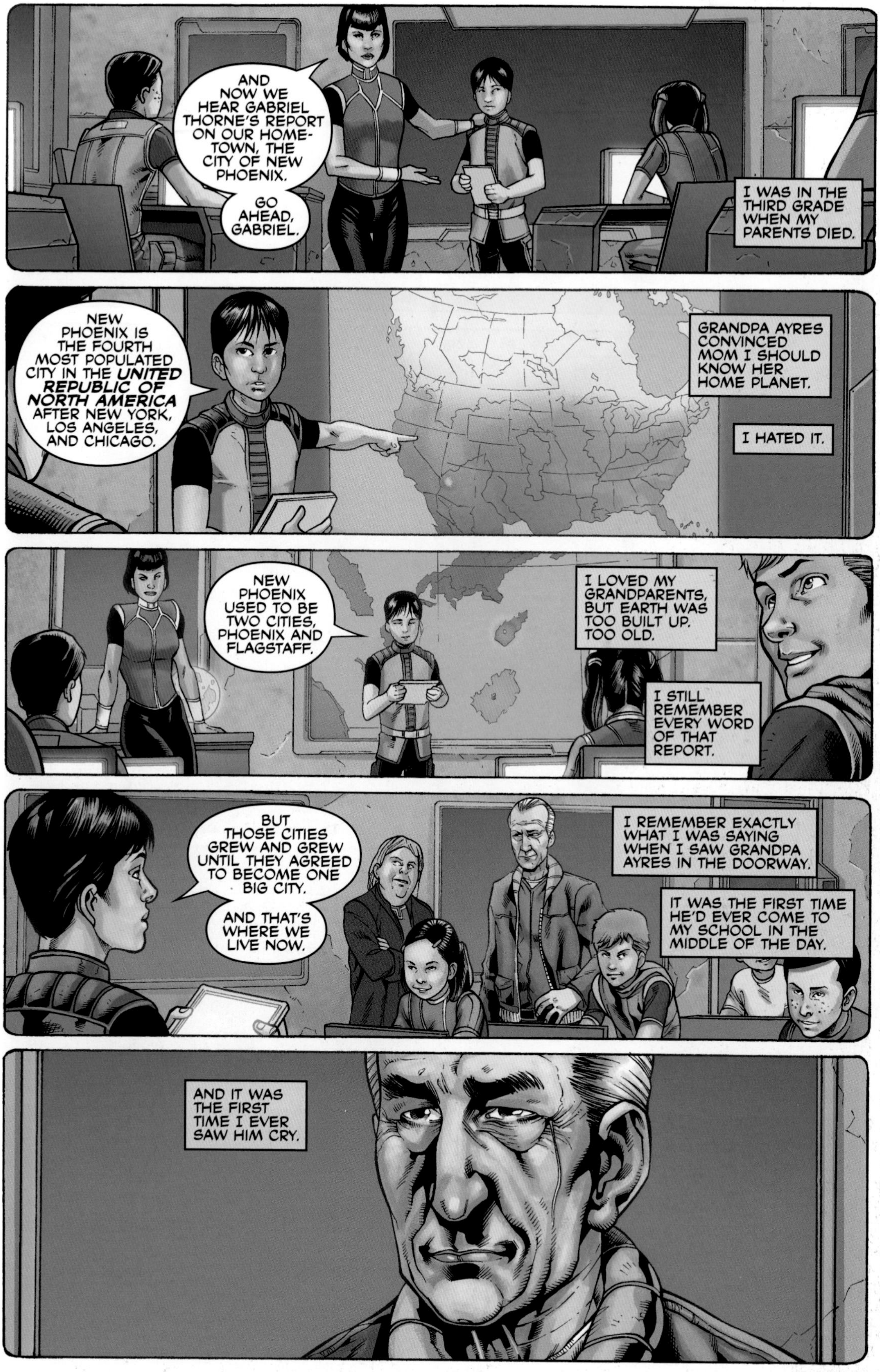
AND NOW WE HEAR GABRIEL THORNE'S REPORT ON OUR HOME-TOWN, THE CITY OF NEW PHOENIX.
GO AHEAD, GABRIEL.
I WAS IN THE THIRD GRADE WHEN MY PARENTS DIED.
NEW PHOENIX IS THE FOURTH MOST POPULATED CITY IN THE UNITED REPUBLIC OF NORTH AMERICA AFTER NEW YORK, LOS ANGELES, AND CHICAGO.
GRANDPA AYRES CONVINCED MOM I SHOULD KNOW HER HOME PLANET.
I HATED IT.
NEW PHOENIX USED TO BE TWO CITIES, PHOENIX AND FLAGSTAFF.
I LOVED MY GRANDPARENTS, BUT EARTH WAS TOO BUILT UP. TOO OLD.
I STILL REMEMBER EVERY WORD OF THAT REPORT.
BUT THOSE CITIES GREW AND GREW UNTIL THEY AGREED TO BECOME ONE BIG CITY.
AND THAT'S WHERE WE LIVE NOW.
I REMEMBER EXACTLY WHAT I WAS SAYING WHEN I SAW GRANDPA AYRES IN THE DOORWAY.
IT WAS THE FIRST TIME HE'D EVER COME TO MY SCHOOL IN THE MIDDLE OF THE DAY.
AND IT WAS THE FIRST TIME I EVER SAW HIM CRY.

MOM AND DAD WERE BOTH ARMY OFFICERS, STATIONED ON THE PLANET *ALLUVION.*

THOSE WHO SERVED UNDER THEM SPOKE HIGHLY OF BOTH.

WHEN THE COVENANT FOUND ALLUVION, THE SAME OLD STORY PLAYED OUT...

THEY GLASSED ALLUVION, BURNING HUMANITY FROM ITS SURFACE.

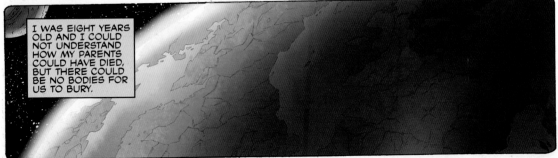

I WAS EIGHT YEARS OLD AND I COULD NOT UNDERSTAND HOW MY PARENTS COULD HAVE DIED, BUT THERE COULD BE NO BODIES FOR US TO BURY.

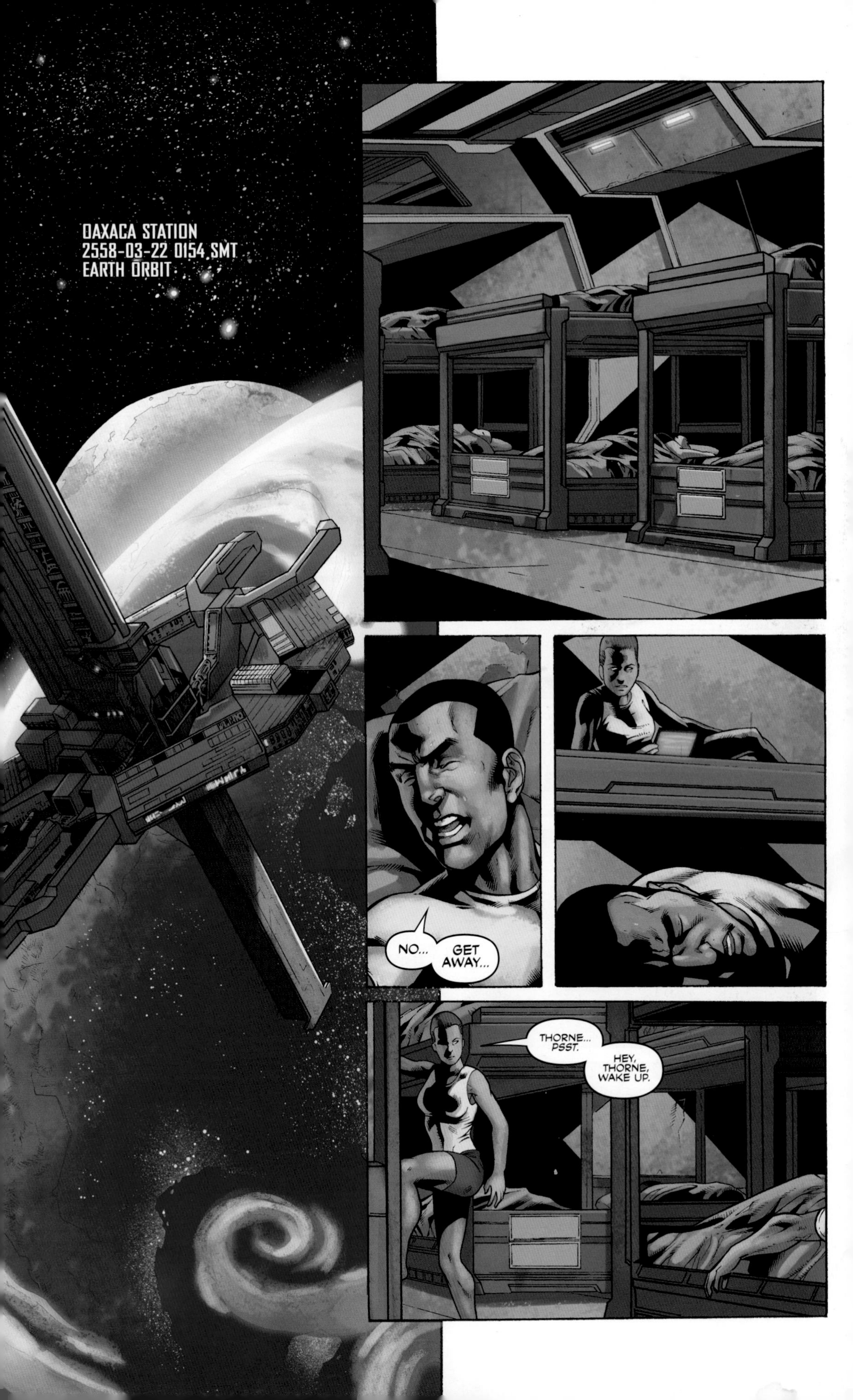
DAXACA STATION
2558-03-22 0154 SMT
EARTH ORBIT
NO... GET AWAY...
THORNE... PSST.
HEY, THORNE, WAKE UP.

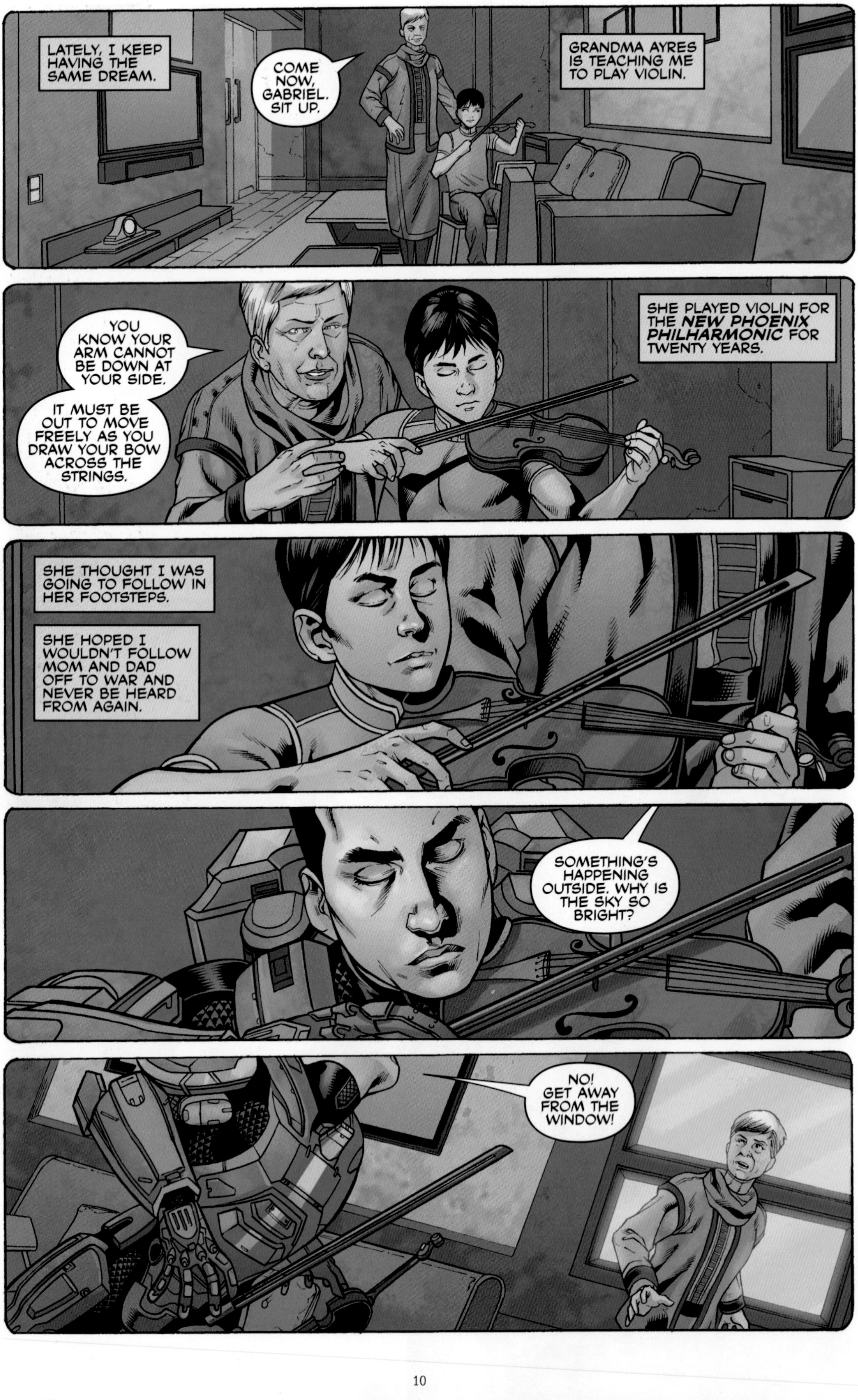

LATELY, I KEEP HAVING THE SAME DREAM.
COME NOW, GABRIEL. SIT UP.
GRANDMA AYRES IS TEACHING ME TO PLAY VIOLIN.
YOU KNOW YOUR ARM CANNOT BE DOWN AT YOUR SIDE.
IT MUST BE OUT TO MOVE FREELY AS YOU DRAW YOUR BOW ACROSS THE STRINGS.
SHE PLAYED VIOLIN FOR THE *NEW PHOENIX PHILHARMONIC* FOR TWENTY YEARS.
SHE THOUGHT I WAS GOING TO FOLLOW IN HER FOOTSTEPS.
SHE HOPED I WOULDN'T FOLLOW MOM AND DAD OFF TO WAR AND NEVER BE HEARD FROM AGAIN.
SOMETHING'S HAPPENING OUTSIDE. WHY IS THE SKY SO BRIGHT?
NO! GET AWAY FROM THE WINDOW!

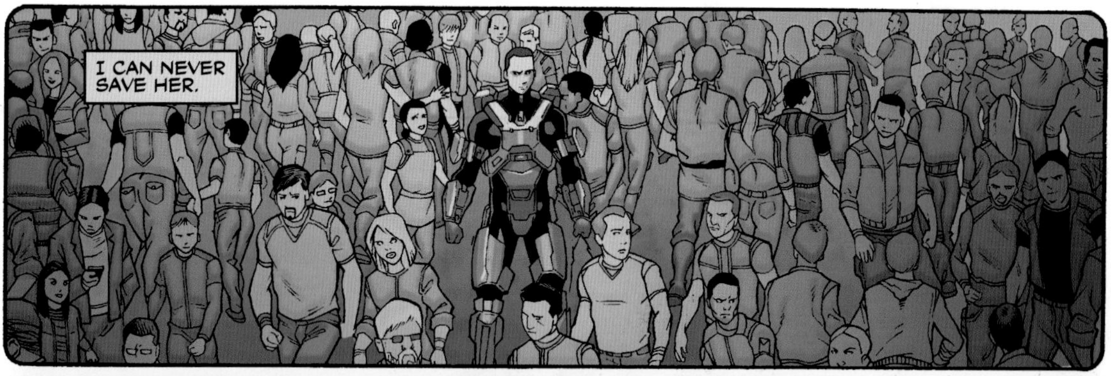
I CAN NEVER SAVE HER.

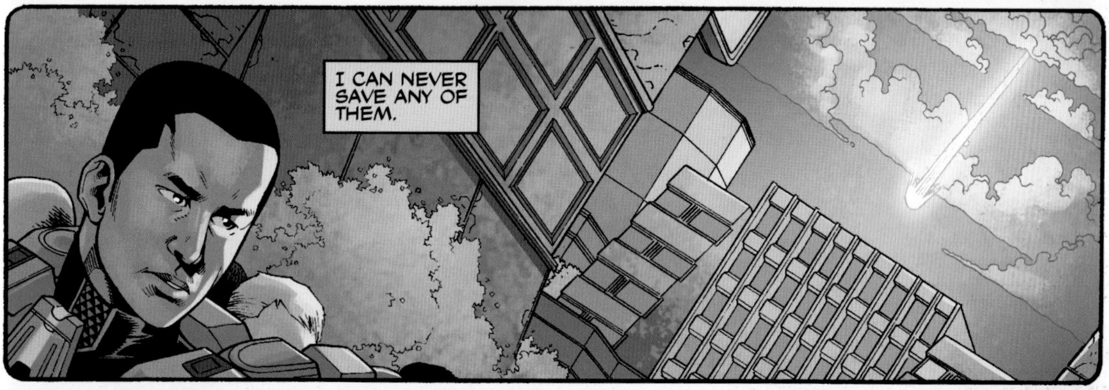
I CAN NEVER SAVE ANY OF THEM.

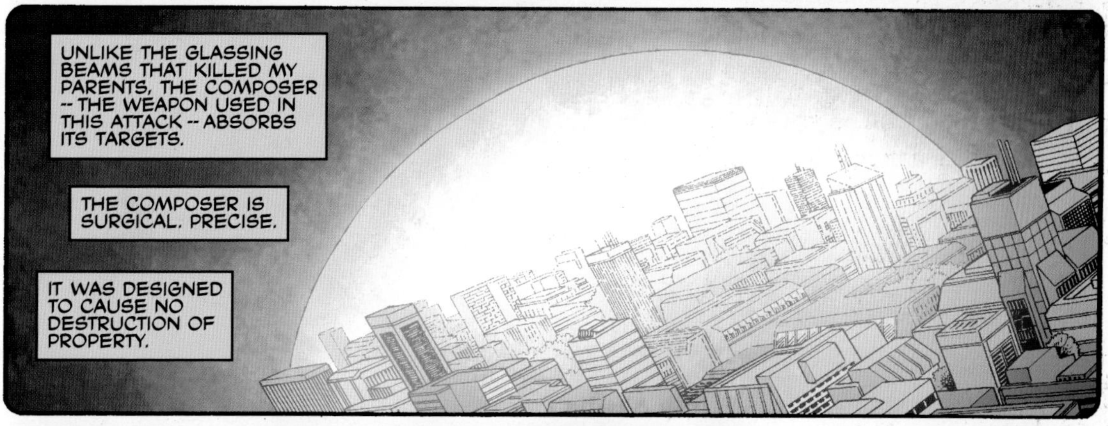
UNLIKE THE GLASSING BEAMS THAT KILLED MY PARENTS, THE COMPOSER -- THE WEAPON USED IN THIS ATTACK -- ABSORBS ITS TARGETS.
THE COMPOSER IS SURGICAL. PRECISE.
IT WAS DESIGNED TO CAUSE NO DESTRUCTION OF PROPERTY.

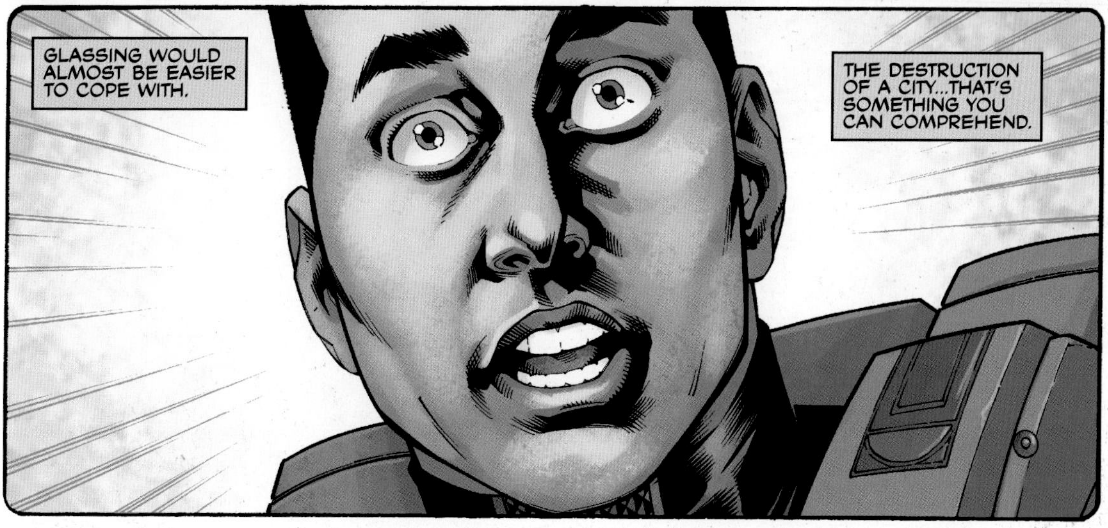
GLASSING WOULD ALMOST BE EASIER TO COPE WITH.
THE DESTRUCTION OF A CITY...THAT'S SOMETHING YOU CAN COMPREHEND.

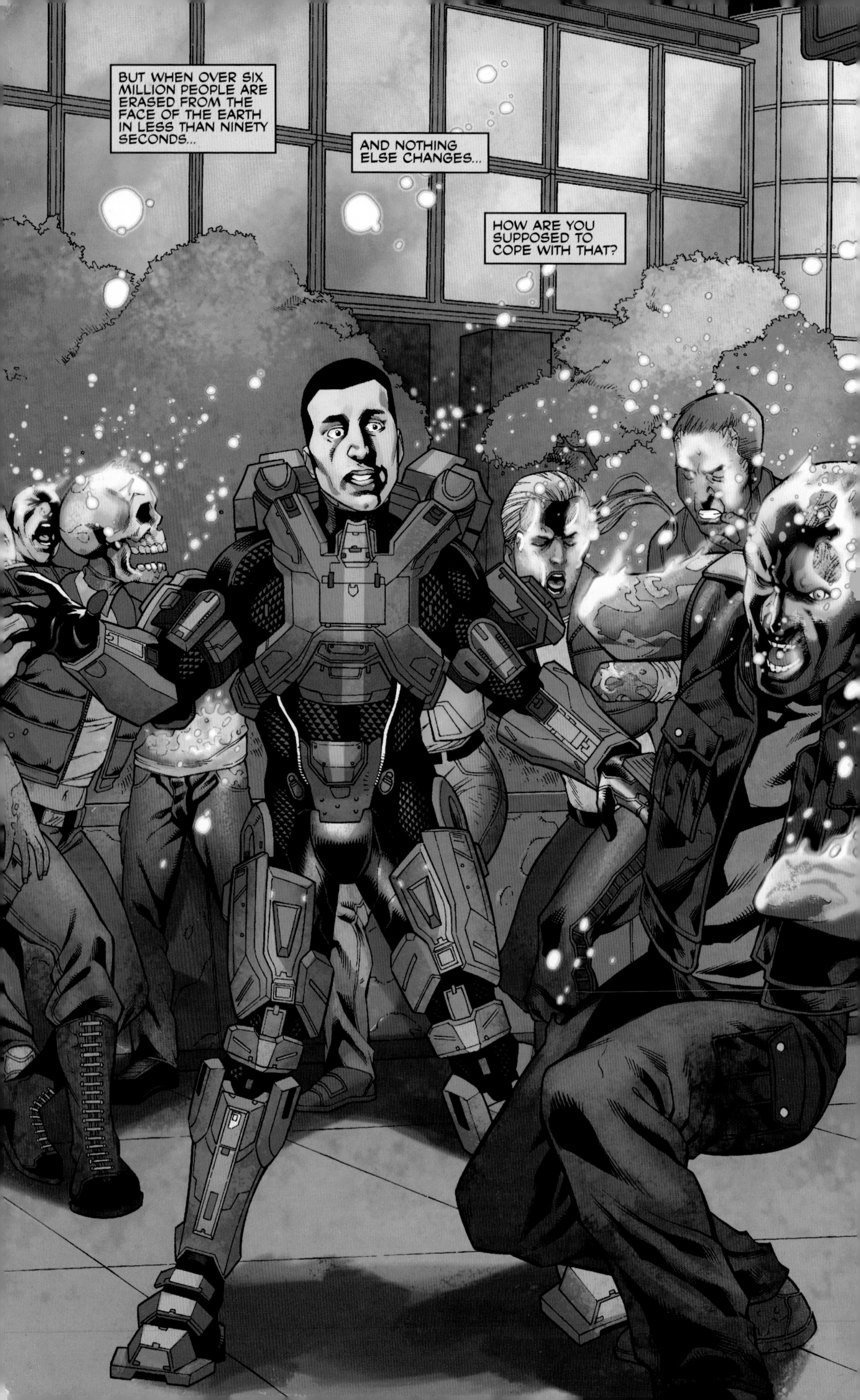
BUT WHEN OVER SIX MILLION PEOPLE ARE ERASED FROM THE FACE OF THE EARTH IN LESS THAN NINETY SECONDS...
AND NOTHING ELSE CHANGES...
HOW ARE YOU SUPPOSED TO COPE WITH THAT?

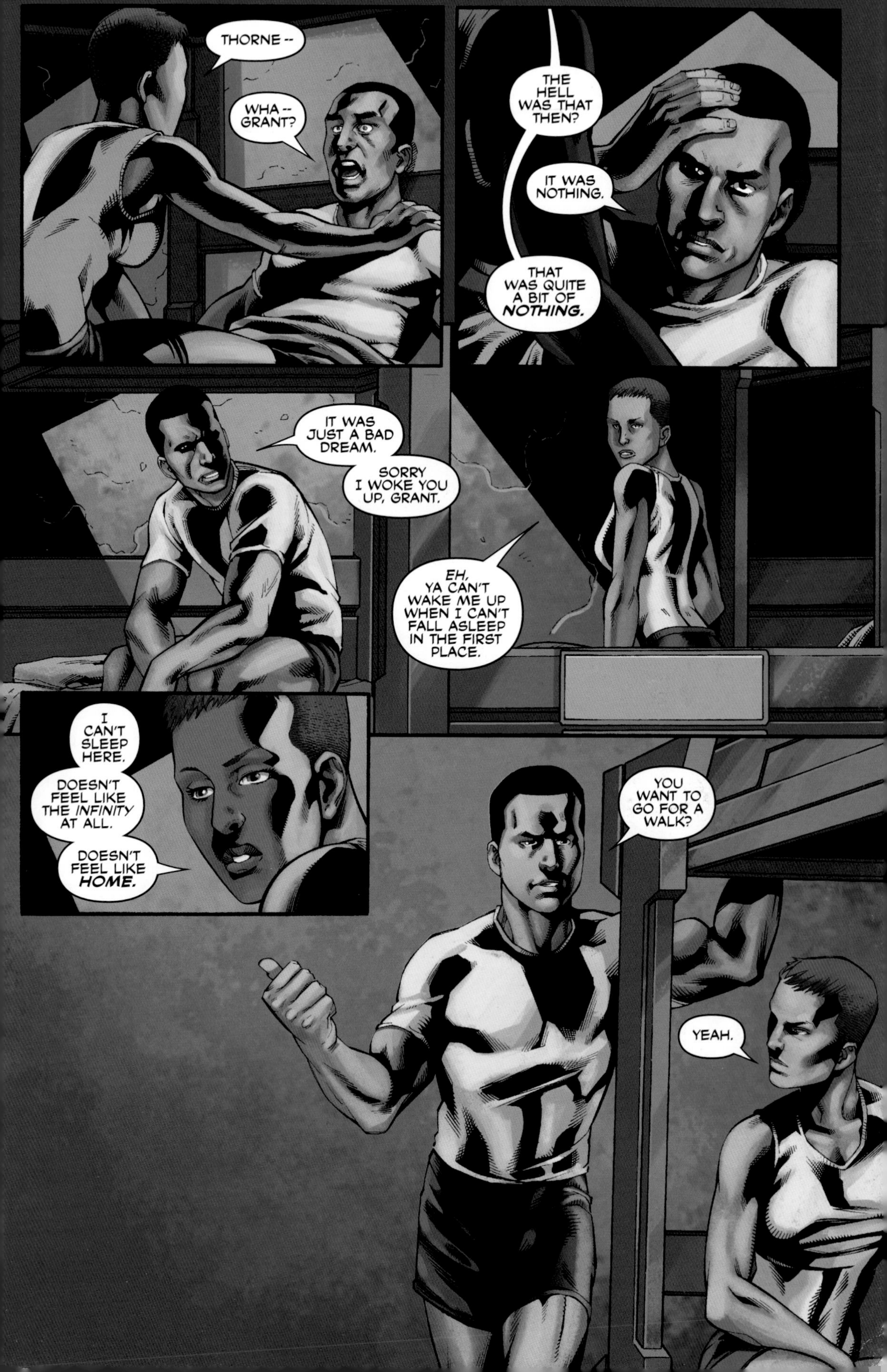
THORNE --
WHA -- GRANT?
THE HELL WAS THAT THEN?
IT WAS NOTHING.
THAT WAS QUITE A BIT OF *NOTHING.*
IT WAS JUST A BAD DREAM.
SORRY I WOKE YOU UP, GRANT.
EH, YA CAN'T WAKE ME UP WHEN I CAN'T FALL ASLEEP IN THE FIRST PLACE.
I CAN'T SLEEP HERE.
DOESN'T FEEL LIKE THE *INFINITY* AT ALL.
DOESN'T FEEL LIKE *HOME.*
YOU WANT TO GO FOR A WALK?
YEAH.

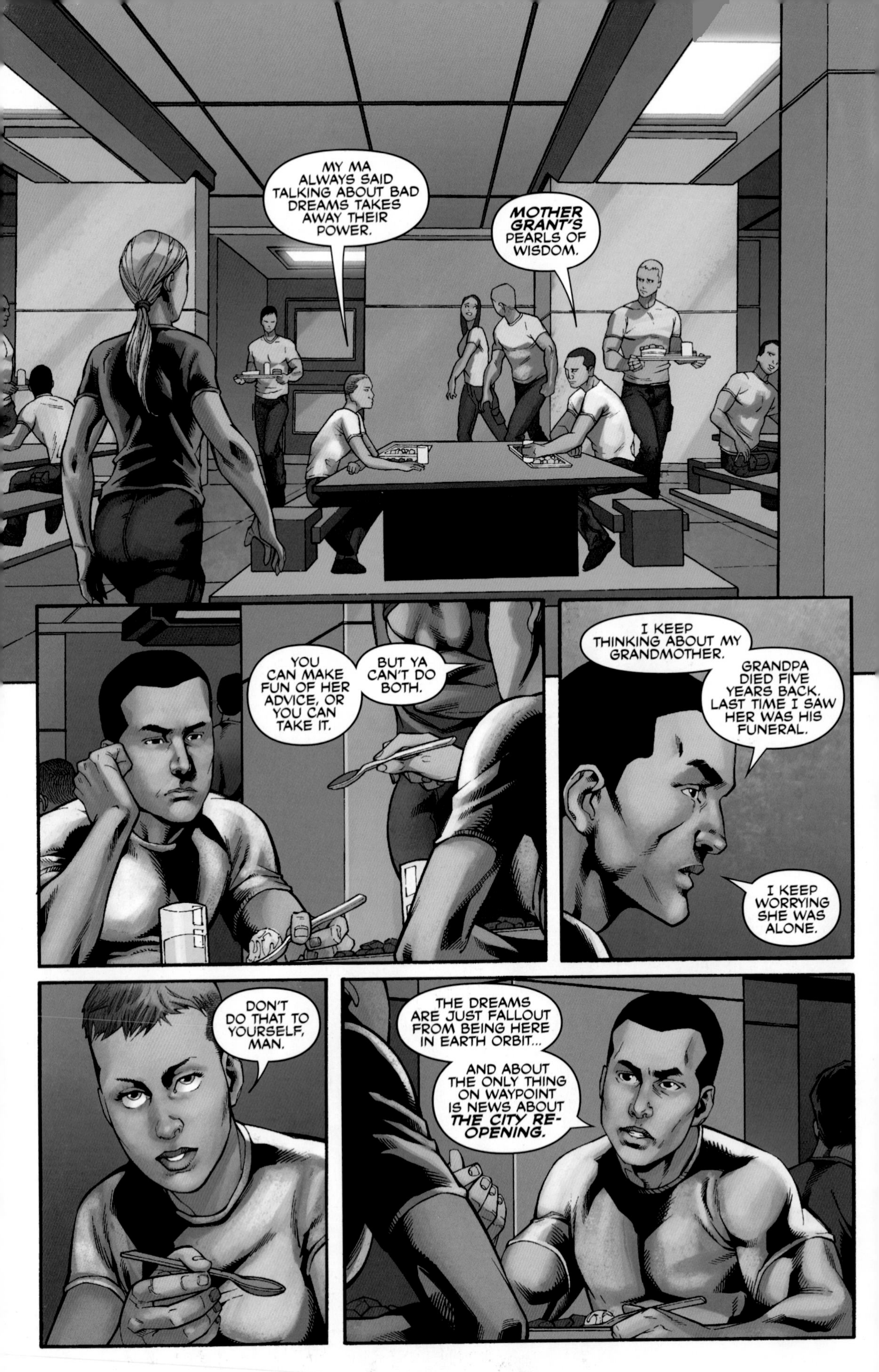
MY MA ALWAYS SAID TALKING ABOUT BAD DREAMS TAKES AWAY THEIR POWER.
MOTHER GRANT'S PEARLS OF WISDOM.
YOU CAN MAKE FUN OF HER ADVICE, OR YOU CAN TAKE IT.
BUT YA CAN'T DO BOTH.
I KEEP THINKING ABOUT MY GRANDMOTHER.
GRANDPA DIED FIVE YEARS BACK. LAST TIME I SAW HER WAS HIS FUNERAL.
I KEEP WORRYING SHE WAS ALONE.
DON'T DO THAT TO YOURSELF, MAN.
THE DREAMS ARE JUST FALLOUT FROM BEING HERE IN EARTH ORBIT...
AND ABOUT THE ONLY THING ON WAYPOINT IS NEWS ABOUT THE CITY RE-OPENING.

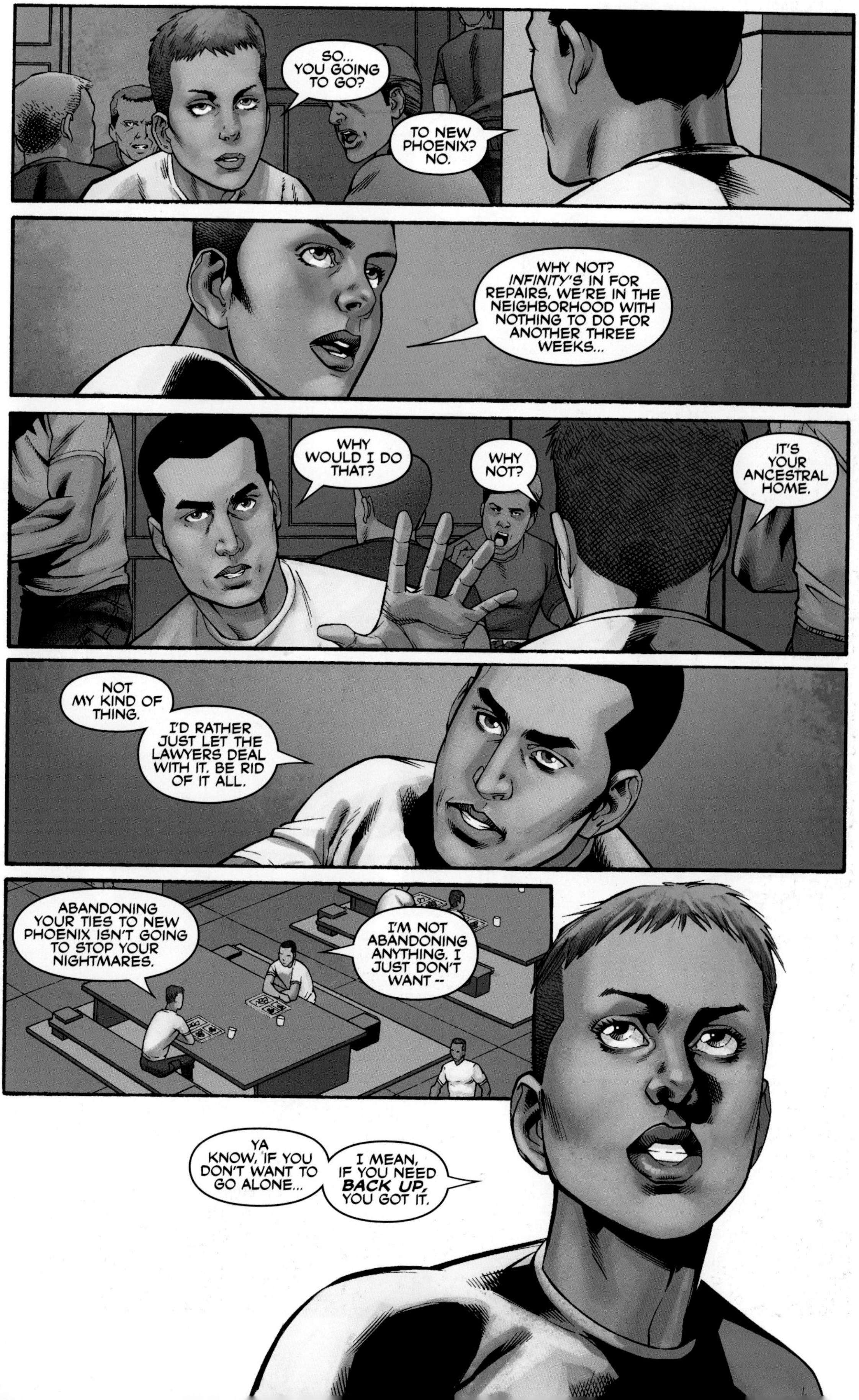
SO... YOU GOING TO GO?
TO NEW PHOENIX? NO.
WHY NOT? *INFINITY*'S IN FOR REPAIRS, WE'RE IN THE NEIGHBORHOOD WITH NOTHING TO DO FOR ANOTHER THREE WEEKS...
WHY WOULD I DO THAT?
WHY NOT?
IT'S YOUR ANCESTRAL HOME.
NOT MY KIND OF THING.
I'D RATHER JUST LET THE LAWYERS DEAL WITH IT. BE RID OF IT ALL.
ABANDONING YOUR TIES TO NEW PHOENIX ISN'T GOING TO STOP YOUR NIGHTMARES.
I'M NOT ABANDONING ANYTHING. I JUST DON'T WANT --
YA KNOW, IF YOU DON'T WANT TO GO ALONE...
I MEAN, IF YOU NEED **BACK UP,** YOU GOT IT.

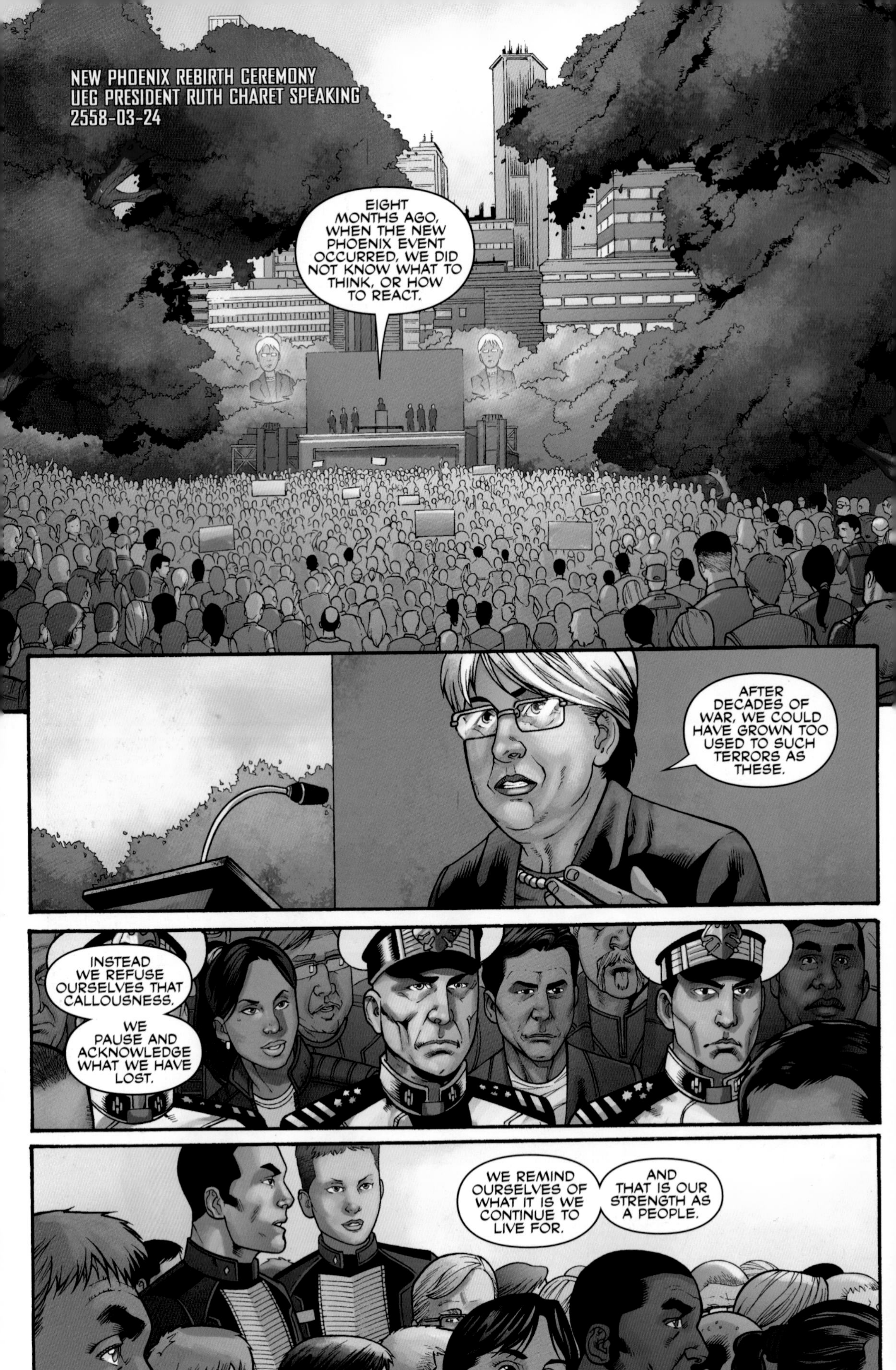
NEW PHOENIX REBIRTH CEREMONY
UEG PRESIDENT RUTH CHARET SPEAKING
2558-03-24
EIGHT MONTHS AGO, WHEN THE NEW PHOENIX EVENT OCCURRED, WE DID NOT KNOW WHAT TO THINK, OR HOW TO REACT.
AFTER DECADES OF WAR, WE COULD HAVE GROWN TOO USED TO SUCH TERRORS AS THESE.
INSTEAD WE REFUSE OURSELVES THAT CALLOUSNESS.
WE PAUSE AND ACKNOWLEDGE WHAT WE HAVE LOST.
WE REMIND OURSELVES OF WHAT IT IS WE CONTINUE TO LIVE FOR.
AND THAT IS OUR STRENGTH AS A PEOPLE.

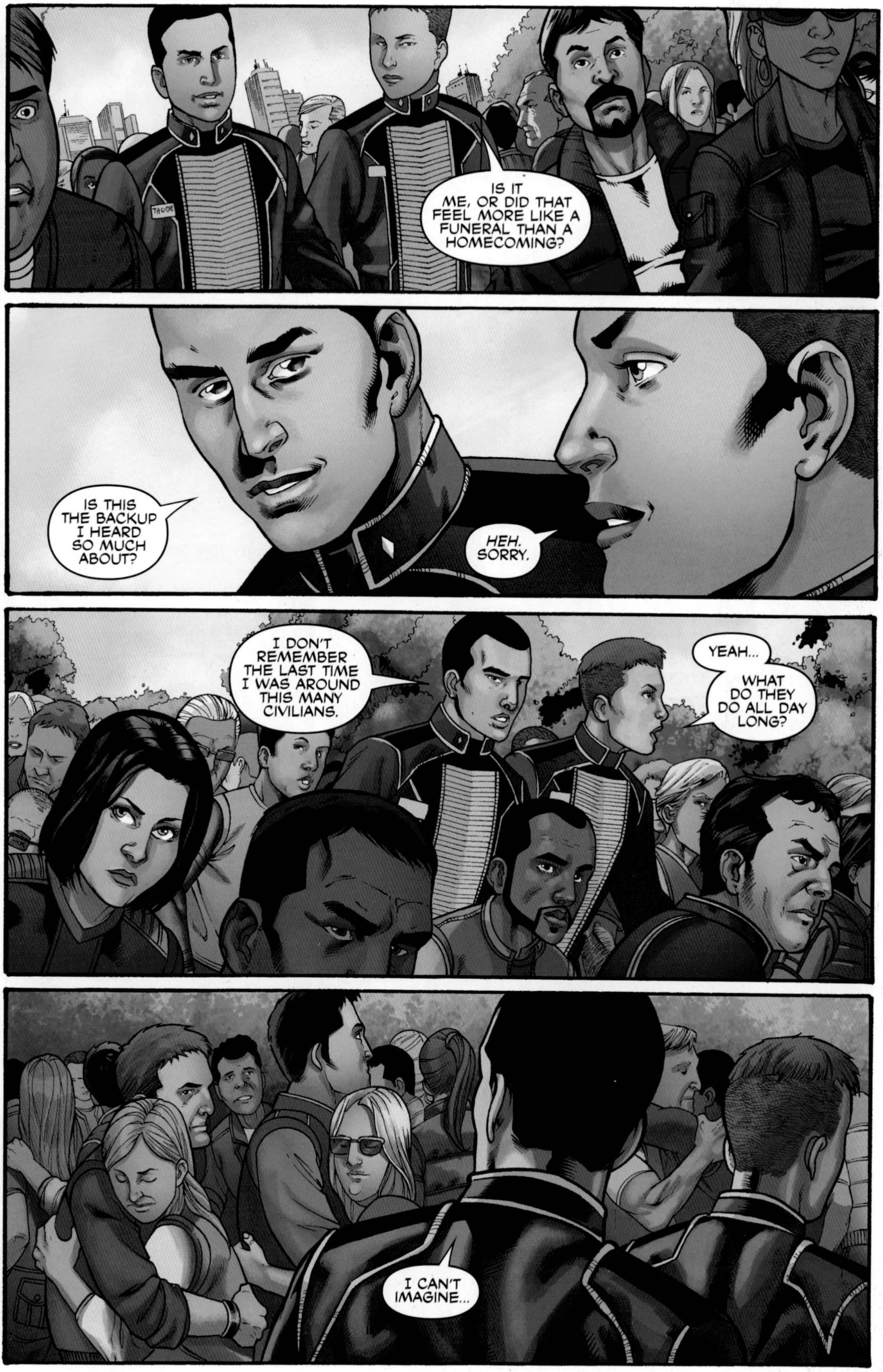
IS IT ME, OR DID THAT FEEL MORE LIKE A FUNERAL THAN A HOMECOMING?
IS THIS THE BACKUP I HEARD SO MUCH ABOUT?
HEH. SORRY.
I DON'T REMEMBER THE LAST TIME I WAS AROUND THIS MANY CIVILIANS.
YEAH...
WHAT DO THEY DO ALL DAY LONG?
I CAN'T IMAGINE...

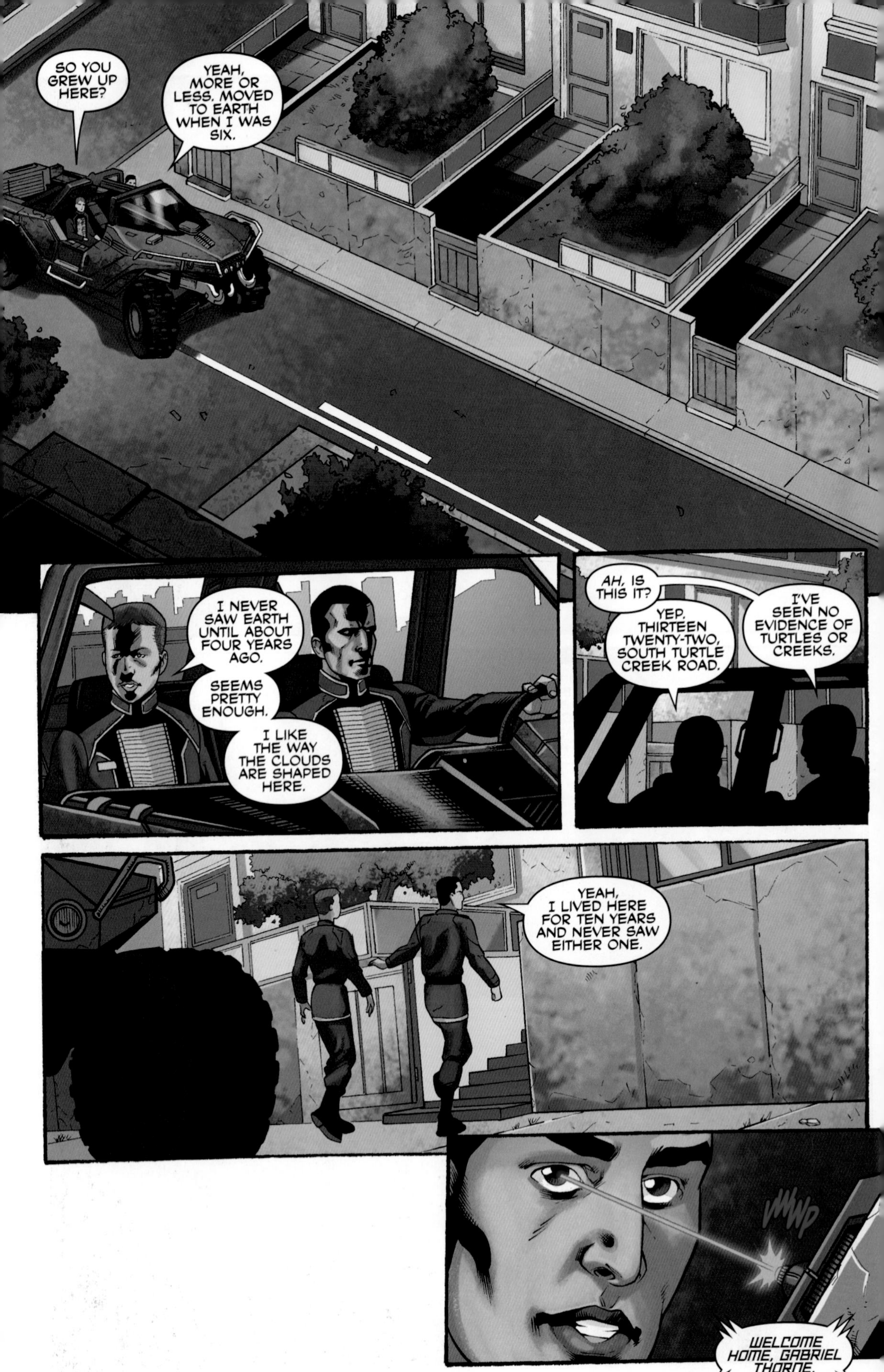
SO YOU GREW UP HERE?
YEAH, MORE OR LESS. MOVED TO EARTH WHEN I WAS SIX.
I NEVER SAW EARTH UNTIL ABOUT FOUR YEARS AGO.
SEEMS PRETTY ENOUGH.
I LIKE THE WAY THE CLOUDS ARE SHAPED HERE.
AH, IS THIS IT?
YEP. THIRTEEN TWENTY-TWO, SOUTH TURTLE CREEK ROAD.
I'VE SEEN NO EVIDENCE OF TURTLES OR CREEKS.
YEAH, I LIVED HERE FOR TEN YEARS AND NEVER SAW EITHER ONE.
VWWP
WELCOME HOME, GABRIEL THORNE.

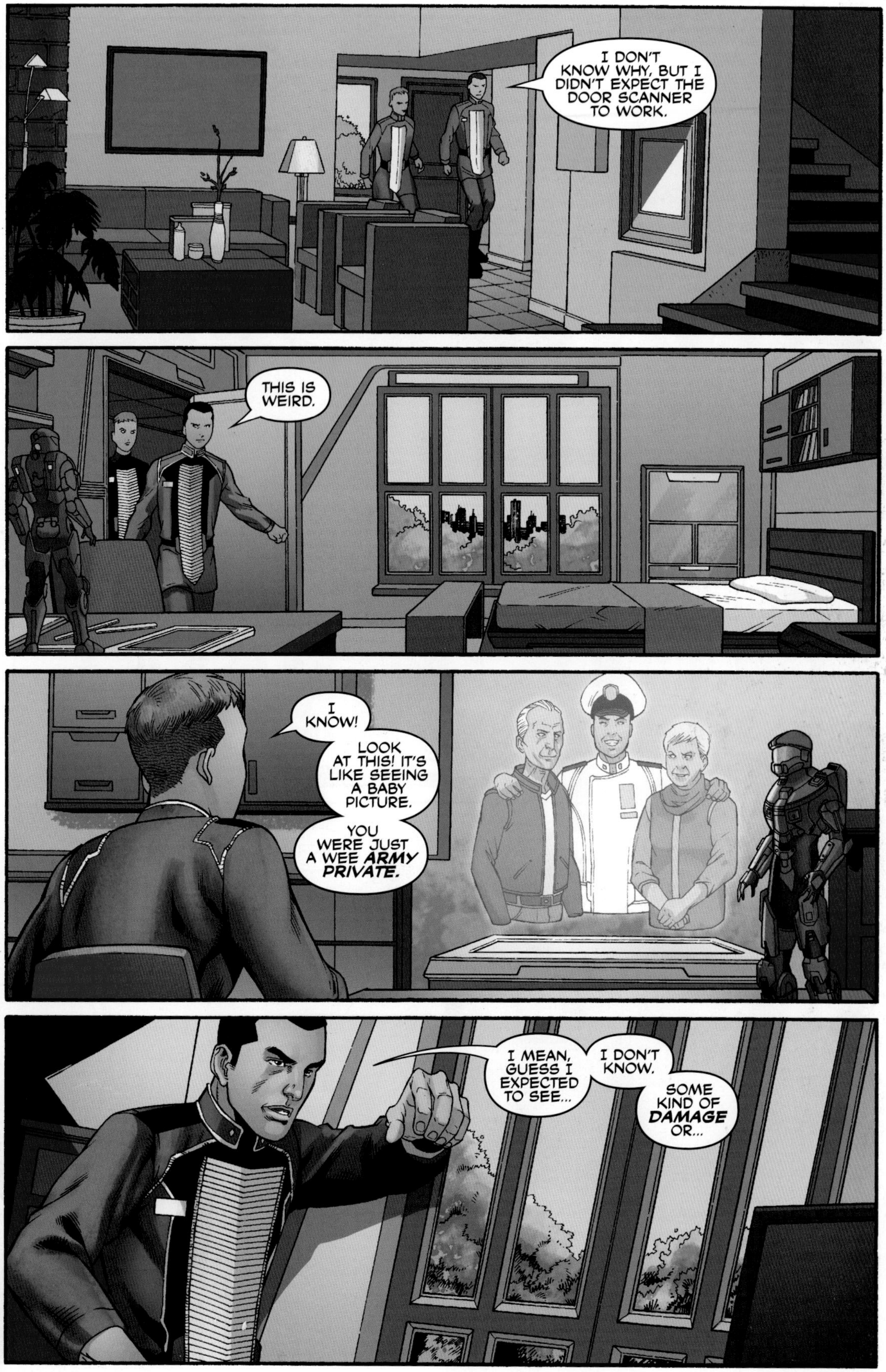
I DON'T KNOW WHY, BUT I DIDN'T EXPECT THE DOOR SCANNER TO WORK.
THIS IS WEIRD.
I KNOW!
LOOK AT THIS! IT'S LIKE SEEING A BABY PICTURE.
YOU WERE JUST A WEE **ARMY PRIVATE.**
I MEAN, GUESS I EXPECTED TO SEE...
I DON'T KNOW.
SOME KIND OF **DAMAGE** OR...

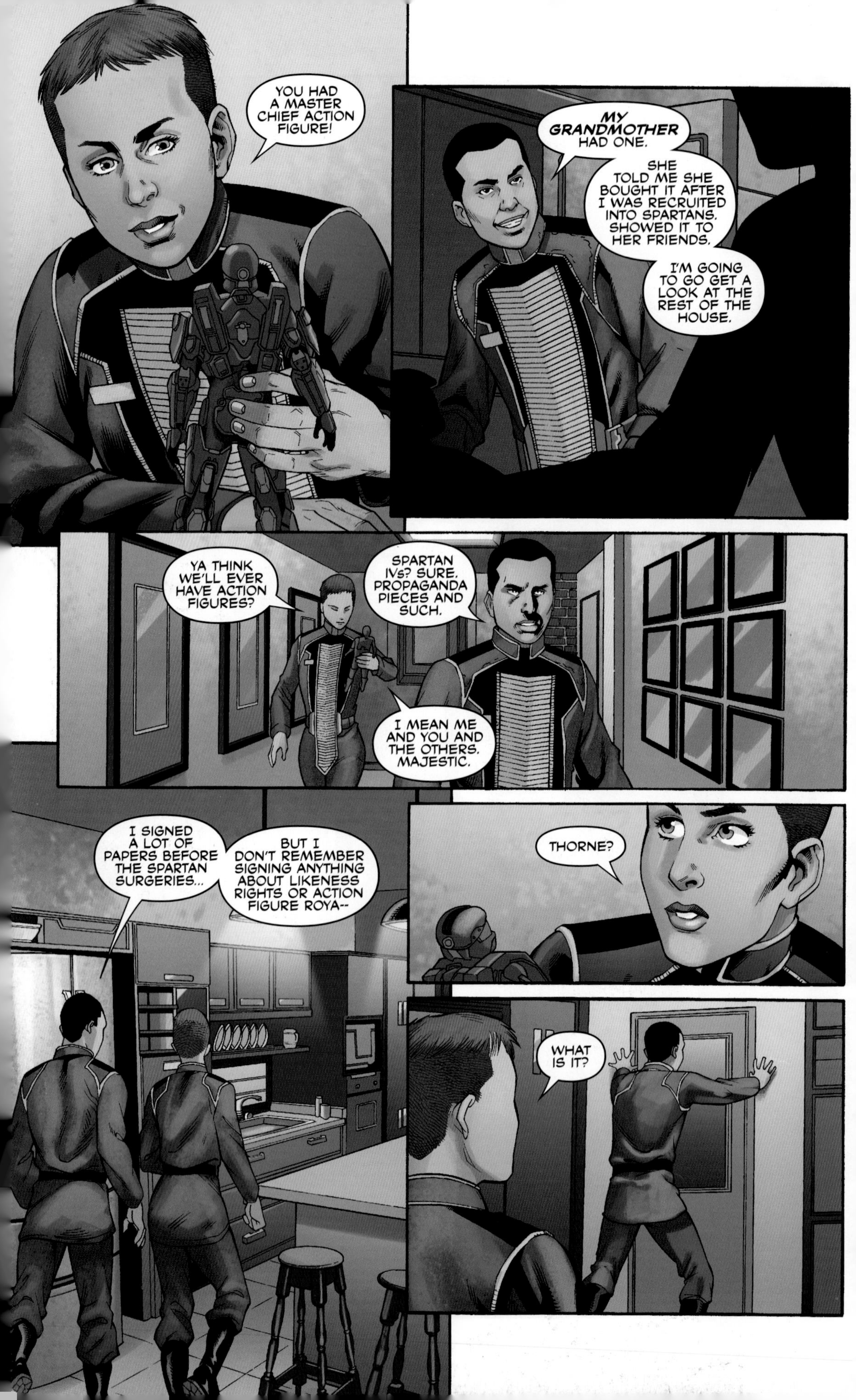
YOU HAD A MASTER CHIEF ACTION FIGURE!
MY GRANDMOTHER HAD ONE.
SHE TOLD ME SHE BOUGHT IT AFTER I WAS RECRUITED INTO SPARTANS. SHOWED IT TO HER FRIENDS.
I'M GOING TO GO GET A LOOK AT THE REST OF THE HOUSE.
YA THINK WE'LL EVER HAVE ACTION FIGURES?
SPARTAN IVs? SURE. PROPAGANDA PIECES AND SUCH.
I MEAN ME AND YOU AND THE OTHERS. MAJESTIC.
I SIGNED A LOT OF PAPERS BEFORE THE SPARTAN SURGERIES...
BUT I DON'T REMEMBER SIGNING ANYTHING ABOUT LIKENESS RIGHTS OR ACTION FIGURE ROYA--
THORNE?
WHAT IS IT?

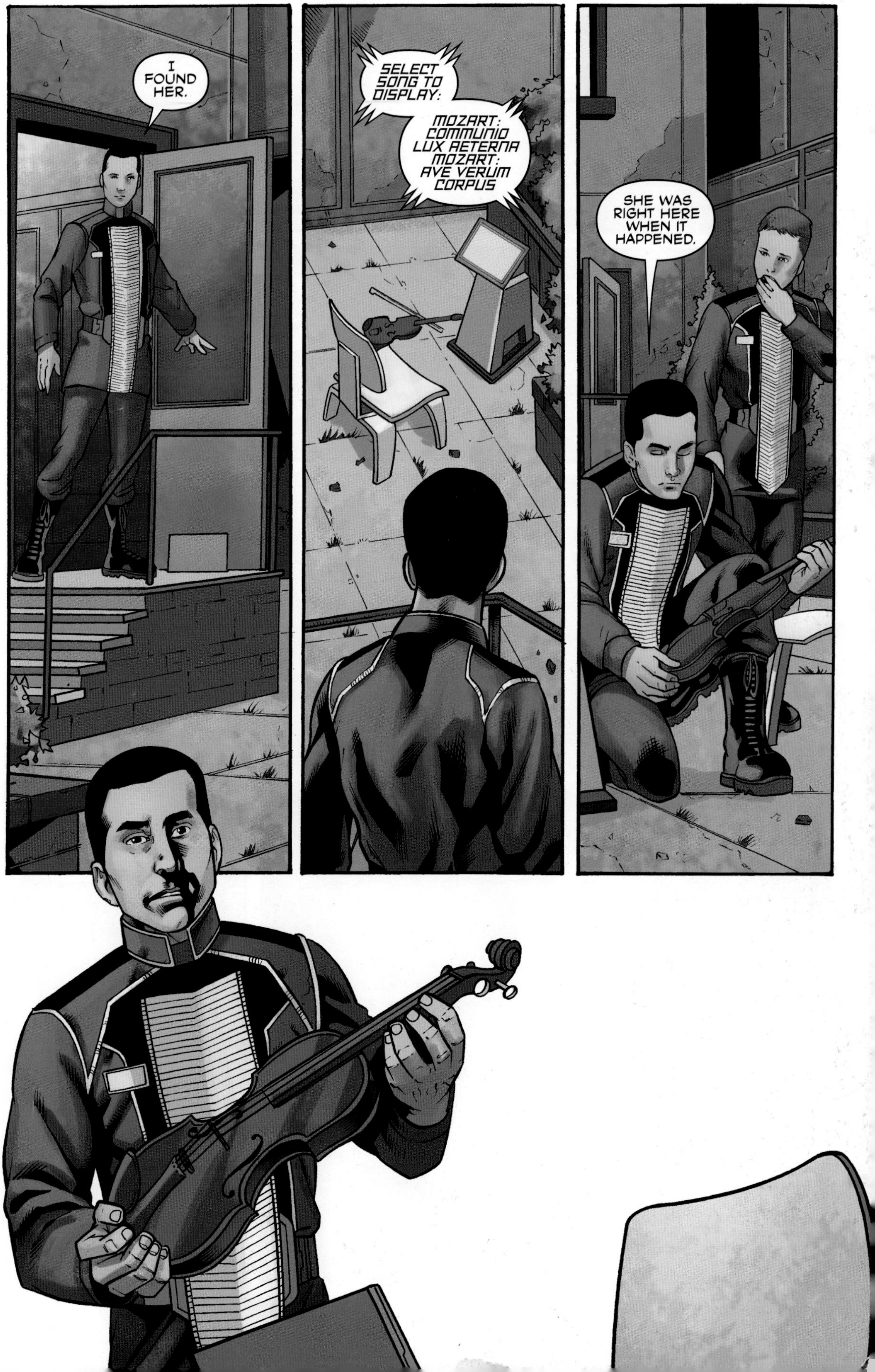
I FOUND HER.
SELECT SONG TO DISPLAY:
MOZART: COMMUNIO LUX AETERNA MOZART: AVE VERUM CORPUS
SHE WAS RIGHT HERE WHEN IT HAPPENED.

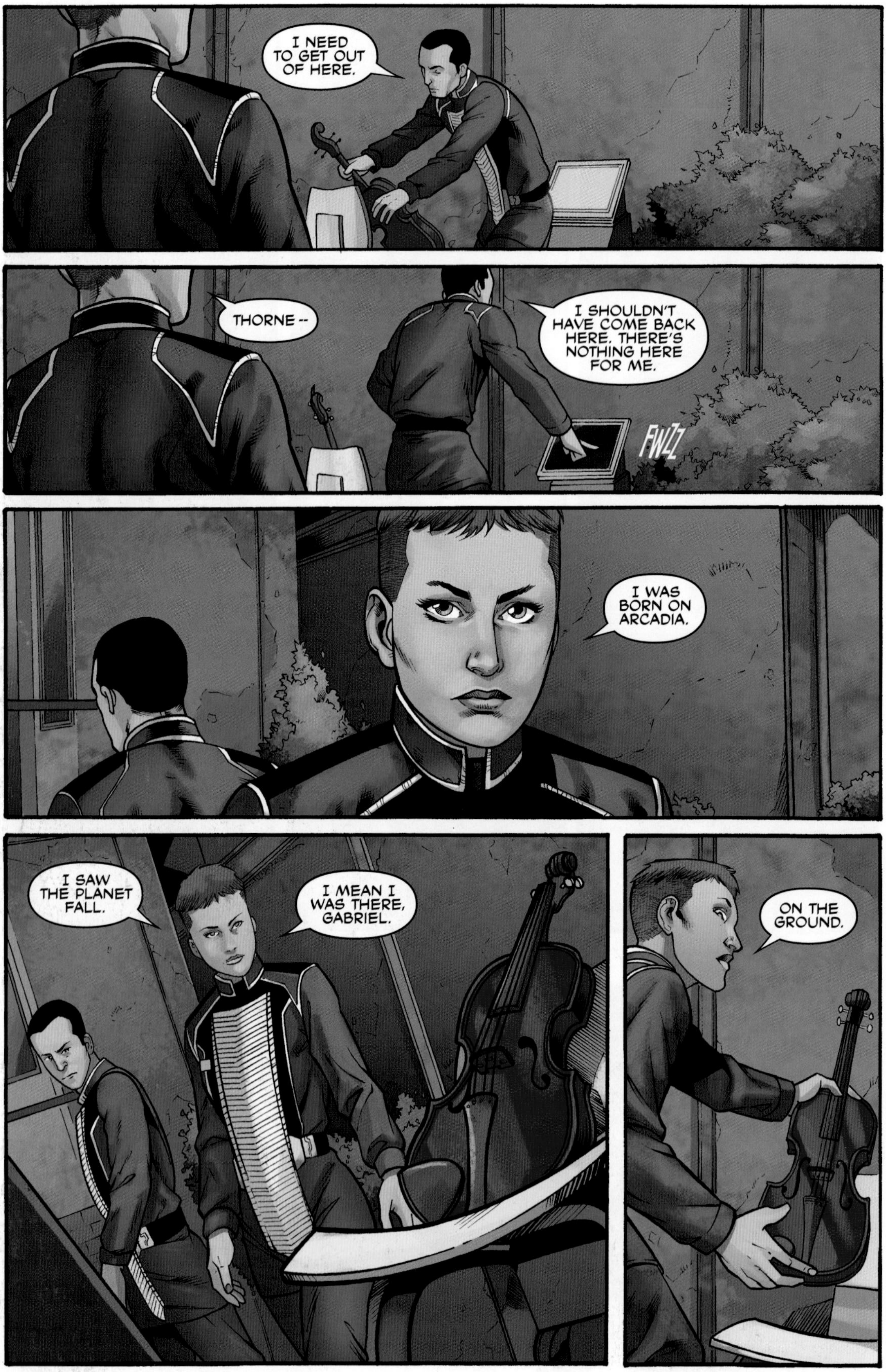
I NEED TO GET OUT OF HERE.
THORNE --
I SHOULDN'T HAVE COME BACK HERE. THERE'S NOTHING HERE FOR ME.
FWZZ
I WAS BORN ON ARCADIA.
I SAW THE PLANET FALL.
I MEAN I WAS THERE, GABRIEL.
ON THE GROUND.

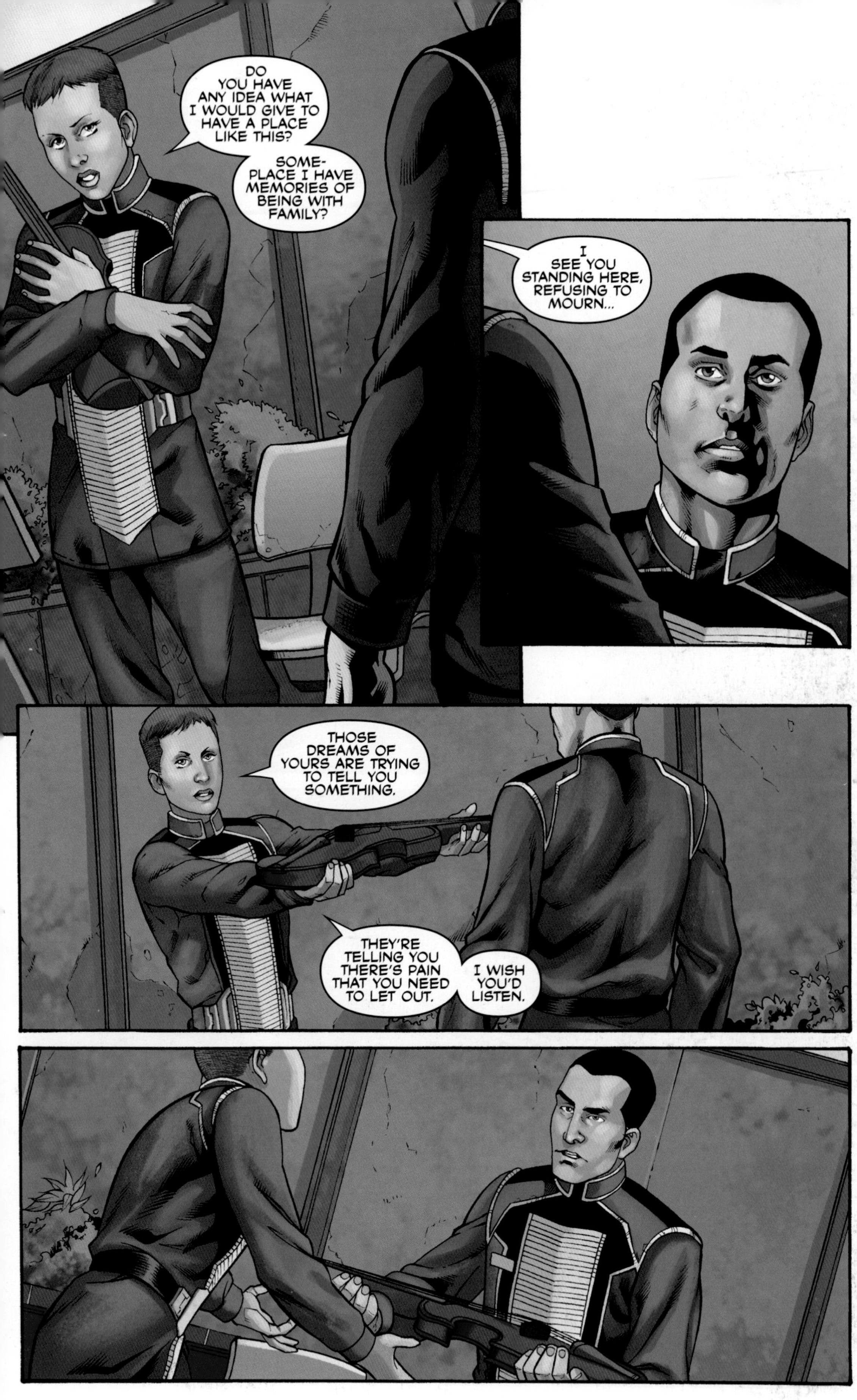
DO YOU HAVE ANY IDEA WHAT I WOULD GIVE TO HAVE A PLACE LIKE THIS?
SOME-PLACE I HAVE MEMORIES OF BEING WITH FAMILY?
I SEE YOU STANDING HERE, REFUSING TO MOURN...
THOSE DREAMS OF YOURS ARE TRYING TO TELL YOU SOMETHING.
THEY'RE TELLING YOU THERE'S PAIN THAT YOU NEED TO LET OUT.
I WISH YOU'D LISTEN.

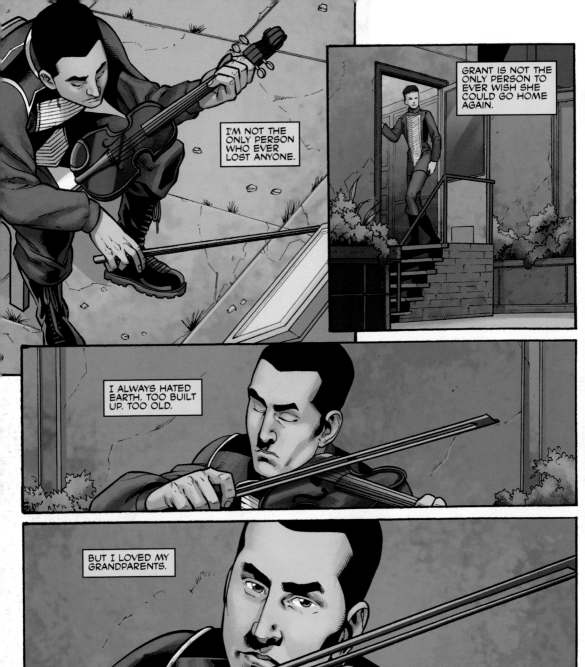

I'M NOT THE ONLY PERSON WHO EVER LOST ANYONE.

GRANT IS NOT THE ONLY PERSON TO EVER WISH SHE COULD GO HOME AGAIN.

I ALWAYS HATED EARTH. TOO BUILT UP. TOO OLD.

BUT I LOVED MY GRANDPARENTS.

AND GRANT'S RIGHT...

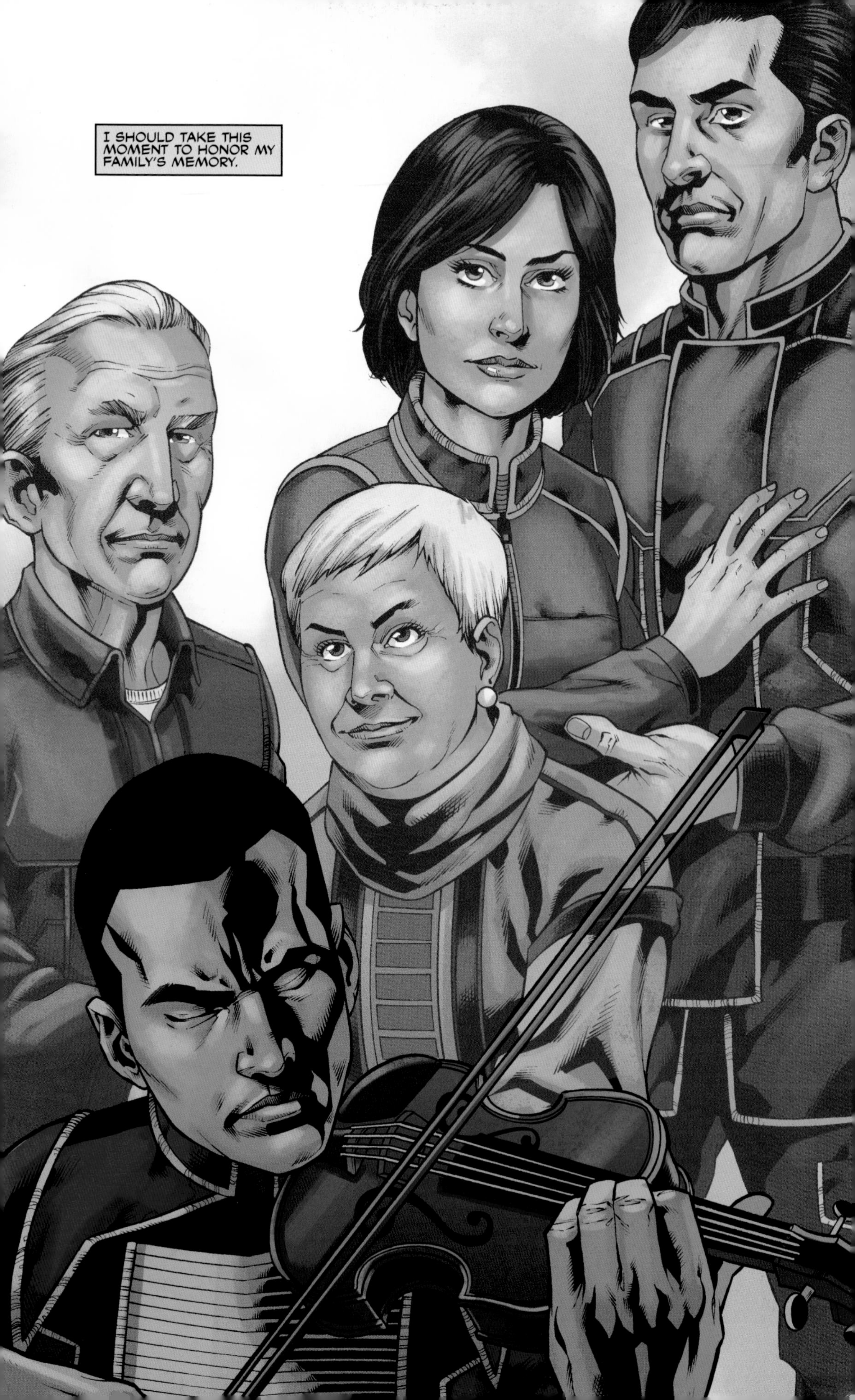
I SHOULD TAKE THIS MOMENT TO HONOR MY FAMILY'S MEMORY.

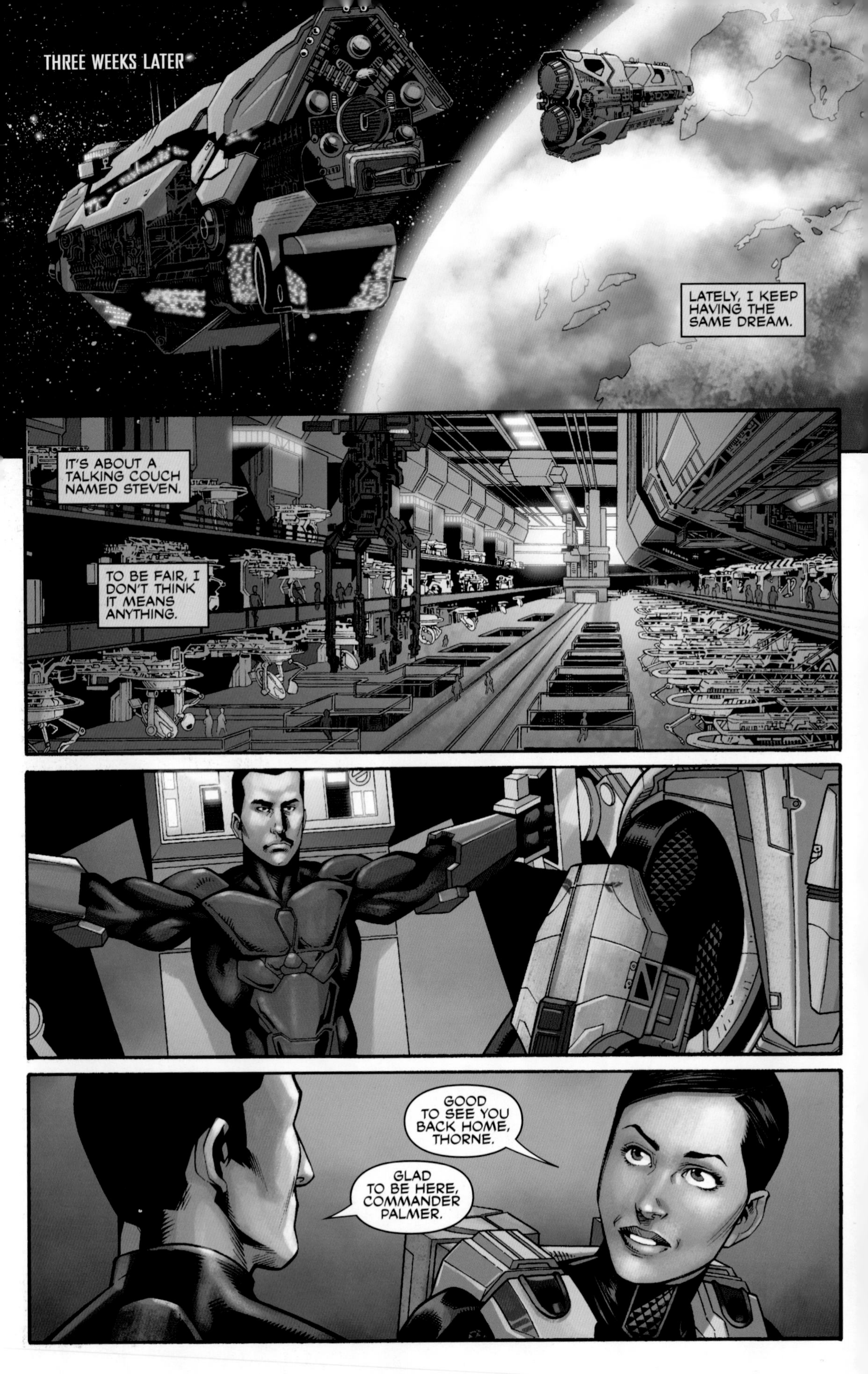
THREE WEEKS LATER
LATELY, I KEEP HAVING THE SAME DREAM.
IT'S ABOUT A TALKING COUCH NAMED STEVEN.
TO BE FAIR, I DON'T THINK IT MEANS ANYTHING.
GOOD TO SEE YOU BACK HOME, THORNE.
GLAD TO BE HERE, COMMANDER PALMER.

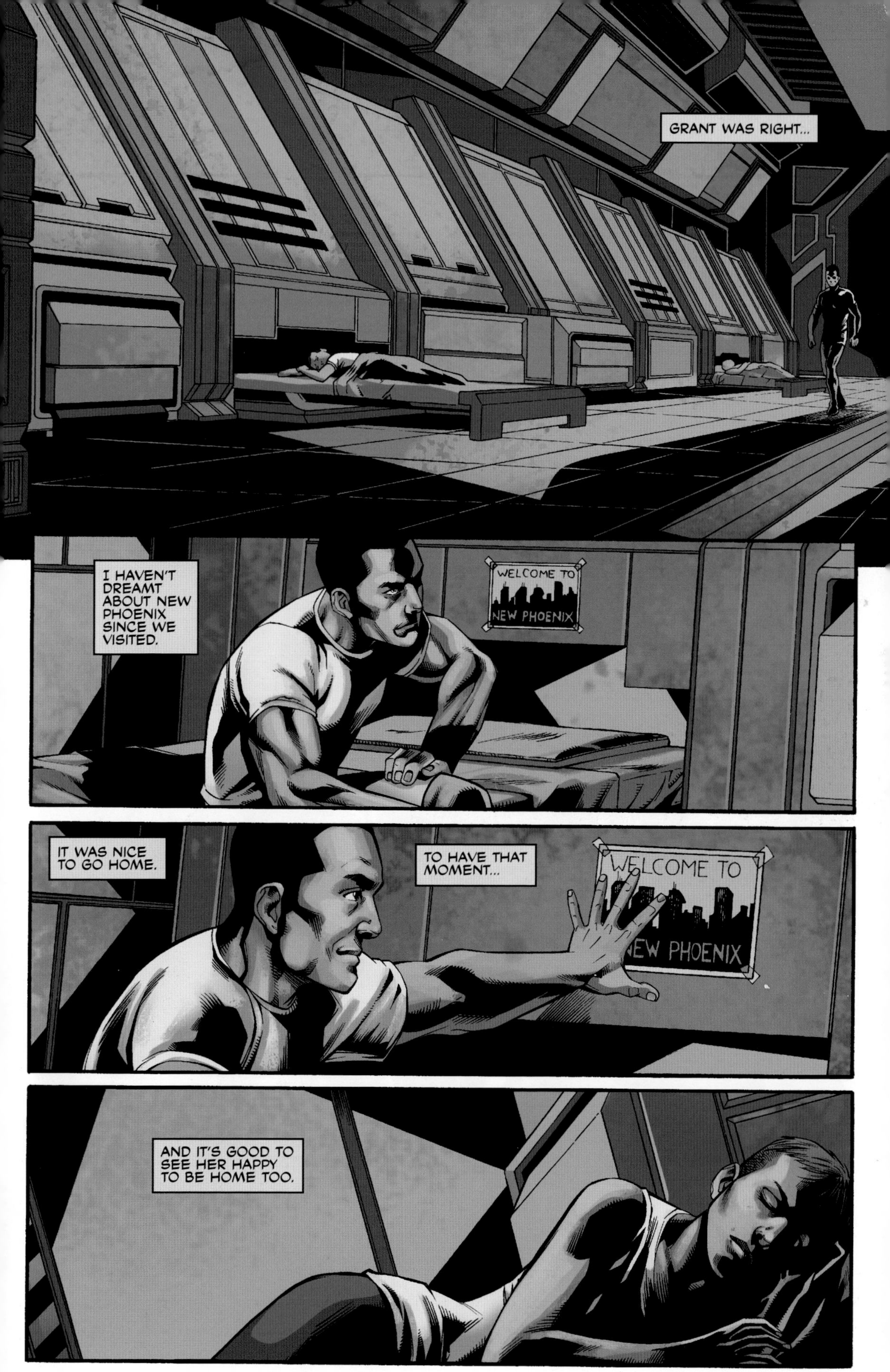
GRANT WAS RIGHT...
I HAVEN'T DREAMT ABOUT NEW PHOENIX SINCE WE VISITED.
WELCOME TO NEW PHOENIX
IT WAS NICE TO GO HOME.
TO HAVE THAT MOMENT...
WELCOME TO NEW PHOENIX
AND IT'S GOOD TO SEE HER HAPPY TO BE HOME TOO.

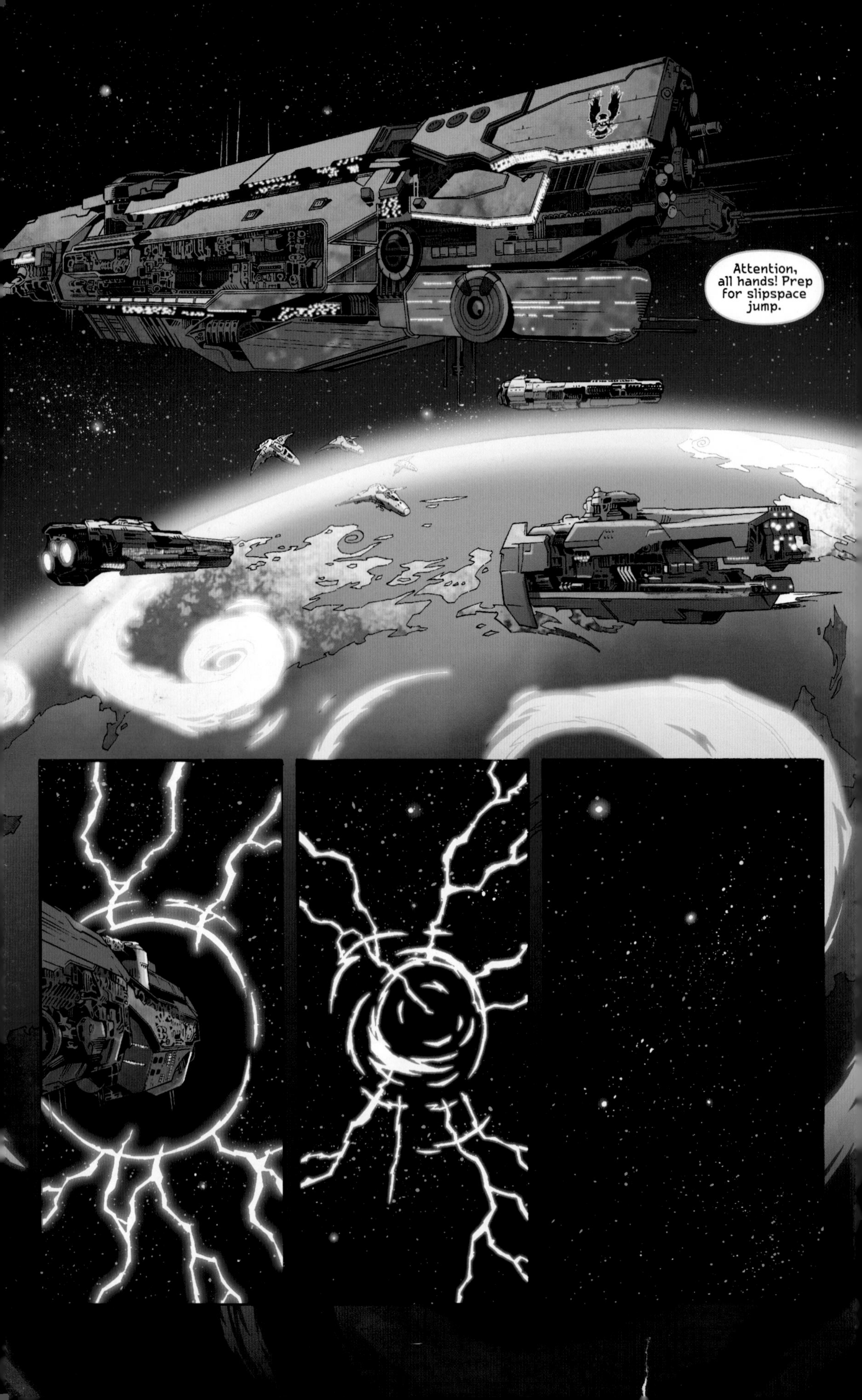
Attention, all hands! Prep for slipspace jump.

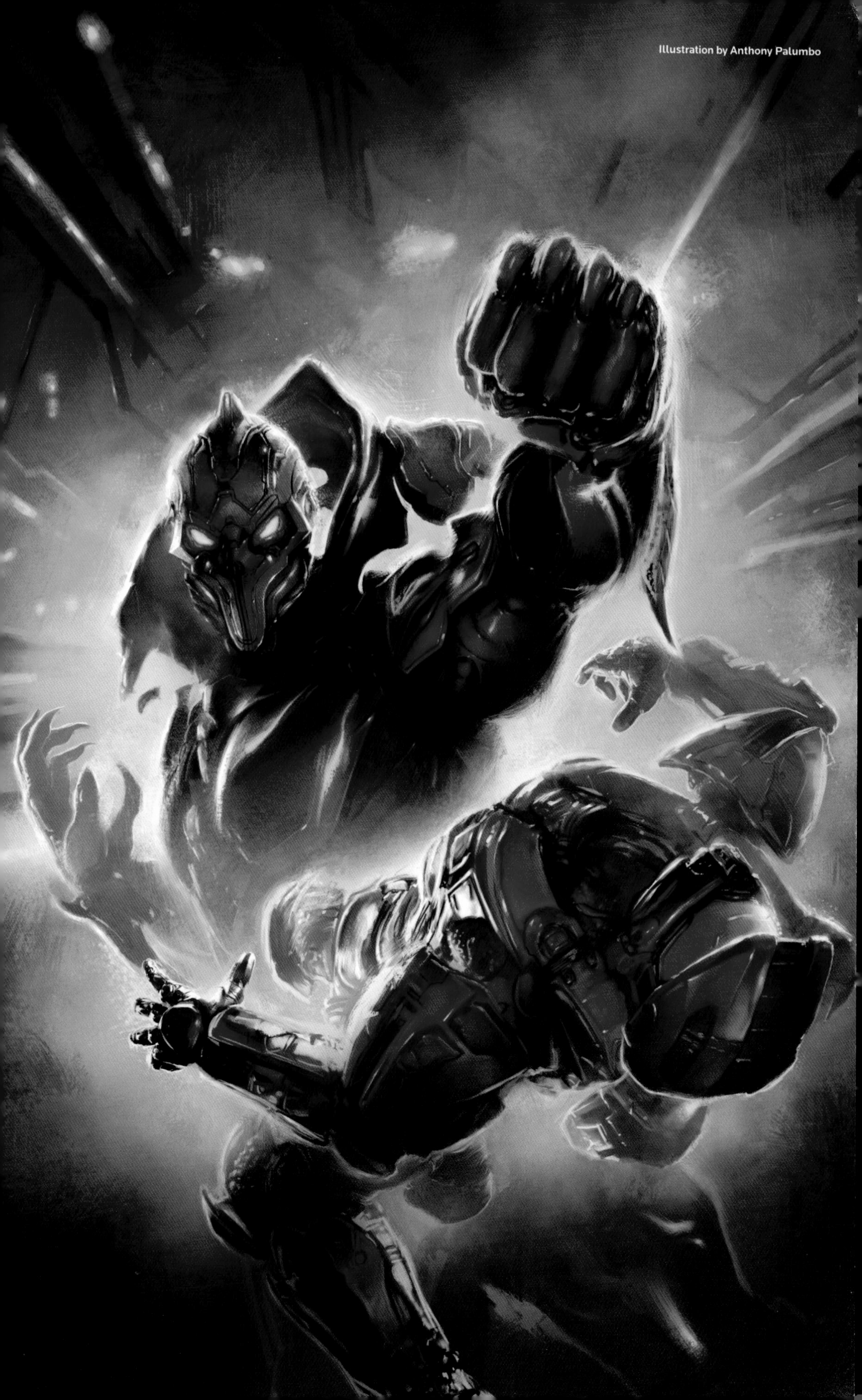

Illustration by Anthony Palumbo

Master Chief Petty Officer of the Navy, Spartan John-117, was adrift in space for the last four years before he was discovered by the UNSC *Infinity* on the surface of the Forerunner shield world Requiem . . .

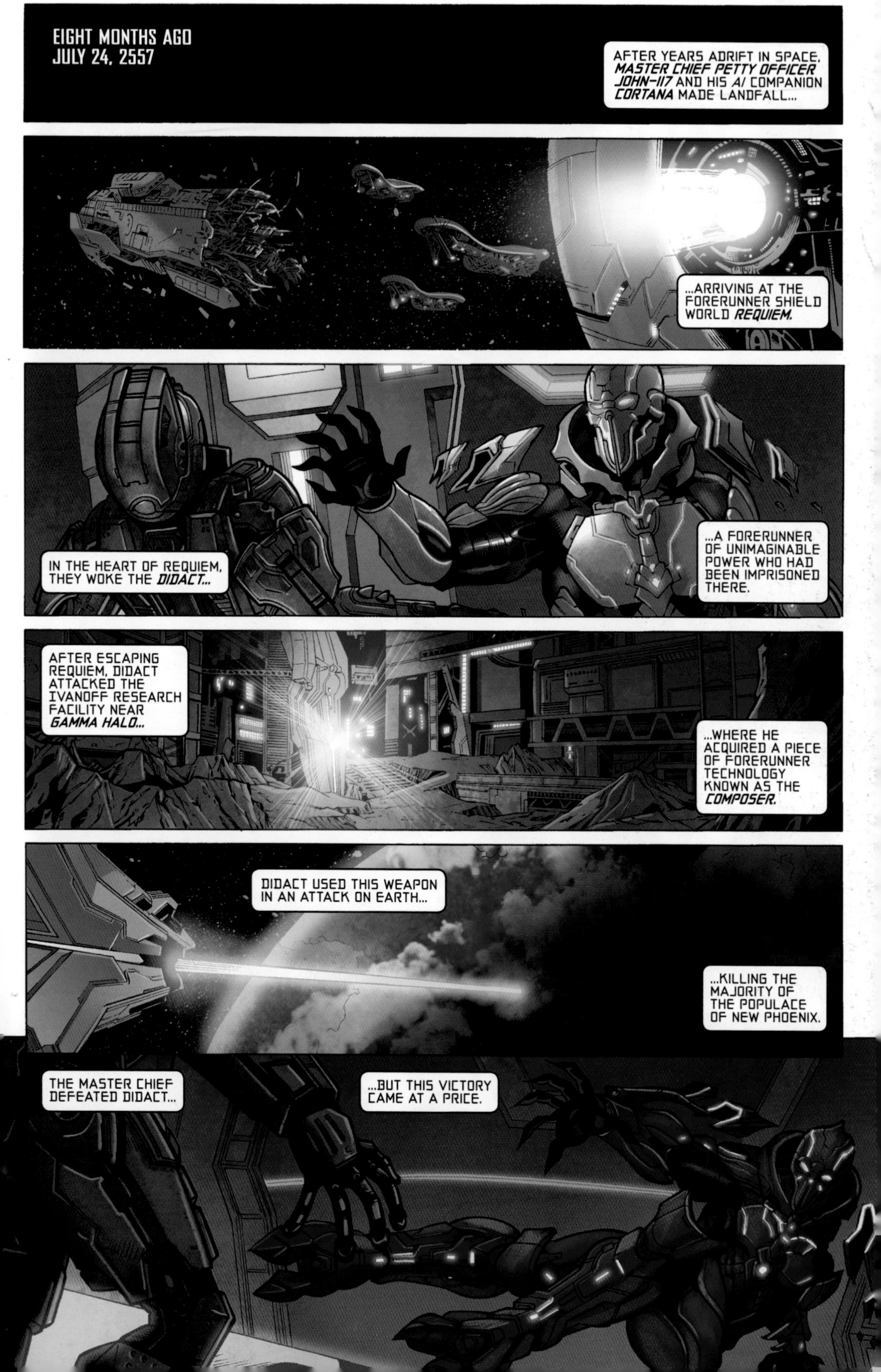
EIGHT MONTHS AGO
JULY 24, 2557
AFTER YEARS ADRIFT IN SPACE, MASTER CHIEF PETTY OFFICER JOHN-117 AND HIS AI COMPANION CORTANA MADE LANDFALL...
...ARRIVING AT THE FORERUNNER SHIELD WORLD REQUIEM.
IN THE HEART OF REQUIEM, THEY WOKE THE DIDACT...
...A FORERUNNER OF UNIMAGINABLE POWER WHO HAD BEEN IMPRISONED THERE.
AFTER ESCAPING REQUIEM, DIDACT ATTACKED THE IVANOFF RESEARCH FACILITY NEAR GAMMA HALO...
...WHERE HE ACQUIRED A PIECE OF FORERUNNER TECHNOLOGY KNOWN AS THE COMPOSER.
DIDACT USED THIS WEAPON IN AN ATTACK ON EARTH...
...KILLING THE MAJORITY OF THE POPULACE OF NEW PHOENIX.
THE MASTER CHIEF DEFEATED DIDACT...
...BUT THIS VICTORY CAME AT A PRICE.

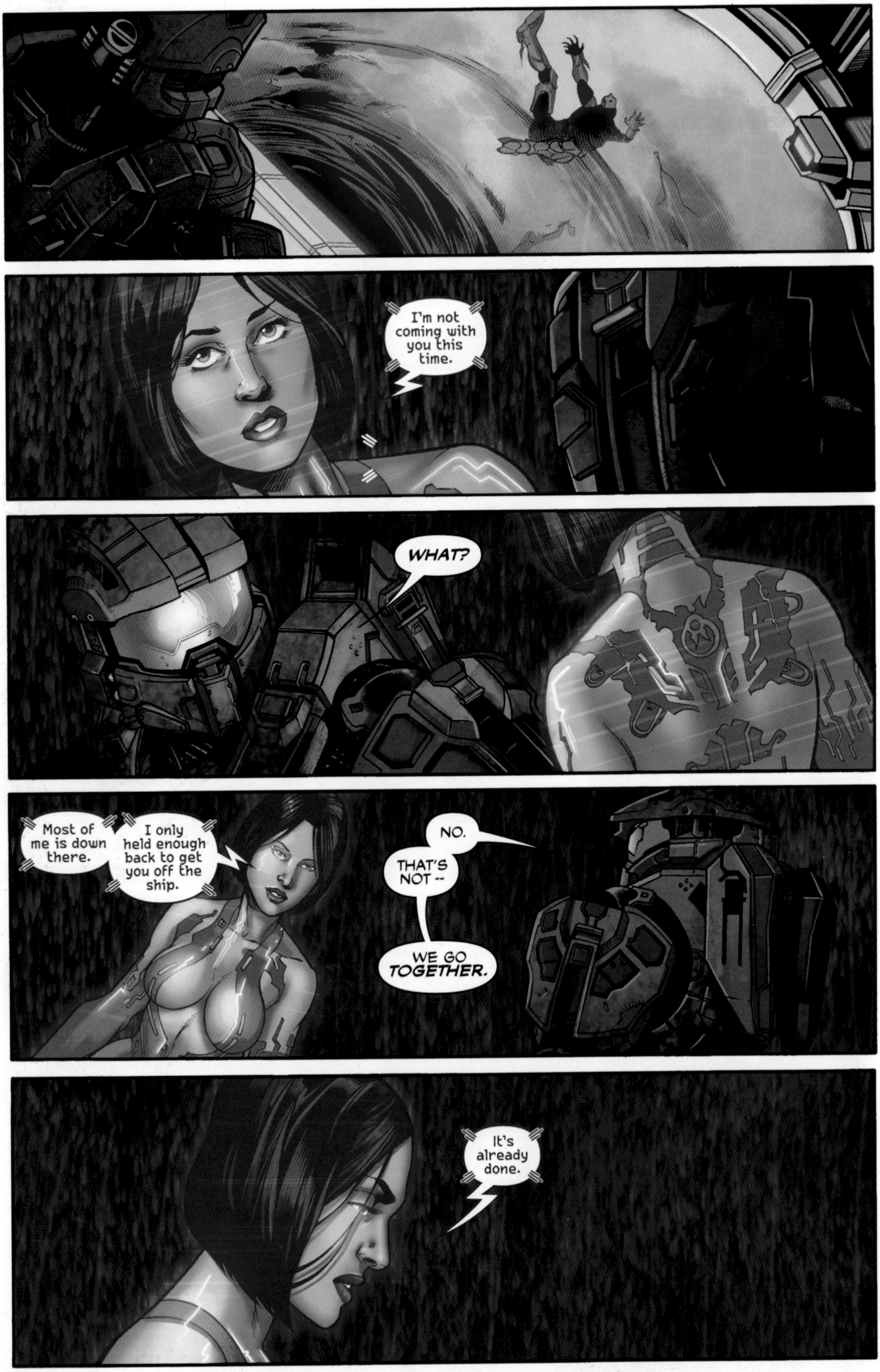
I'm not coming with you this time.
WHAT?
Most of me is down there.
I only held enough back to get you off the ship.
NO.
THAT'S NOT --
WE GO TOGETHER.
It's already done.

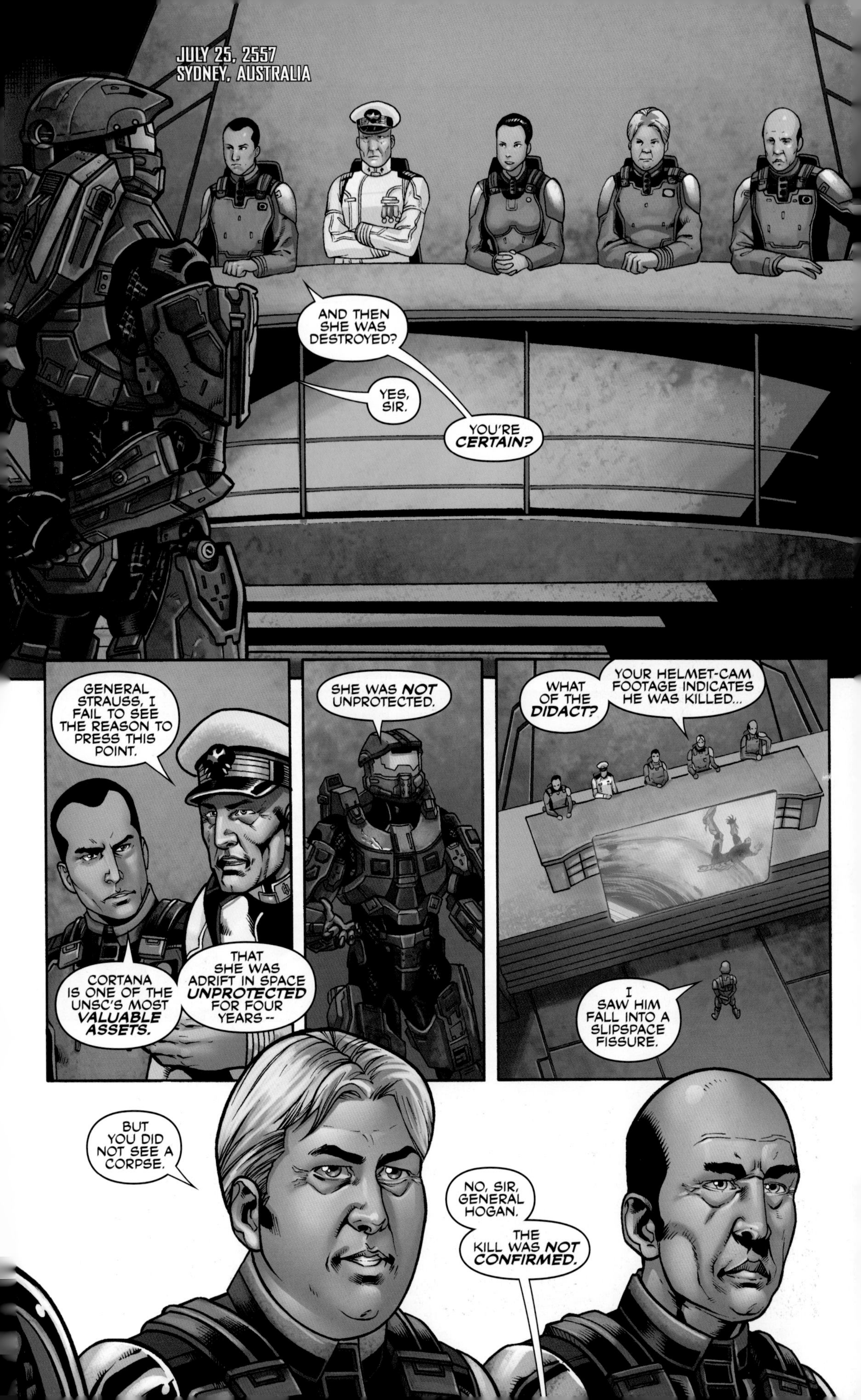
JULY 25, 2557
SYDNEY, AUSTRALIA
AND THEN SHE WAS DESTROYED?
YES, SIR.
YOU'RE *CERTAIN?*
GENERAL STRAUSS, I FAIL TO SEE THE REASON TO PRESS THIS POINT.
CORTANA IS ONE OF THE UNSC'S MOST *VALUABLE ASSETS.*
THAT SHE WAS ADRIFT IN SPACE *UNPROTECTED* FOR FOUR YEARS --
SHE WAS *NOT* UNPROTECTED.
WHAT OF THE *DIDACT?*
YOUR HELMET-CAM FOOTAGE INDICATES HE WAS KILLED...
I SAW HIM FALL INTO A SLIPSPACE FISSURE.
BUT YOU DID NOT SEE A CORPSE.
NO, SIR, GENERAL HOGAN.
THE KILL WAS *NOT CONFIRMED.*

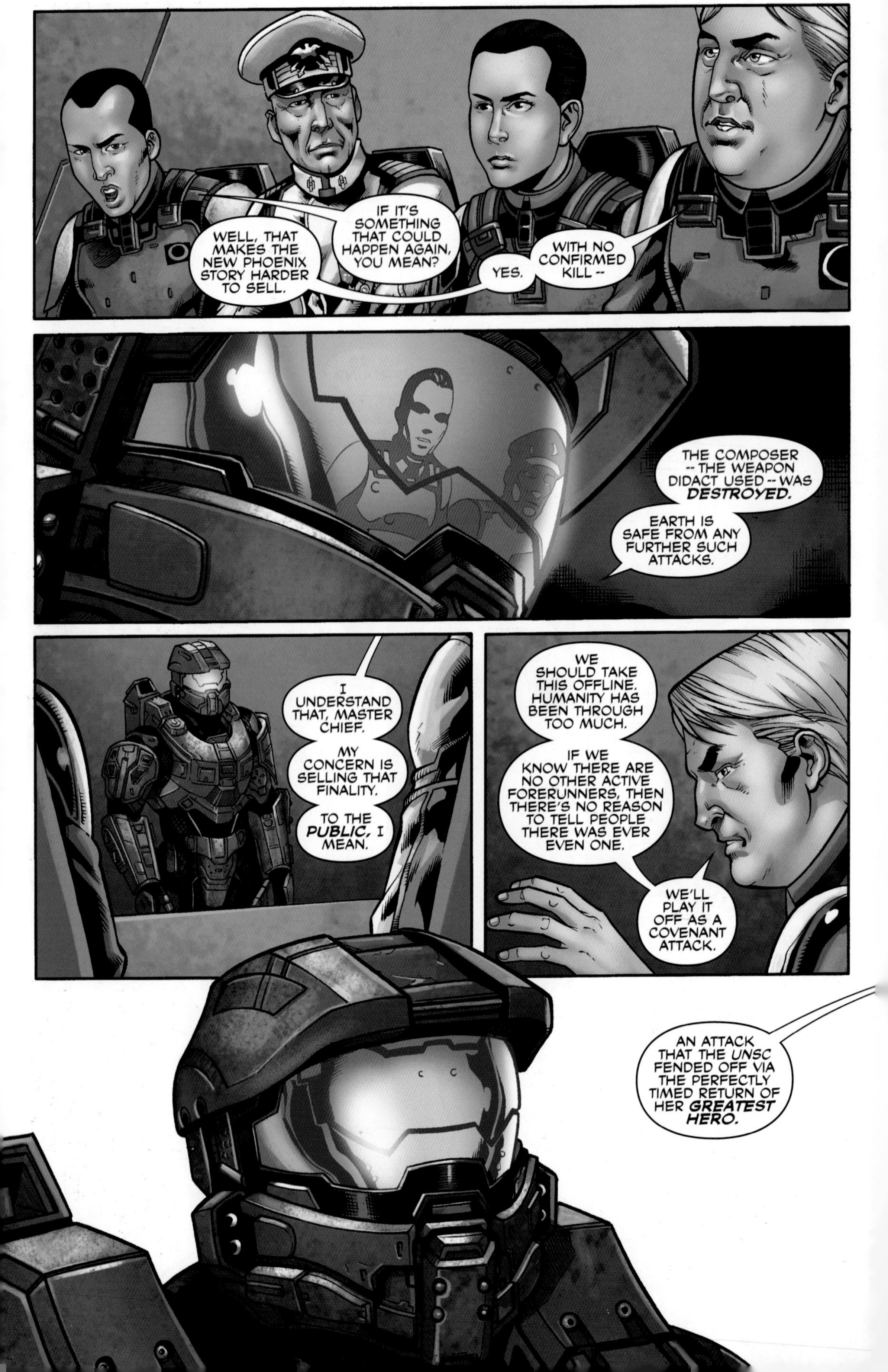
WELL, THAT MAKES THE NEW PHOENIX STORY HARDER TO SELL.
IF IT'S SOMETHING THAT COULD HAPPEN AGAIN, YOU MEAN?
YES.
WITH NO CONFIRMED KILL --
THE COMPOSER -- THE WEAPON DIDACT USED -- WAS *DESTROYED.*
EARTH IS SAFE FROM ANY FURTHER SUCH ATTACKS.
I UNDERSTAND THAT, MASTER CHIEF.
MY CONCERN IS SELLING THAT FINALITY.
TO THE *PUBLIC,* I MEAN.
WE SHOULD TAKE THIS OFFLINE. HUMANITY HAS BEEN THROUGH TOO MUCH.
IF WE KNOW THERE ARE NO OTHER ACTIVE FORERUNNERS, THEN THERE'S NO REASON TO TELL PEOPLE THERE WAS EVER EVEN ONE.
WE'LL PLAY IT OFF AS A COVENANT ATTACK.
AN ATTACK THAT THE *UNSC* FENDED OFF VIA THE PERFECTLY TIMED RETURN OF HER *GREATEST HERO.*

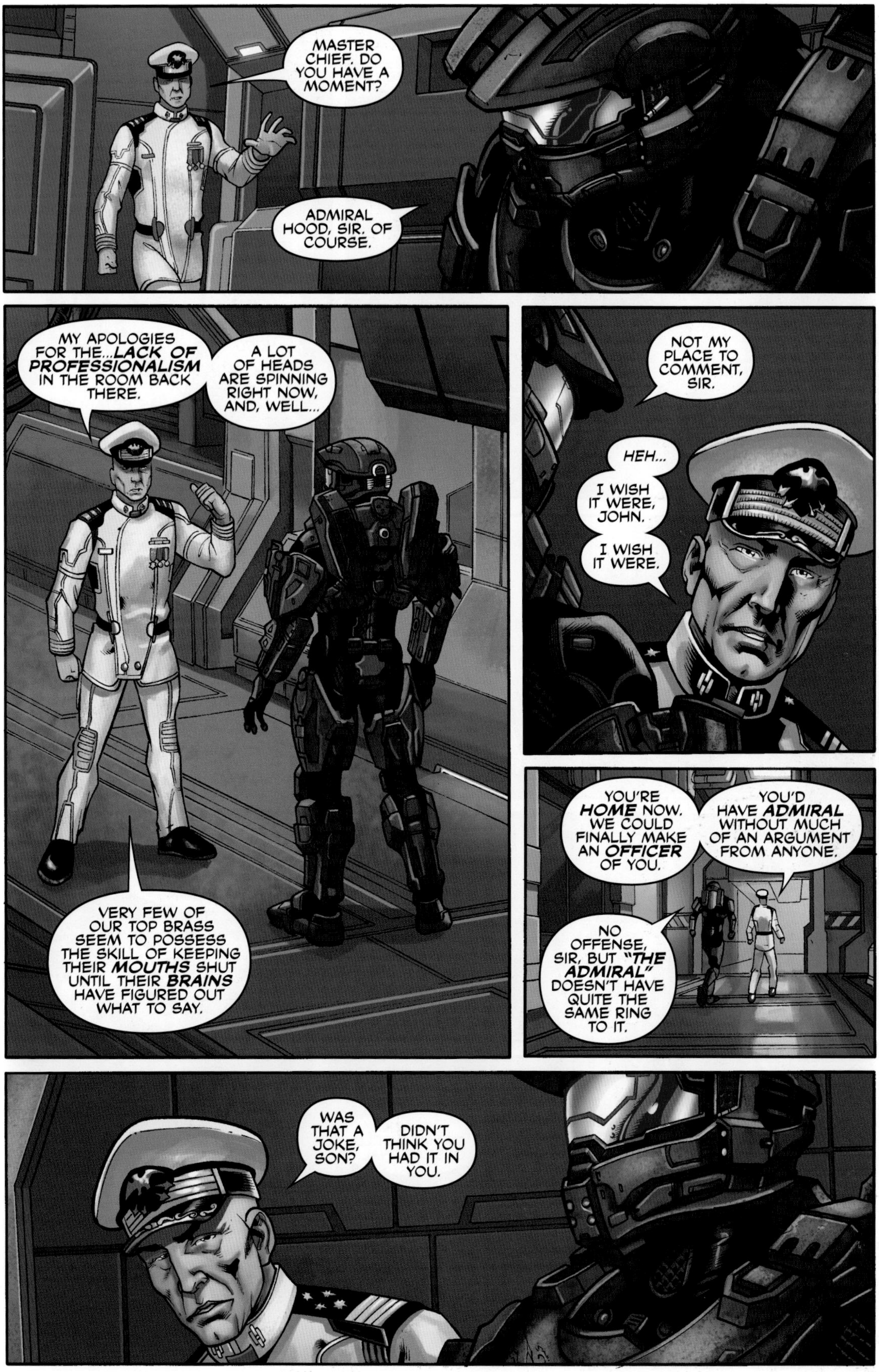
MASTER CHIEF. DO YOU HAVE A MOMENT?
ADMIRAL HOOD, SIR. OF COURSE.
MY APOLOGIES FOR THE...LACK OF PROFESSIONALISM IN THE ROOM BACK THERE.
A LOT OF HEADS ARE SPINNING RIGHT NOW, AND, WELL...
VERY FEW OF OUR TOP BRASS SEEM TO POSSESS THE SKILL OF KEEPING THEIR MOUTHS SHUT UNTIL THEIR BRAINS HAVE FIGURED OUT WHAT TO SAY.
NOT MY PLACE TO COMMENT, SIR.
HEH...
I WISH IT WERE, JOHN.
I WISH IT WERE.
YOU'RE HOME NOW. WE COULD FINALLY MAKE AN OFFICER OF YOU.
YOU'D HAVE ADMIRAL WITHOUT MUCH OF AN ARGUMENT FROM ANYONE.
NO OFFENSE, SIR, BUT "THE ADMIRAL" DOESN'T HAVE QUITE THE SAME RING TO IT.
WAS THAT A JOKE, SON?
DIDN'T THINK YOU HAD IT IN YOU.

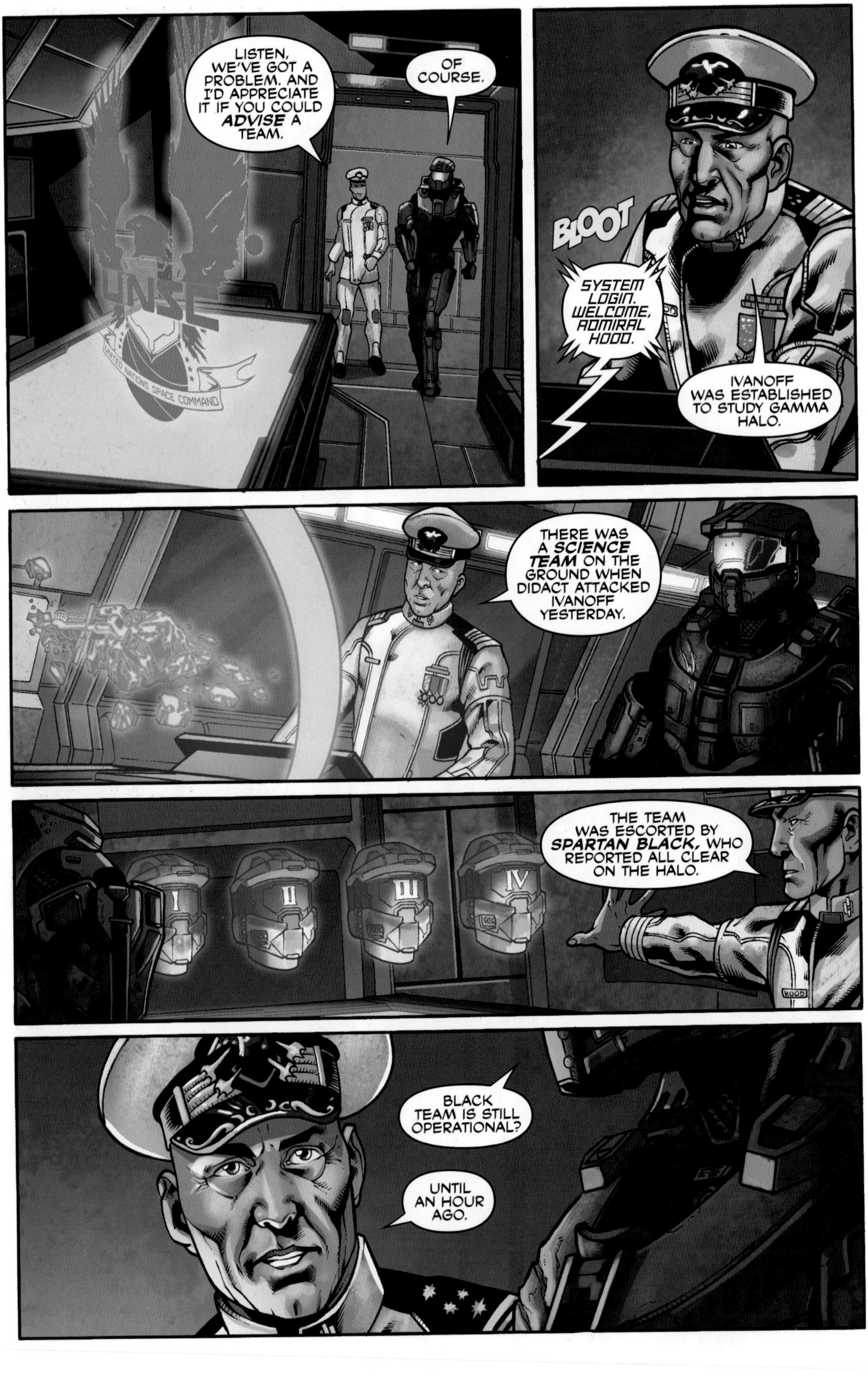
LISTEN, WE'VE GOT A PROBLEM. AND I'D APPRECIATE IT IF YOU COULD ADVISE A TEAM.
OF COURSE.
UNITED NATIONS SPACE COMMAND
BLOOT
SYSTEM LOGIN. WELCOME, ADMIRAL HOOD.
IVANOFF WAS ESTABLISHED TO STUDY GAMMA HALO.
THERE WAS A SCIENCE TEAM ON THE GROUND WHEN DIDACT ATTACKED IVANOFF YESTERDAY.
THE TEAM WAS ESCORTED BY SPARTAN BLACK, WHO REPORTED ALL CLEAR ON THE HALO.
HOOD
BLACK TEAM IS STILL OPERATIONAL?
UNTIL AN HOUR AGO.

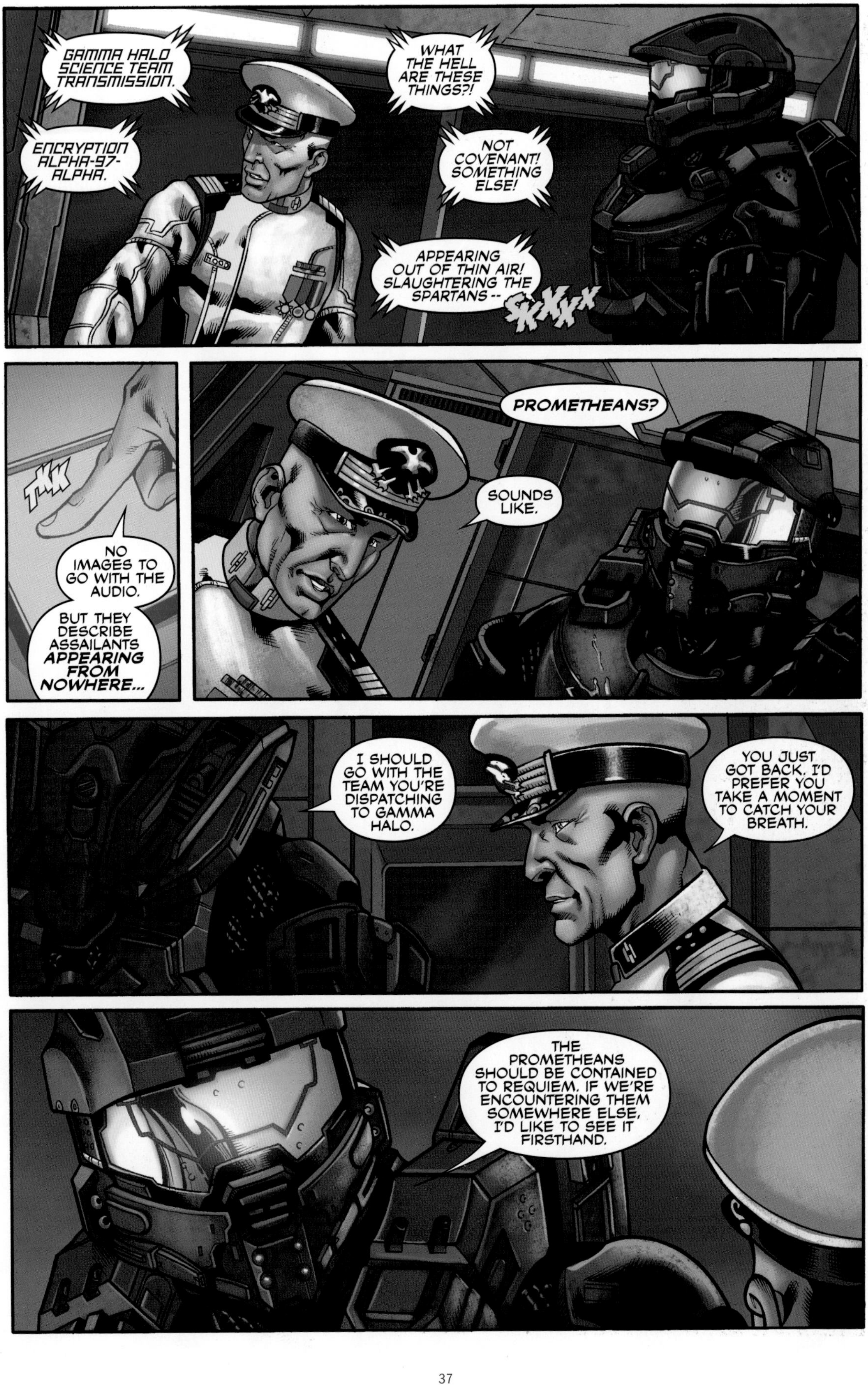
GAMMA HALO SCIENCE TEAM TRANSMISSION.
ENCRYPTION ALPHA-97-ALPHA.
WHAT THE HELL ARE THESE THINGS?!
NOT COVENANT! SOMETHING ELSE!
APPEARING OUT OF THIN AIR! SLAUGHTERING THE SPARTANS --
SKXXX
TKK
NO IMAGES TO GO WITH THE AUDIO.
BUT THEY DESCRIBE ASSAILANTS APPEARING FROM NOWHERE...
PROMETHEANS?
SOUNDS LIKE.
I SHOULD GO WITH THE TEAM YOU'RE DISPATCHING TO GAMMA HALO.
YOU JUST GOT BACK. I'D PREFER YOU TAKE A MOMENT TO CATCH YOUR BREATH.
THE PROMETHEANS SHOULD BE CONTAINED TO REQUIEM. IF WE'RE ENCOUNTERING THEM SOMEWHERE ELSE, I'D LIKE TO SEE IT FIRSTHAND.

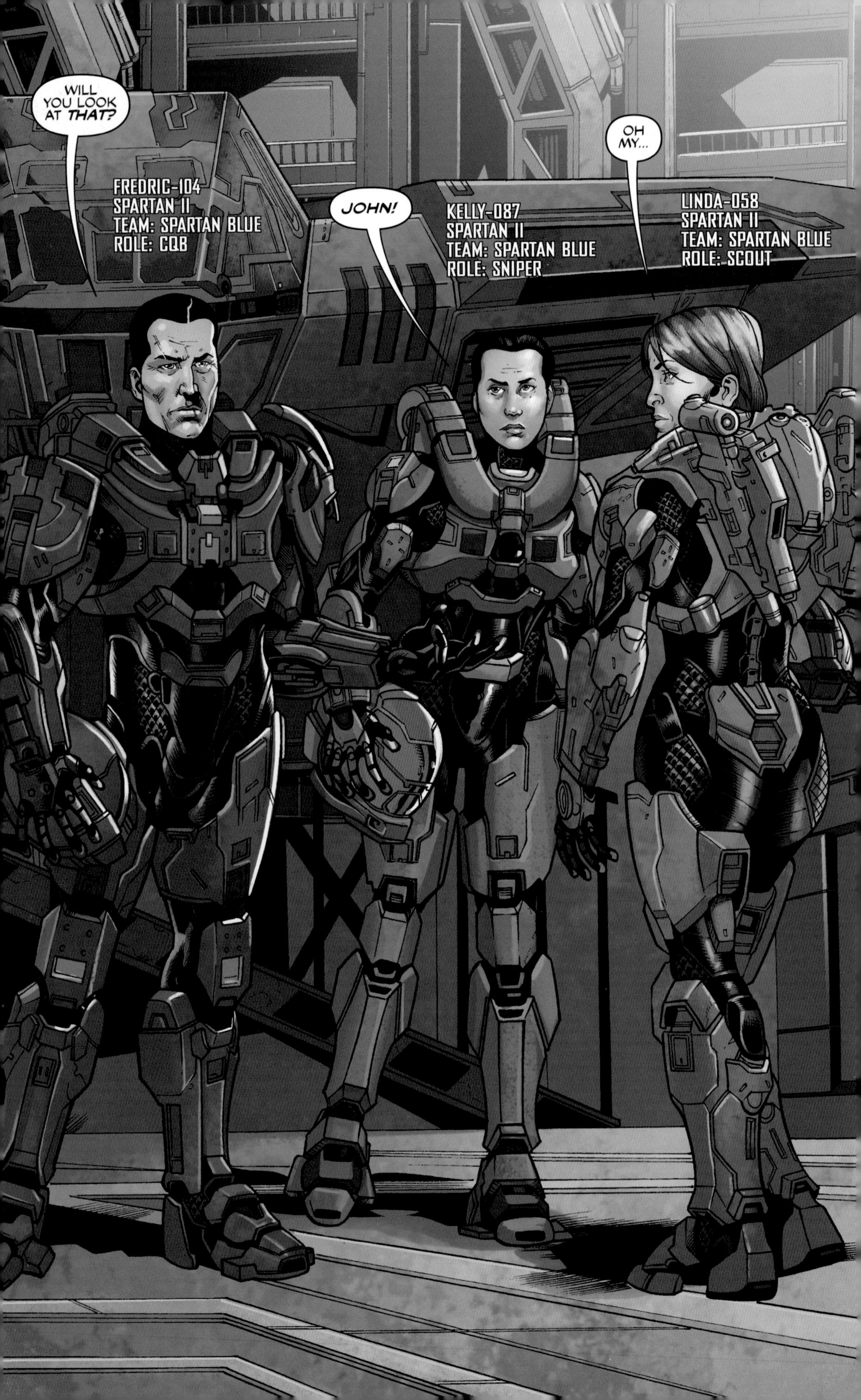
WILL YOU LOOK AT THAT?
FREDRIC-104
SPARTAN II
TEAM: SPARTAN BLUE
ROLE: CQB
JOHN!
KELLY-087
SPARTAN II
TEAM: SPARTAN BLUE
ROLE: SNIPER
OH MY...
LINDA-058
SPARTAN II
TEAM: SPARTAN BLUE
ROLE: SCOUT

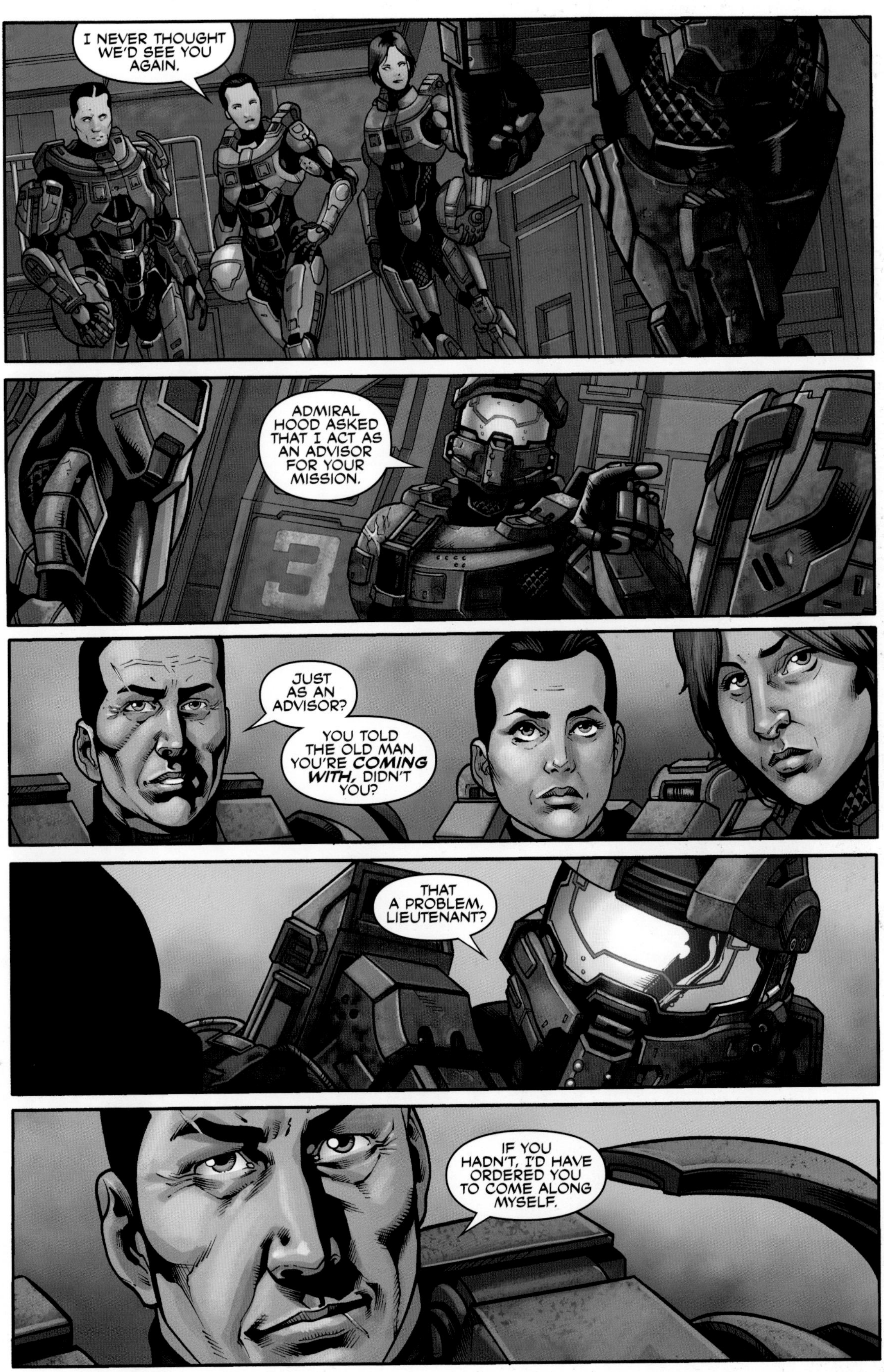
I NEVER THOUGHT WE'D SEE YOU AGAIN.
ADMIRAL HOOD ASKED THAT I ACT AS AN ADVISOR FOR YOUR MISSION.
JUST AS AN ADVISOR?
YOU TOLD THE OLD MAN YOU'RE ***COMING WITH,*** DIDN'T YOU?
THAT A PROBLEM, LIEUTENANT?
IF YOU HADN'T, I'D HAVE ORDERED YOU TO COME ALONG MYSELF.

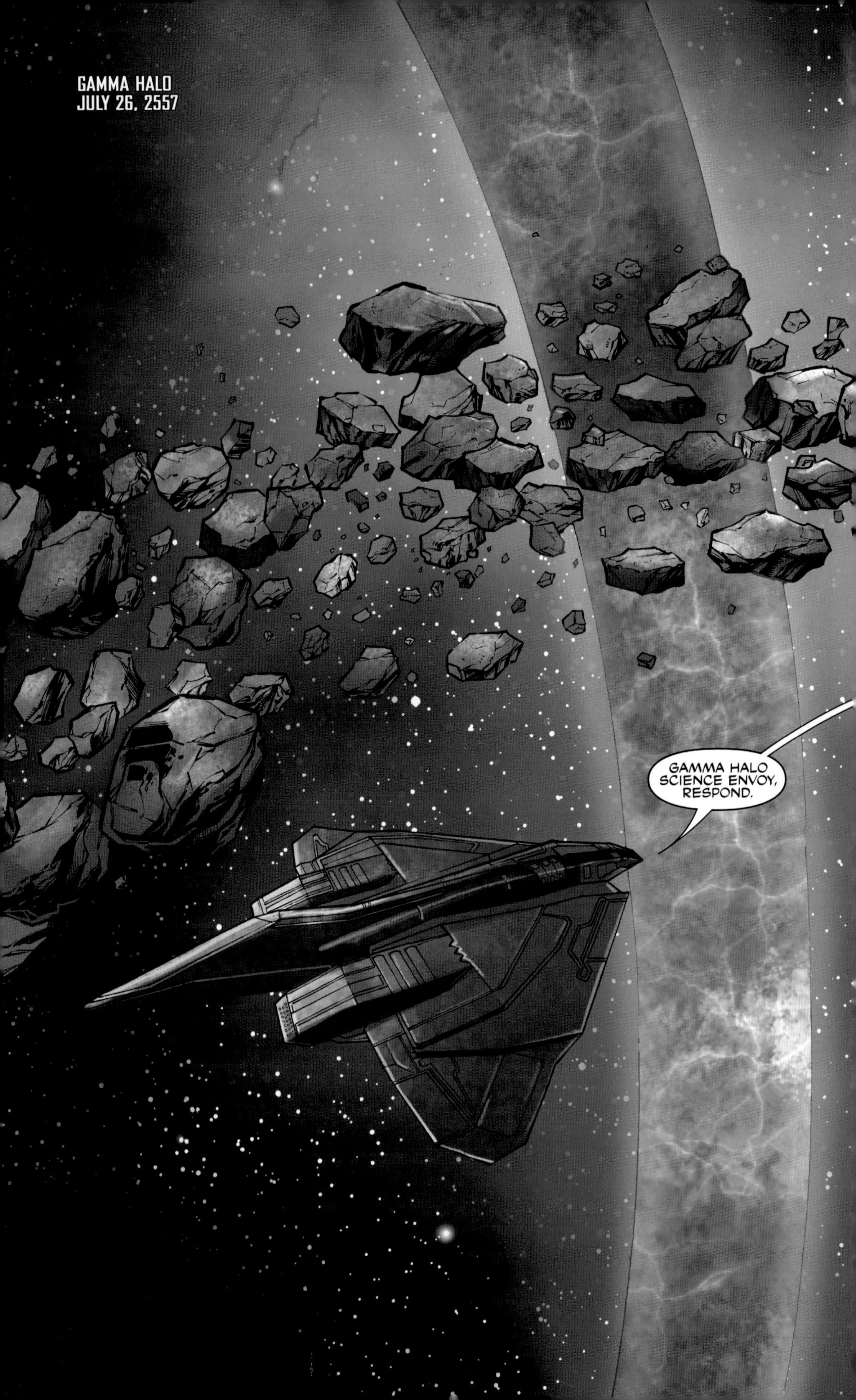
GAMMA HALO
JULY 26, 2557
GAMMA HALO SCIENCE ENVOY, RESPOND.

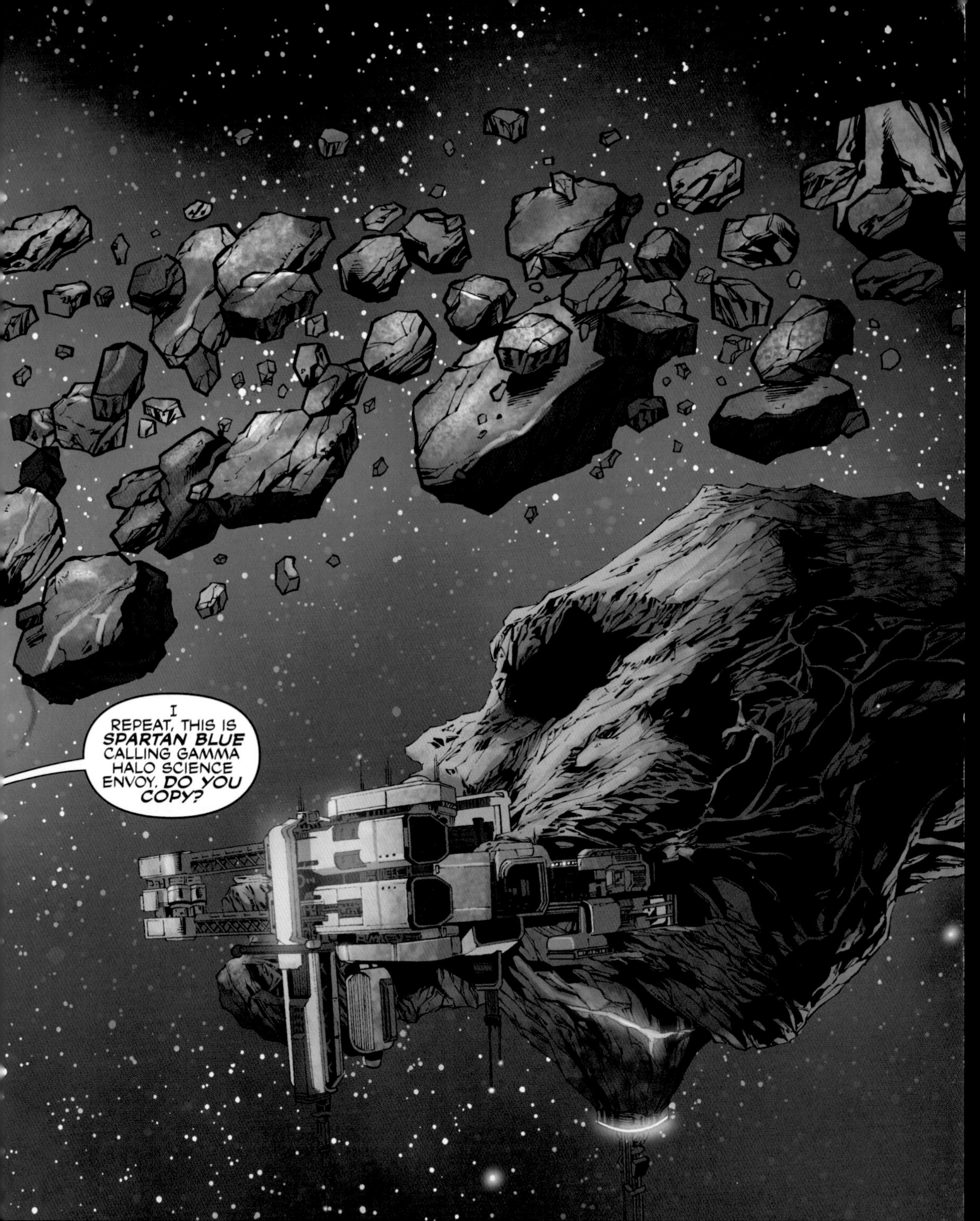
I REPEAT, THIS IS SPARTAN BLUE CALLING GAMMA HALO SCIENCE ENVOY. DO YOU COPY?

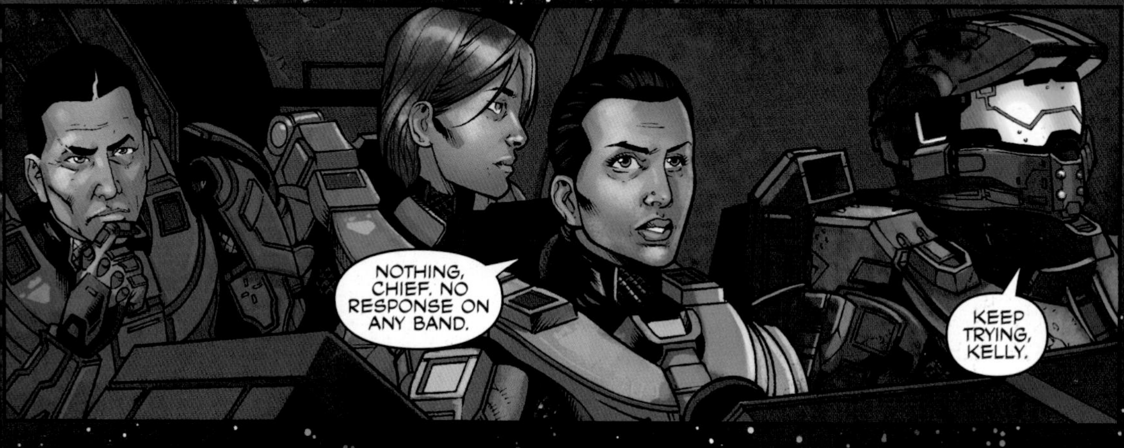
NOTHING, CHIEF. NO RESPONSE ON ANY BAND.
KEEP TRYING, KELLY.

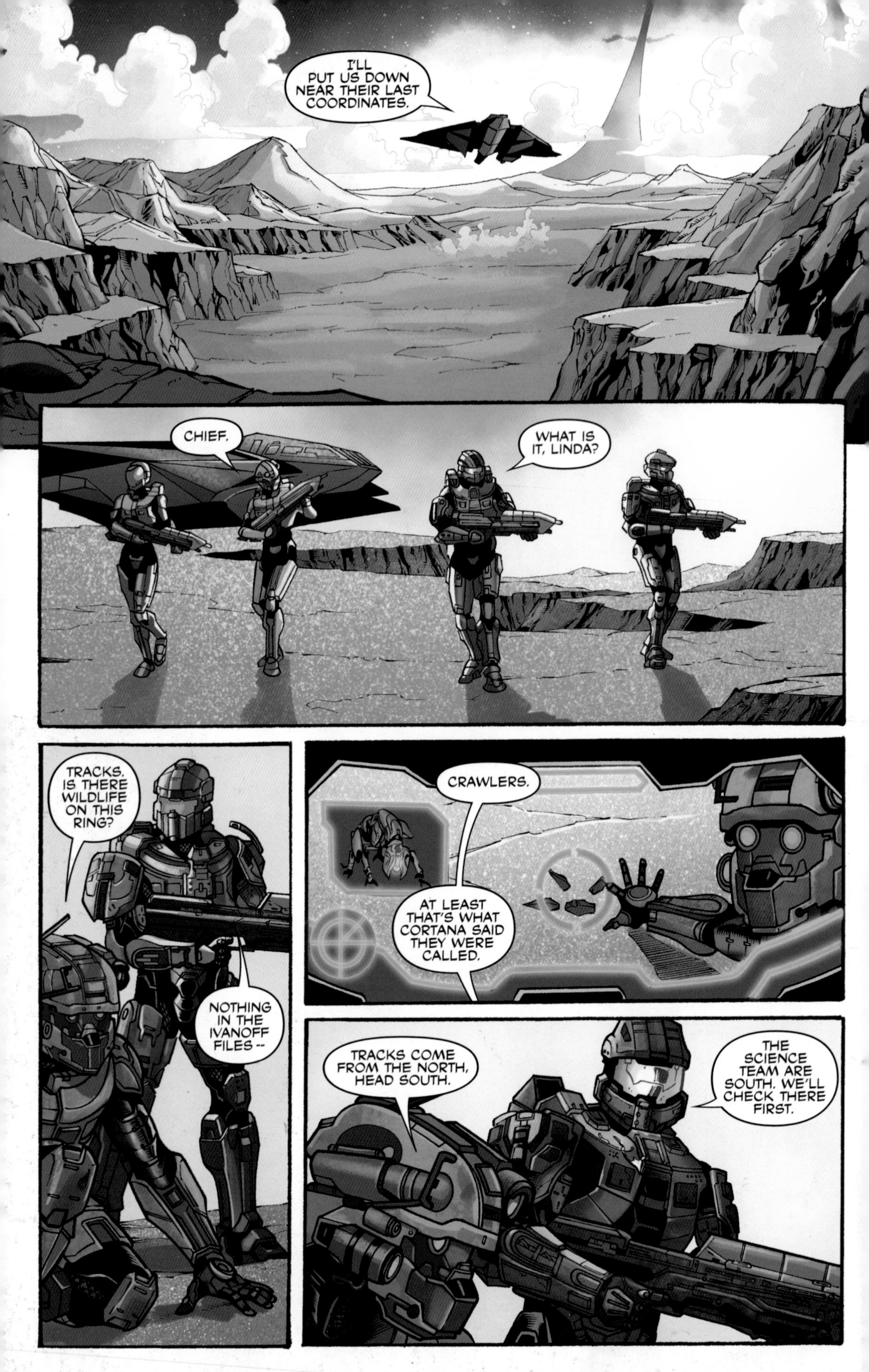
I'LL PUT US DOWN NEAR THEIR LAST COORDINATES.
CHIEF.
WHAT IS IT, LINDA?
TRACKS. IS THERE WILDLIFE ON THIS RING?
NOTHING IN THE IVANOFF FILES --
CRAWLERS.
AT LEAST THAT'S WHAT CORTANA SAID THEY WERE CALLED.
TRACKS COME FROM THE NORTH, HEAD SOUTH.
THE SCIENCE TEAM ARE SOUTH. WE'LL CHECK THERE FIRST.

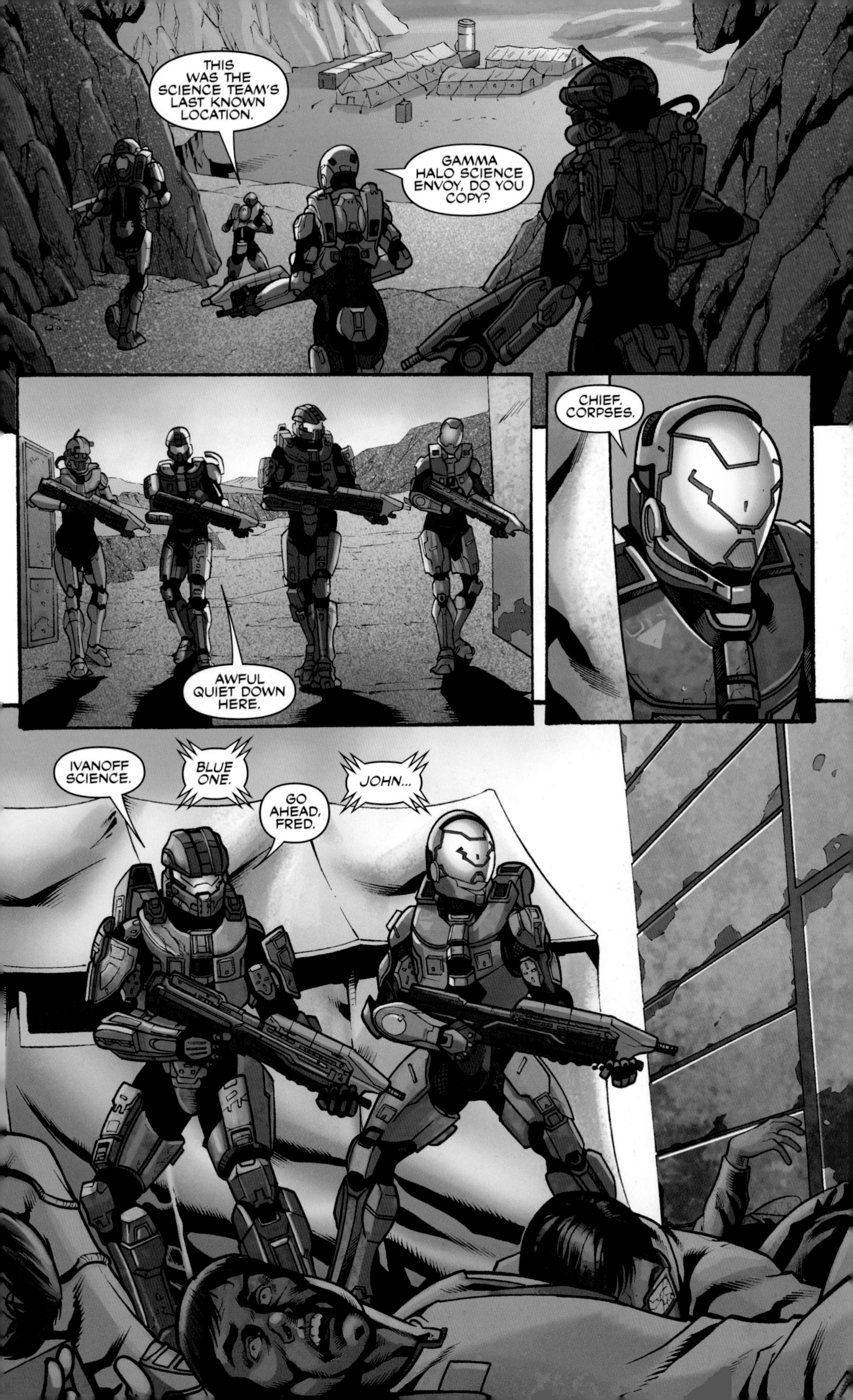
THIS WAS THE SCIENCE TEAM'S LAST KNOWN LOCATION.
GAMMA HALO SCIENCE ENVOY, DO YOU COPY?
AWFUL QUIET DOWN HERE.
CHIEF. CORPSES.
IVANOFF SCIENCE.
BLUE ONE.
GO AHEAD, FRED.
JOHN...

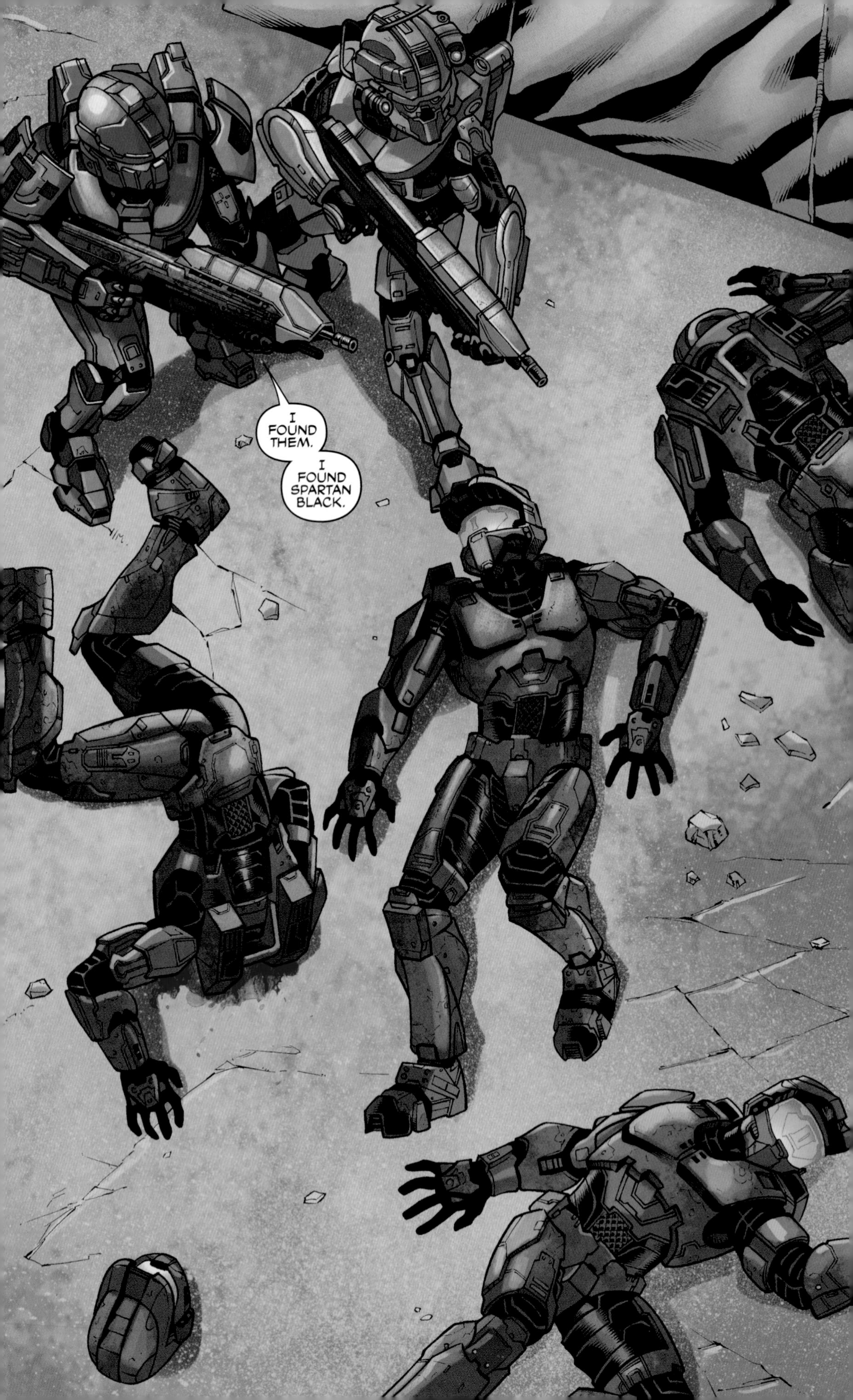
I FOUND THEM.
I FOUND SPARTAN BLACK.

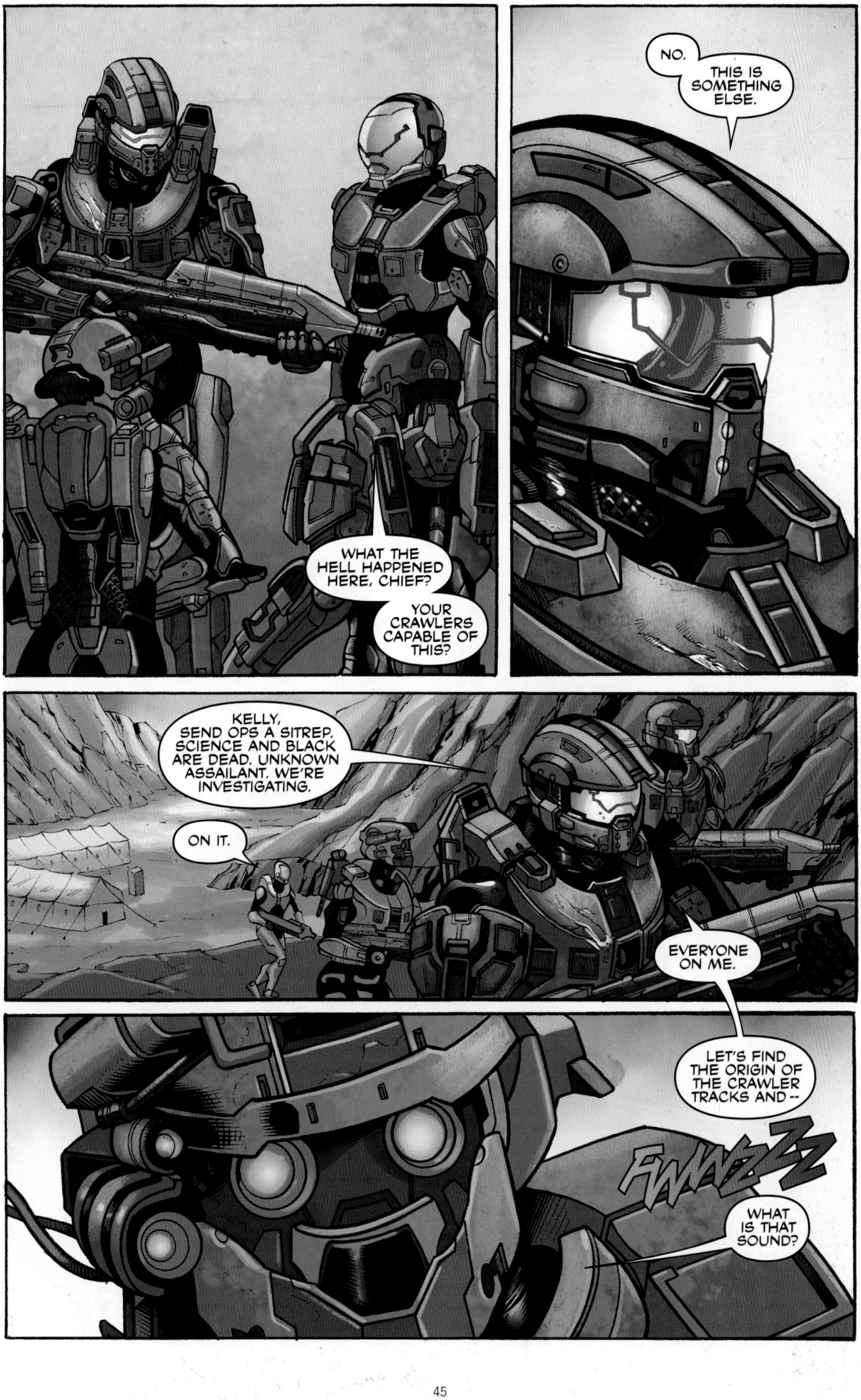
WHAT THE HELL HAPPENED HERE, CHIEF?
YOUR CRAWLERS CAPABLE OF THIS?
NO.
THIS IS SOMETHING ELSE.
KELLY, SEND OPS A SITREP. SCIENCE AND BLACK ARE DEAD. UNKNOWN ASSAILANT. WE'RE INVESTIGATING.
ON IT.
EVERYONE ON ME.
LET'S FIND THE ORIGIN OF THE CRAWLER TRACKS AND --
FWNNZZZ
WHAT IS THAT SOUND?

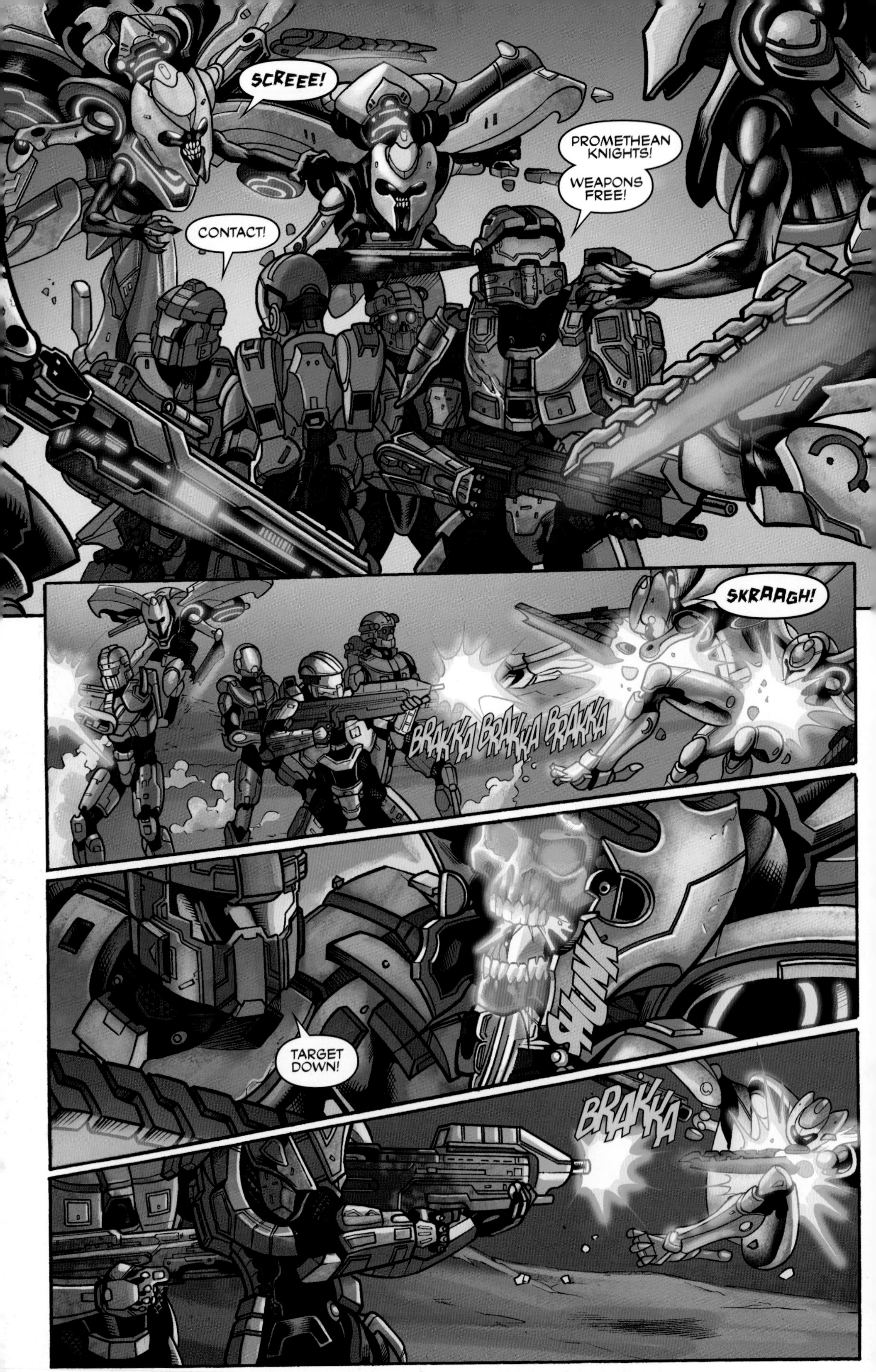
SCREEE!
PROMETHEAN KNIGHTS!
WEAPONS FREE!
CONTACT!
SKRAAGH!
BRAKKA BRAKKA BRAKKA
SHUNK
TARGET DOWN!
BRAKKA

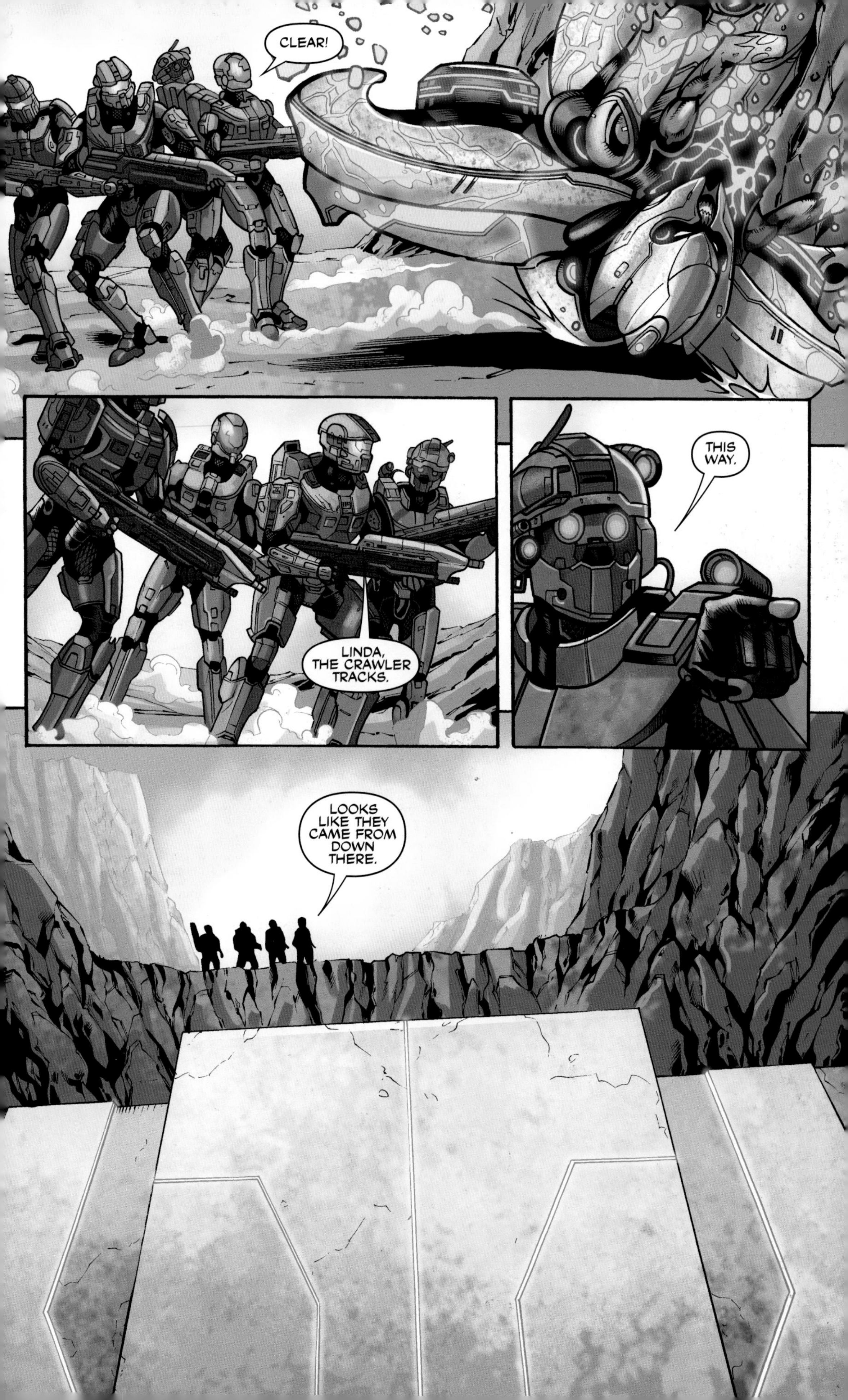
CLEAR!
LINDA, THE CRAWLER TRACKS.
THIS WAY.
LOOKS LIKE THEY CAME FROM DOWN THERE.

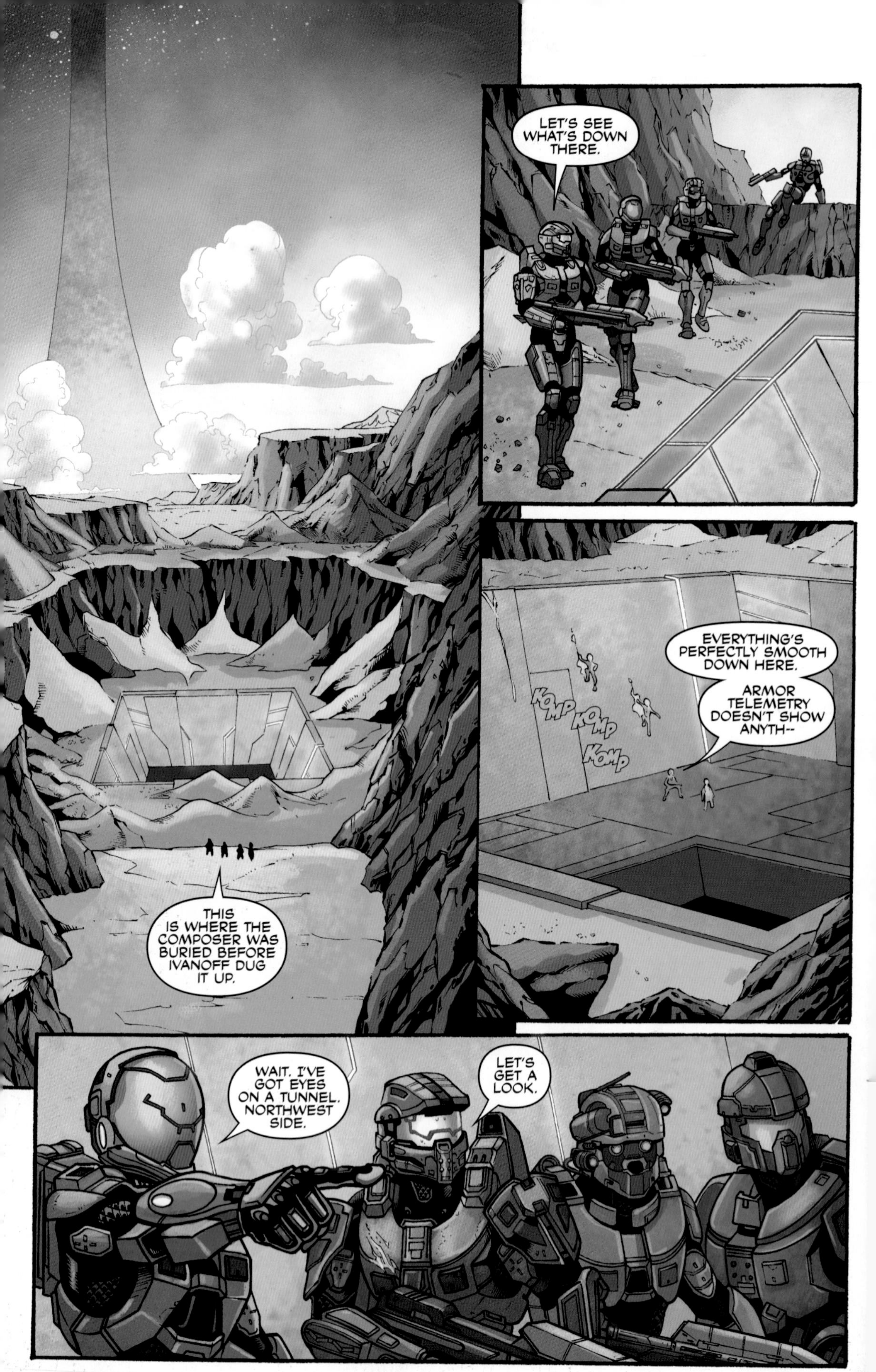
THIS IS WHERE THE COMPOSER WAS BURIED BEFORE IVANOFF DUG IT UP.
LET'S SEE WHAT'S DOWN THERE.
EVERYTHING'S PERFECTLY SMOOTH DOWN HERE.
ARMOR TELEMETRY DOESN'T SHOW ANYTH--
KOMP KOMP KOMP
WAIT. I'VE GOT EYES ON A TUNNEL. NORTHWEST SIDE.
LET'S GET A LOOK.

HRMMM...

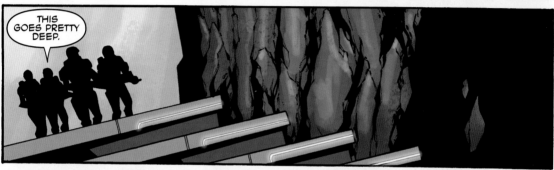

THIS GOES PRETTY DEEP.

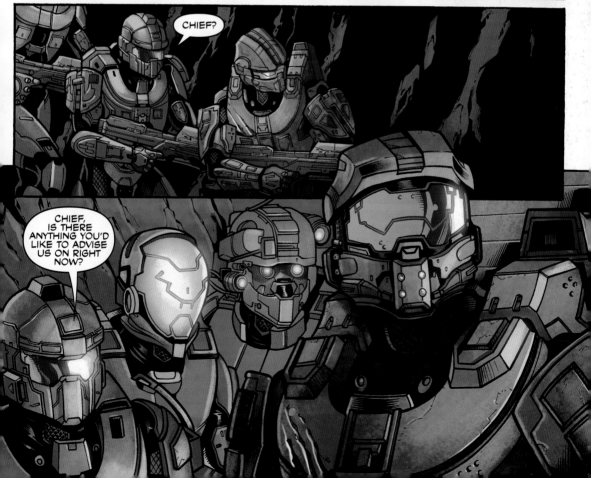

CHIEF?

CHIEF, IS THERE ANYTHING YOU'D LIKE TO ADVISE US ON RIGHT NOW?

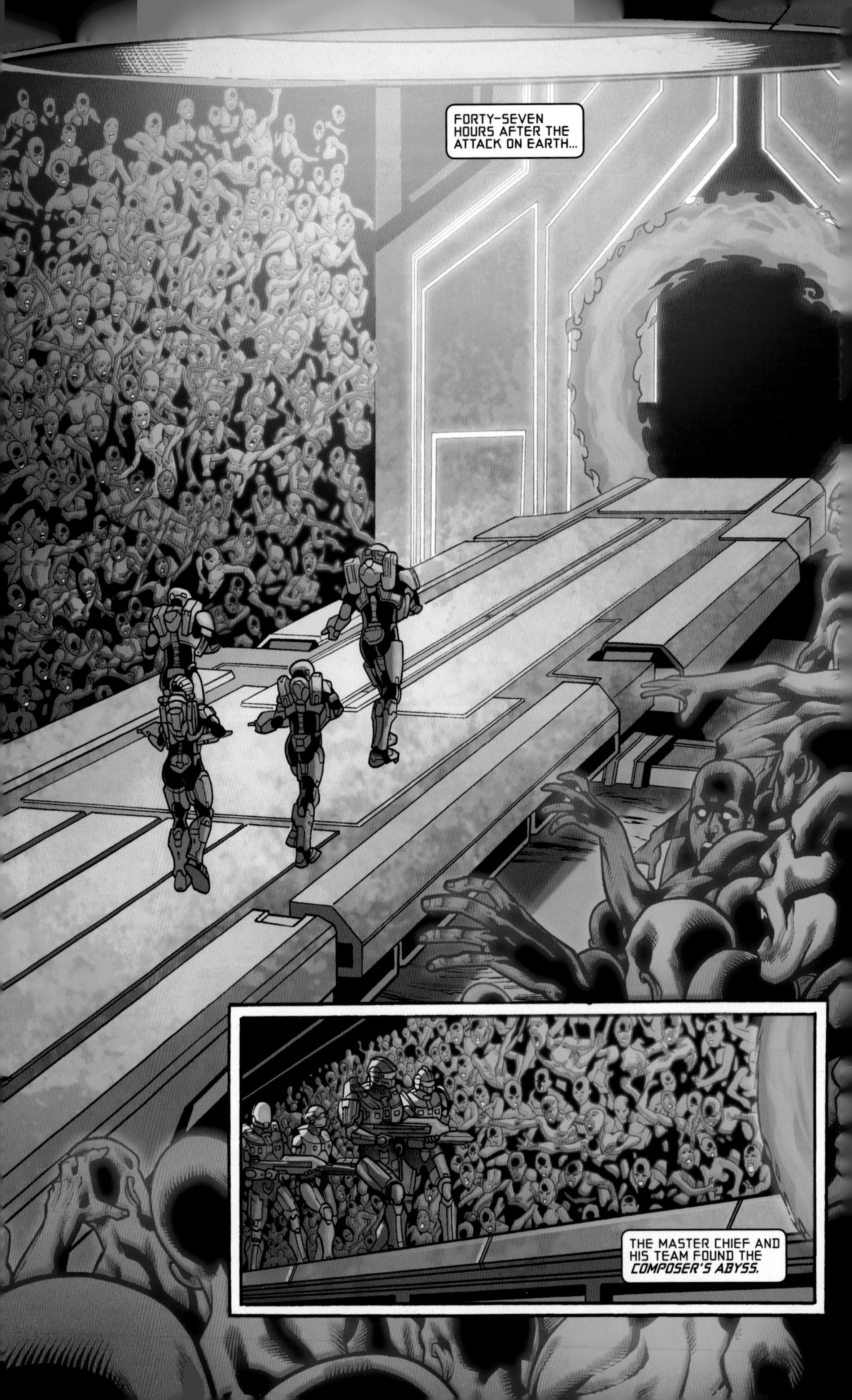
FORTY-SEVEN HOURS AFTER THE ATTACK ON EARTH...
THE MASTER CHIEF AND HIS TEAM FOUND THE *COMPOSER'S ABYSS.*

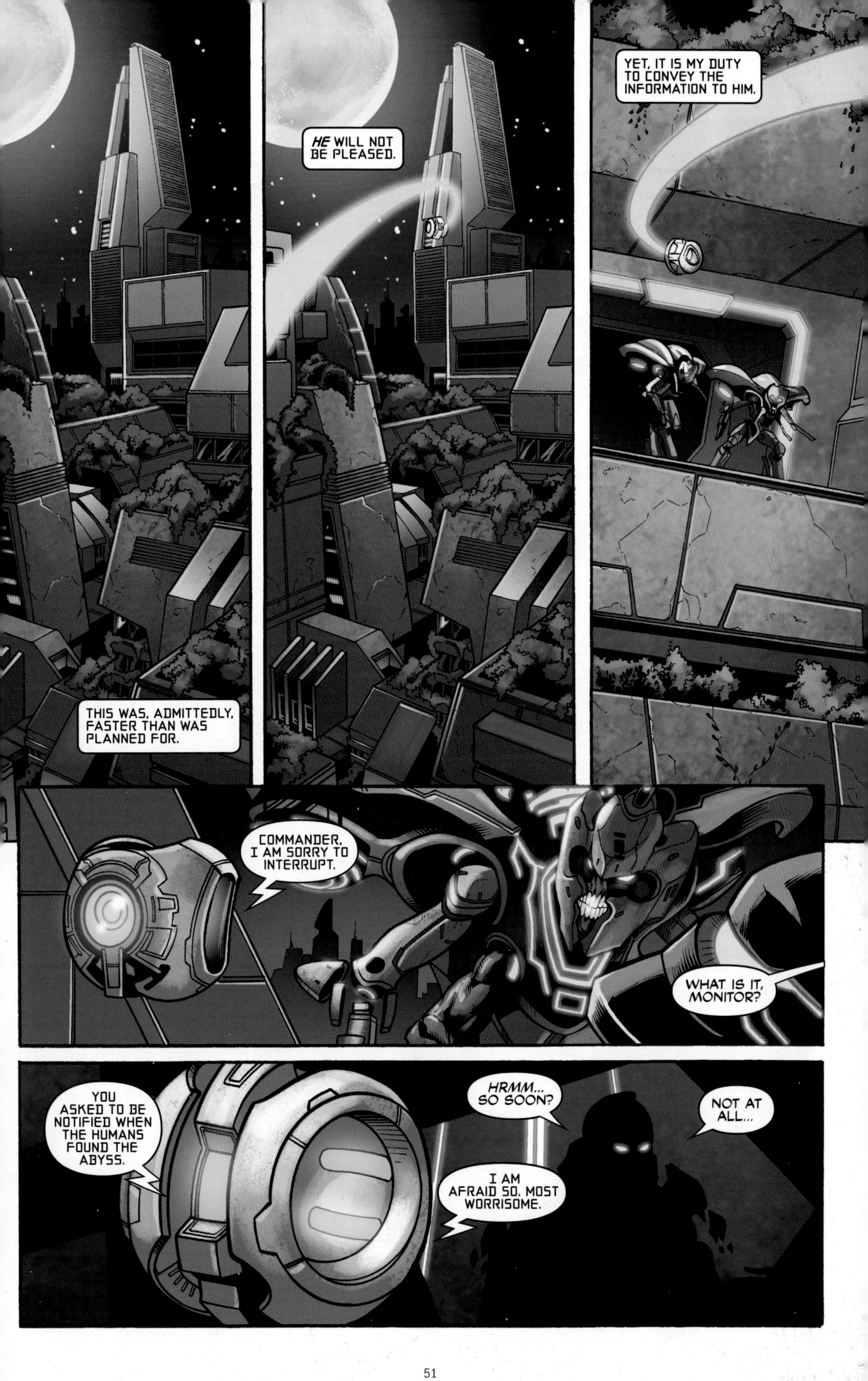
THIS WAS, ADMITTEDLY, FASTER THAN WAS PLANNED FOR.
HE WILL NOT BE PLEASED.
YET, IT IS MY DUTY TO CONVEY THE INFORMATION TO HIM.
COMMANDER, I AM SORRY TO INTERRUPT.
WHAT IS IT, MONITOR?
YOU ASKED TO BE NOTIFIED WHEN THE HUMANS FOUND THE ABYSS.
HRMM... SO SOON?
I AM AFRAID SO. MOST WORRISOME.
NOT AT ALL...

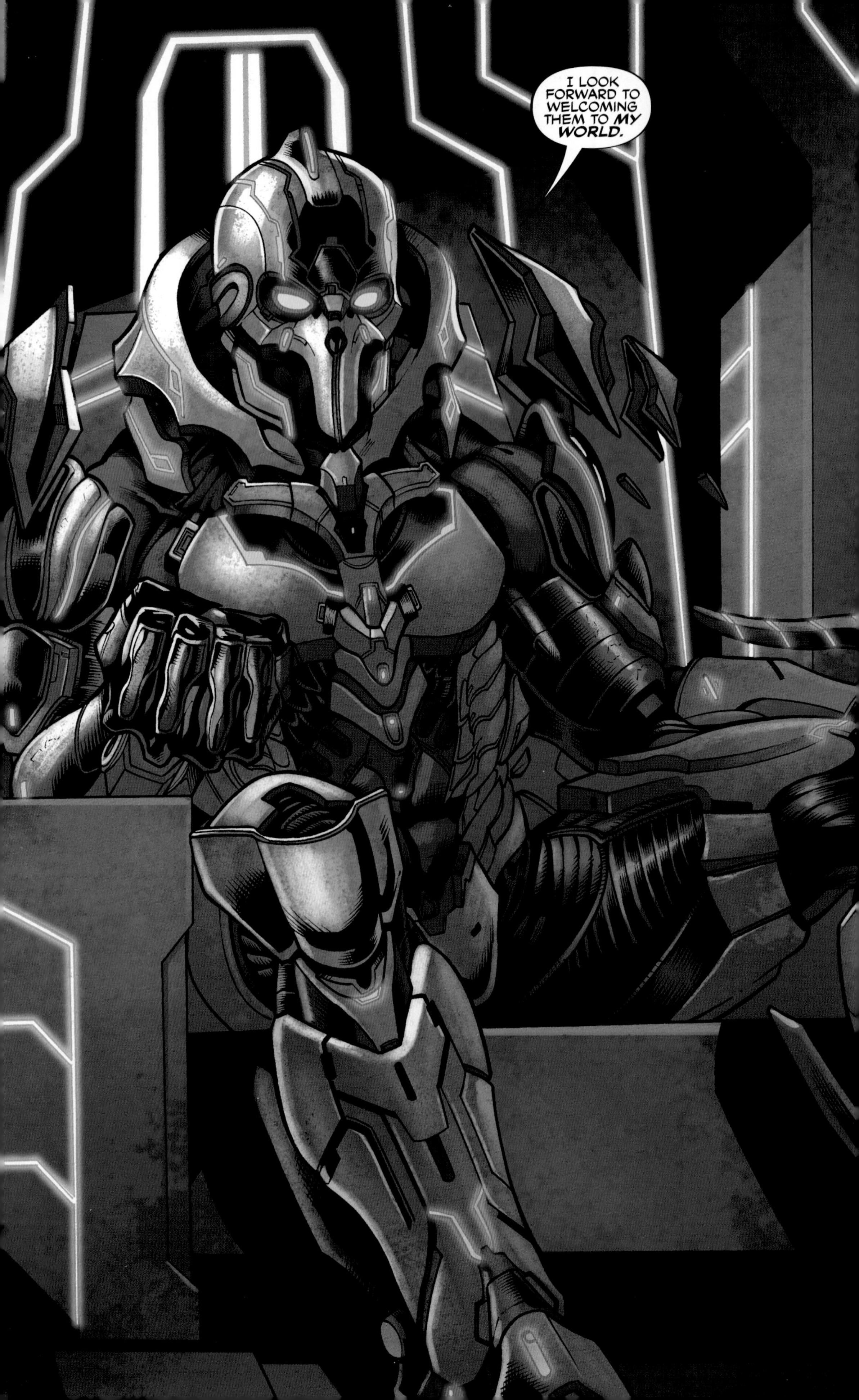
I LOOK FORWARD TO WELCOMING THEM TO *MY WORLD.*

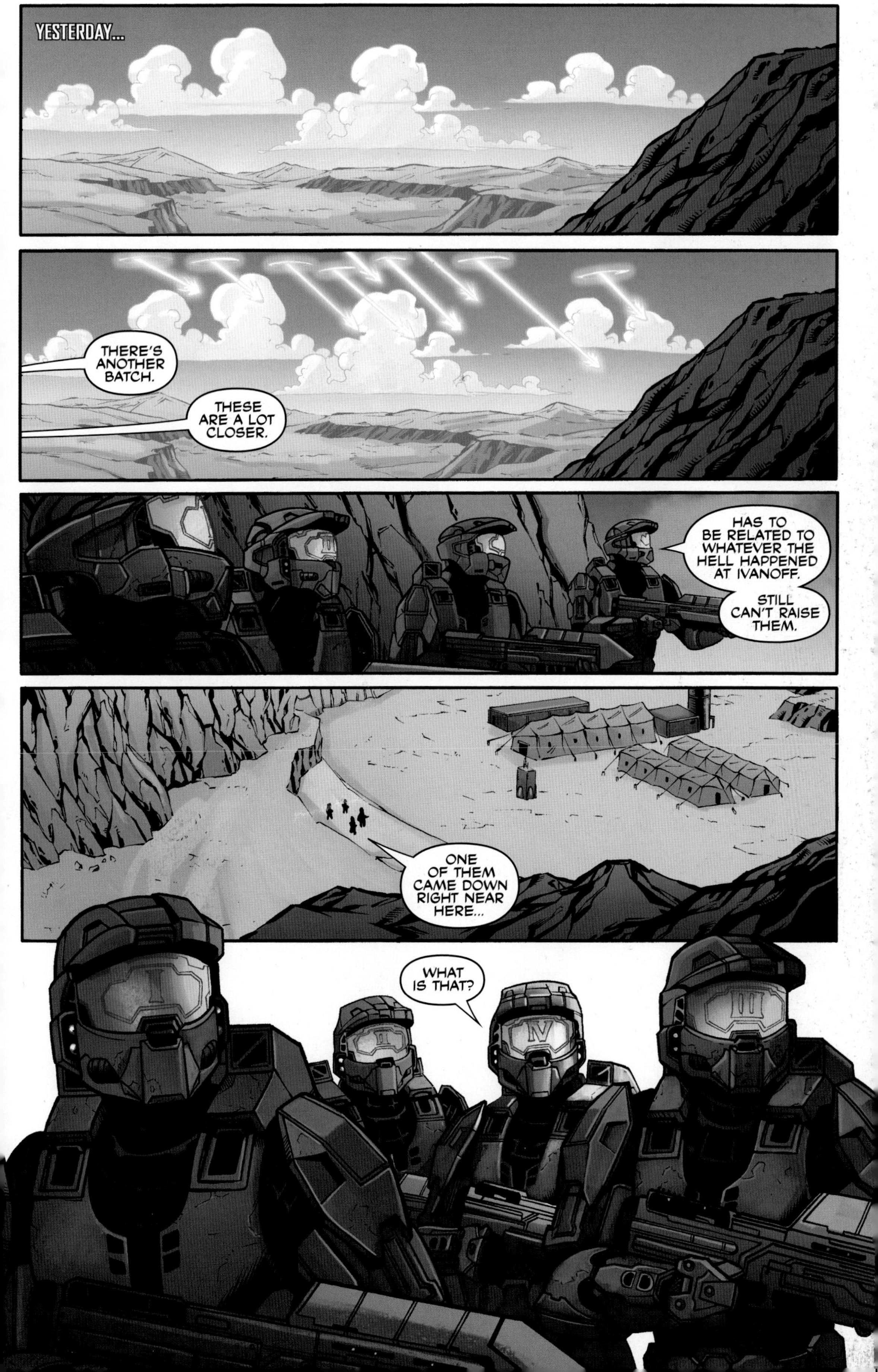
YESTERDAY...
THERE'S ANOTHER BATCH.
THESE ARE A LOT CLOSER.
HAS TO BE RELATED TO WHATEVER THE HELL HAPPENED AT IVANOFF.
STILL CAN'T RAISE THEM.
ONE OF THEM CAME DOWN RIGHT NEAR HERE...
WHAT IS THAT?

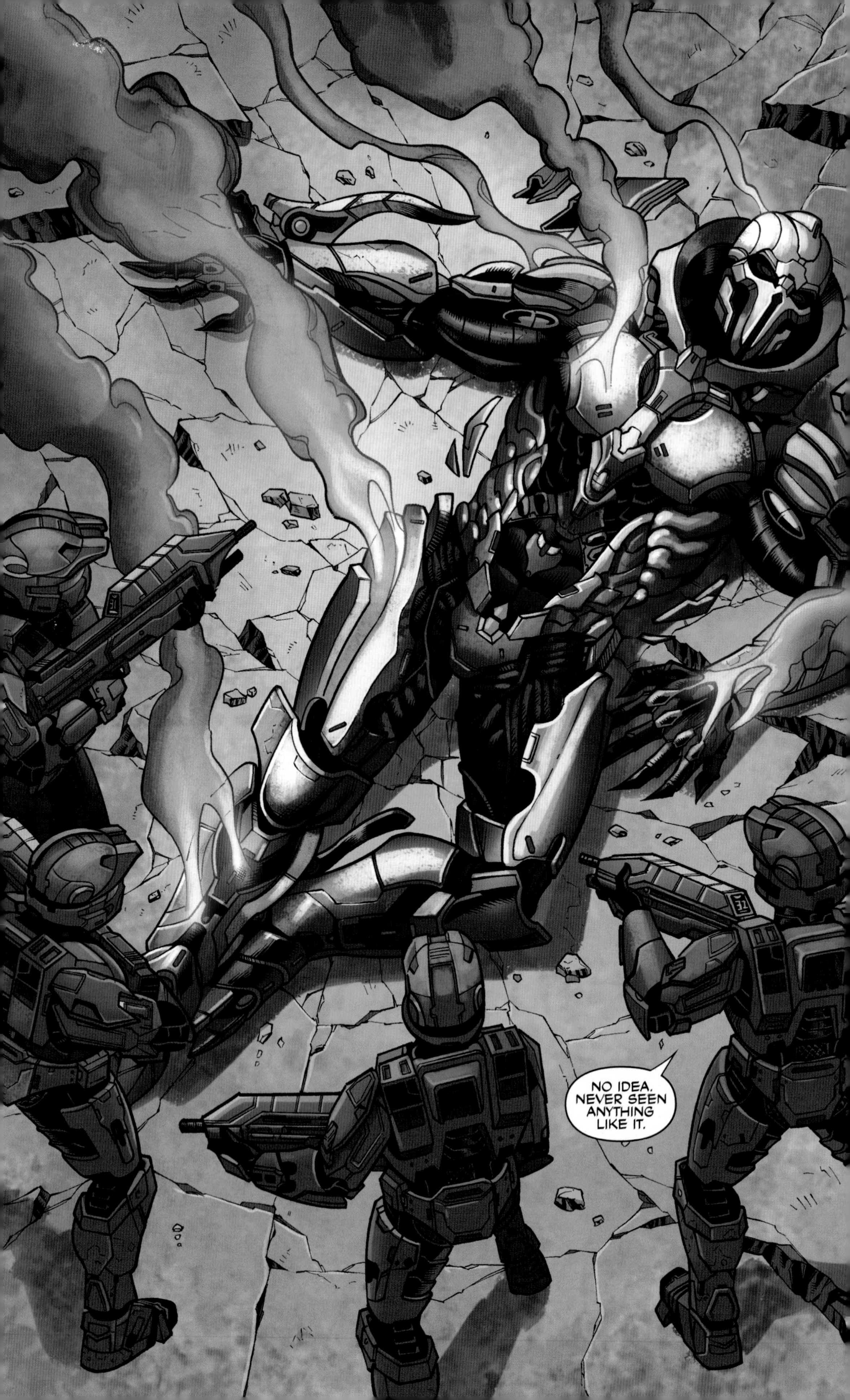
NO IDEA. NEVER SEEN ANYTHING LIKE IT.

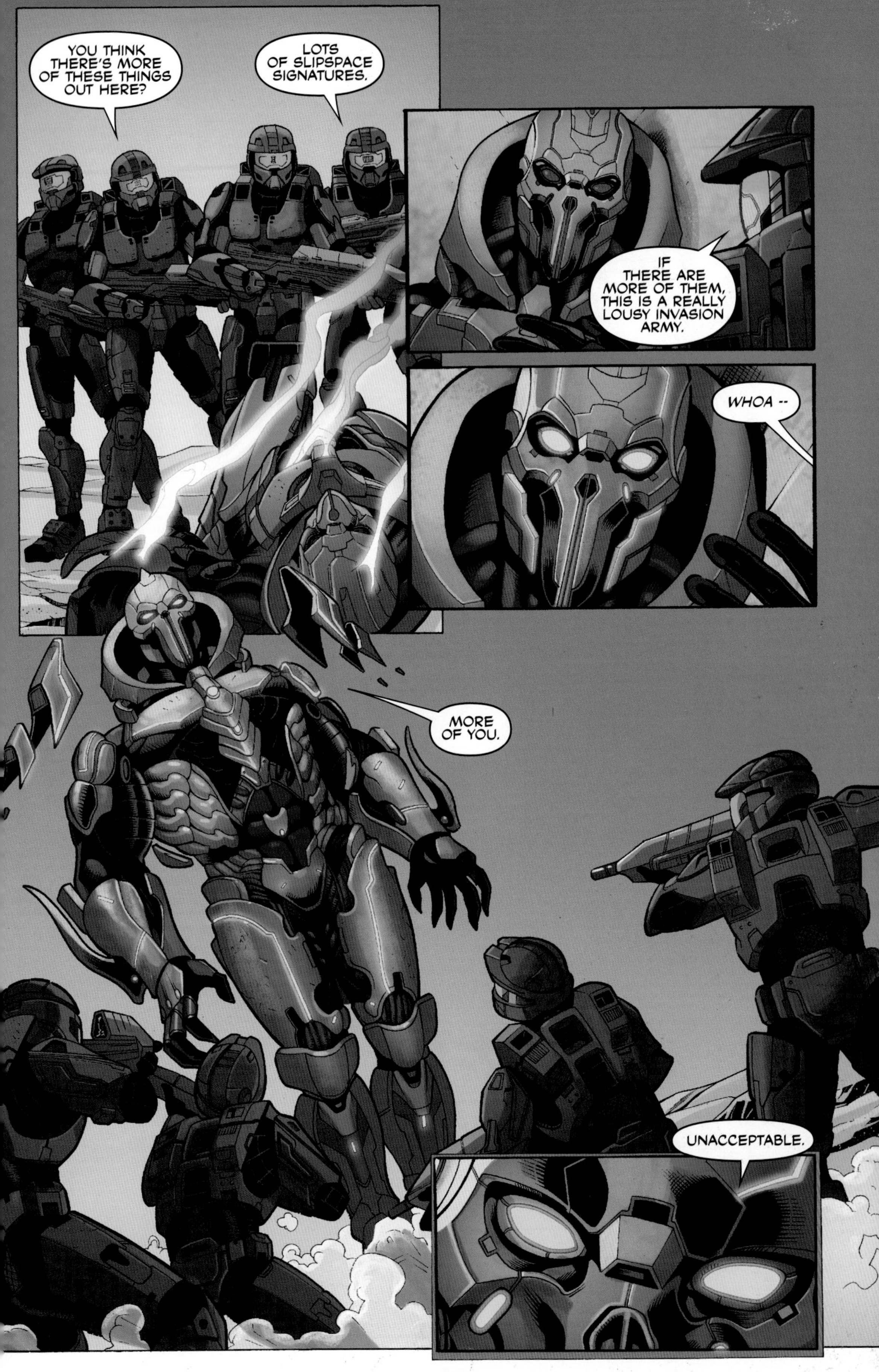
YOU THINK THERE'S MORE OF THESE THINGS OUT HERE?
LOTS OF SLIPSPACE SIGNATURES.
IF THERE ARE MORE OF THEM, THIS IS A REALLY LOUSY INVASION ARMY.
WHOA --
MORE OF YOU.
UNACCEPTABLE.

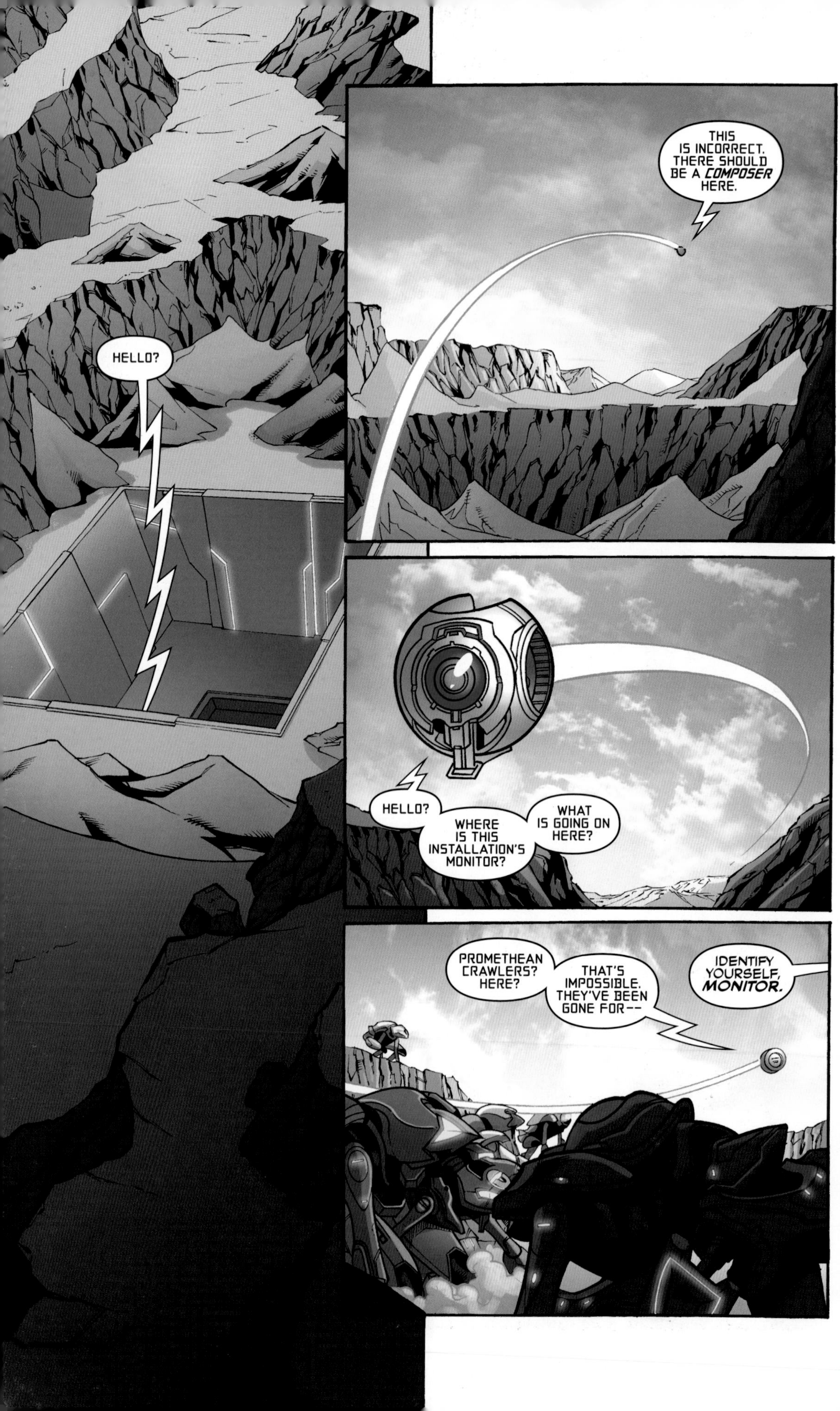
HELLO?
THIS IS INCORRECT. THERE SHOULD BE A COMPOSER HERE.
HELLO?
WHERE IS THIS INSTALLATION'S MONITOR?
WHAT IS GOING ON HERE?
PROMETHEAN CRAWLERS? HERE?
THAT'S IMPOSSIBLE. THEY'VE BEEN GONE FOR--
IDENTIFY YOURSELF, MONITOR.

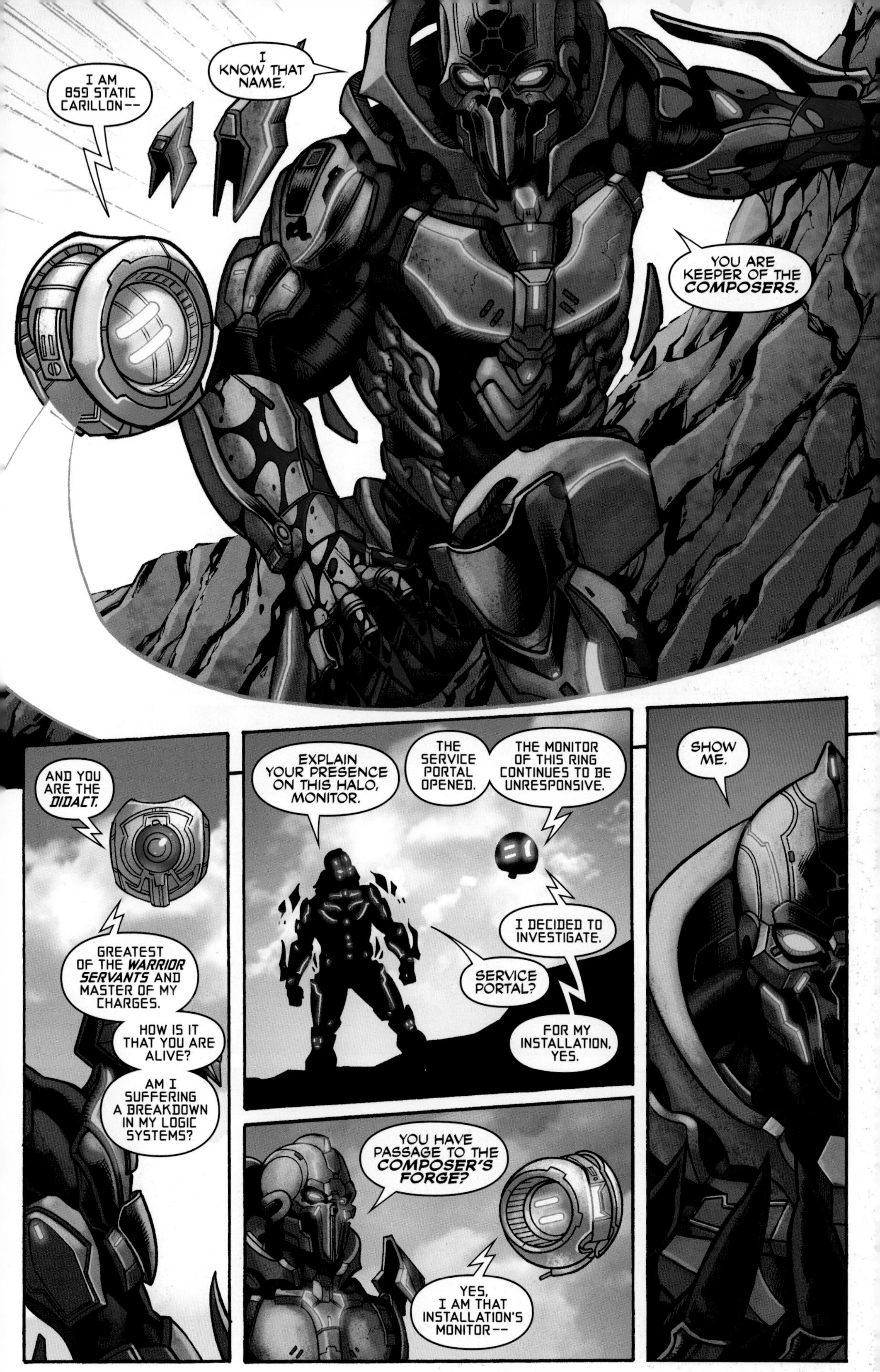
I AM
859 STATIC
CARILLON--
I KNOW THAT NAME.
YOU ARE KEEPER OF THE COMPOSERS.
AND YOU ARE THE DIDACT.
GREATEST OF THE WARRIOR SERVANTS AND MASTER OF MY CHARGES.
HOW IS IT THAT YOU ARE ALIVE?
AM I SUFFERING A BREAKDOWN IN MY LOGIC SYSTEMS?
EXPLAIN YOUR PRESENCE ON THIS HALO, MONITOR.
THE SERVICE PORTAL OPENED.
THE MONITOR OF THIS RING CONTINUES TO BE UNRESPONSIVE.
I DECIDED TO INVESTIGATE.
SERVICE PORTAL?
FOR MY INSTALLATION, YES.
YOU HAVE PASSAGE TO THE COMPOSER'S FORGE?
YES, I AM THAT INSTALLATION'S MONITOR--
SHOW ME.

TODAY...

WE'RE NOT ON THE HALO ANY MORE.

NO, KELLY.

FORERUNNER PORTAL SYSTEM.

WE COULD BE ANYWHERE IN THE GALAXY, JOHN.

AS LONG AS THE PORTAL'S OPEN, WE HAVE A WAY HOME.

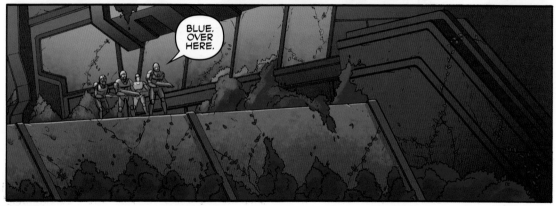

BLUE. OVER HERE.

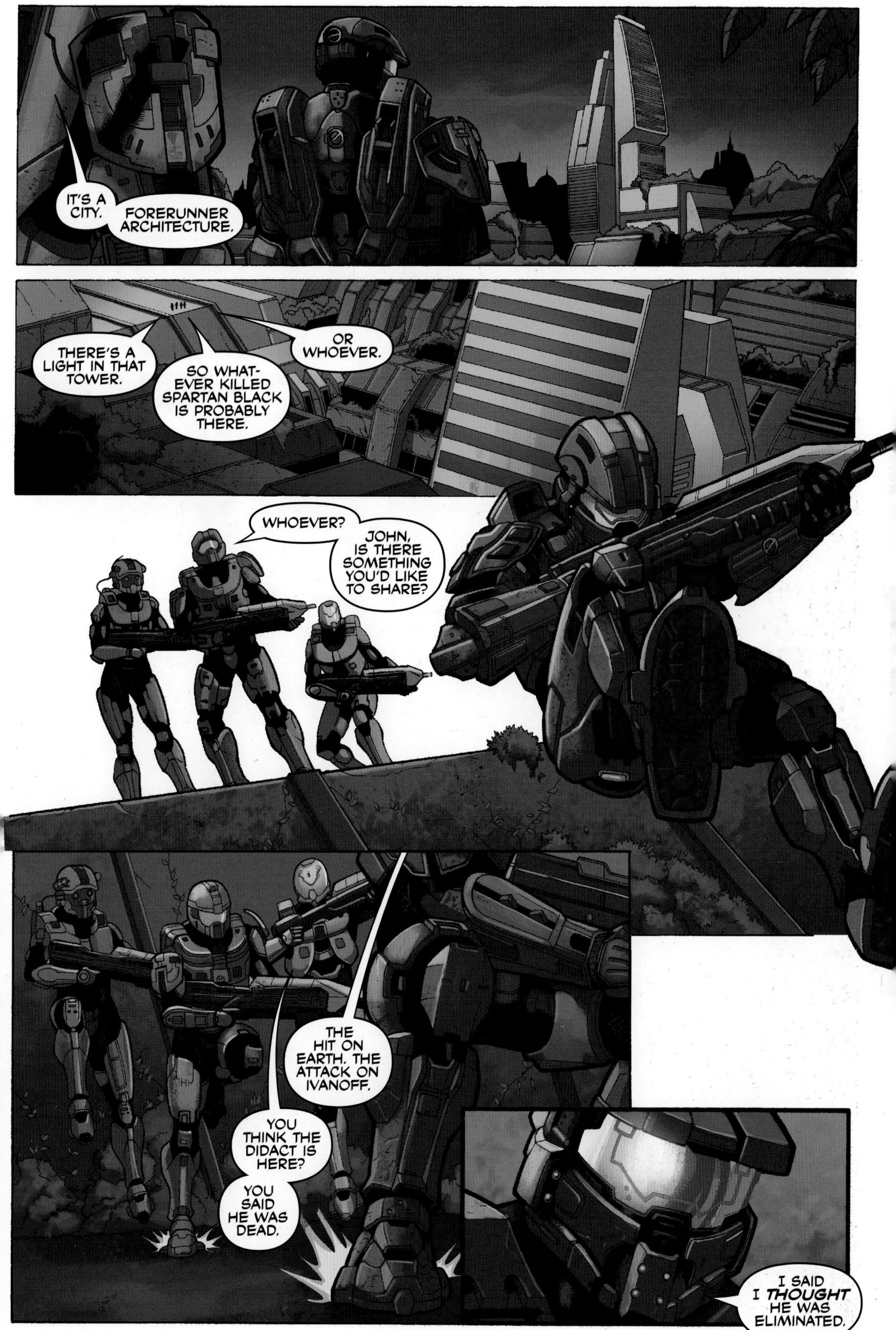
IT'S A CITY.
FORERUNNER ARCHITECTURE.
THERE'S A LIGHT IN THAT TOWER.
SO WHATEVER KILLED SPARTAN BLACK IS PROBABLY THERE.
OR WHOEVER.
WHOEVER?
JOHN, IS THERE SOMETHING YOU'D LIKE TO SHARE?
THE HIT ON EARTH. THE ATTACK ON IVANOFF.
YOU THINK THE DIDACT IS HERE?
YOU SAID HE WAS DEAD.
I SAID I *THOUGHT* HE WAS ELIMINATED.

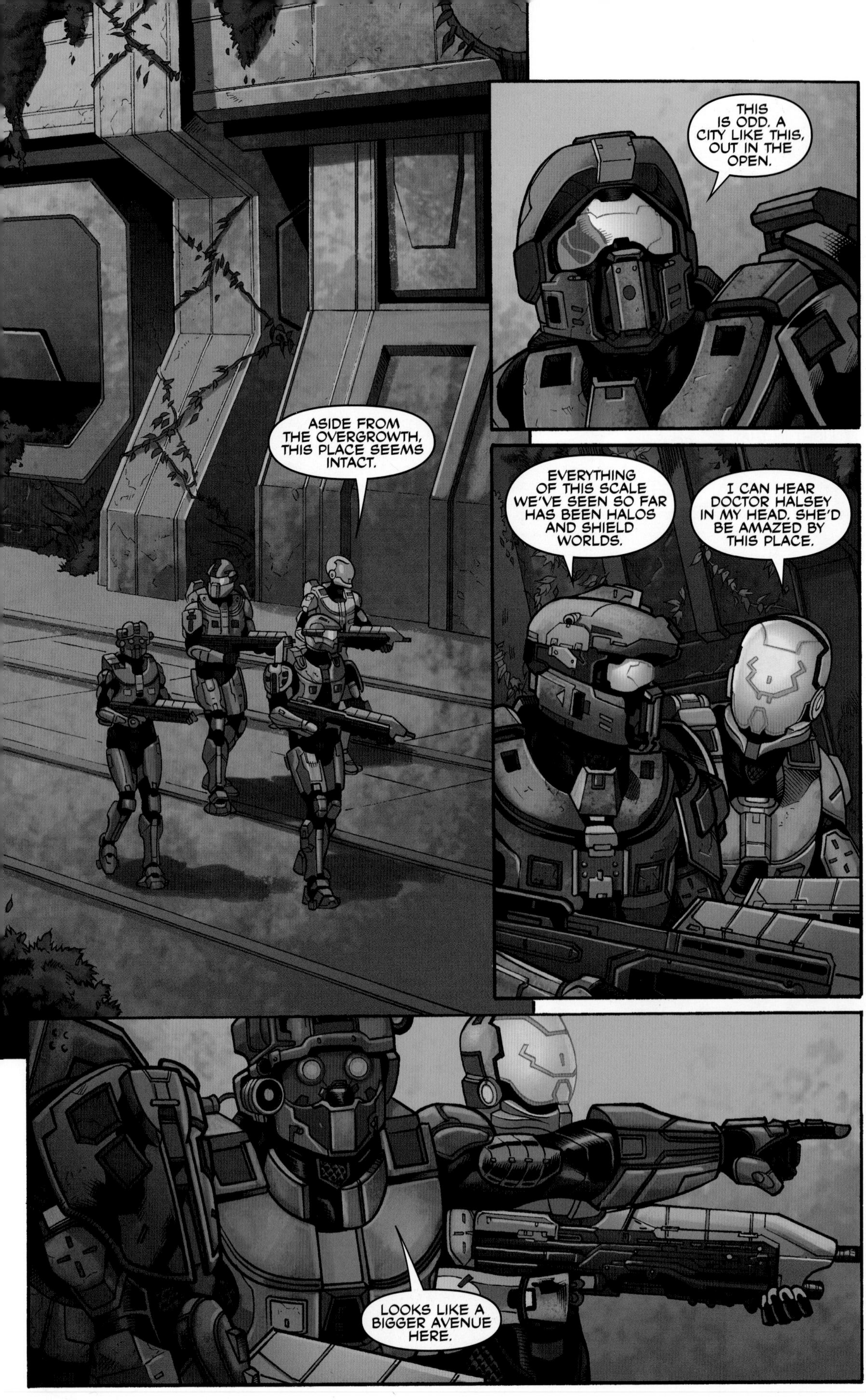
ASIDE FROM THE OVERGROWTH, THIS PLACE SEEMS INTACT.
THIS IS ODD. A CITY LIKE THIS, OUT IN THE OPEN.
EVERYTHING OF THIS SCALE WE'VE SEEN SO FAR HAS BEEN HALOS AND SHIELD WORLDS.
I CAN HEAR DOCTOR HALSEY IN MY HEAD. SHE'D BE AMAZED BY THIS PLACE.
LOOKS LIKE A BIGGER AVENUE HERE.

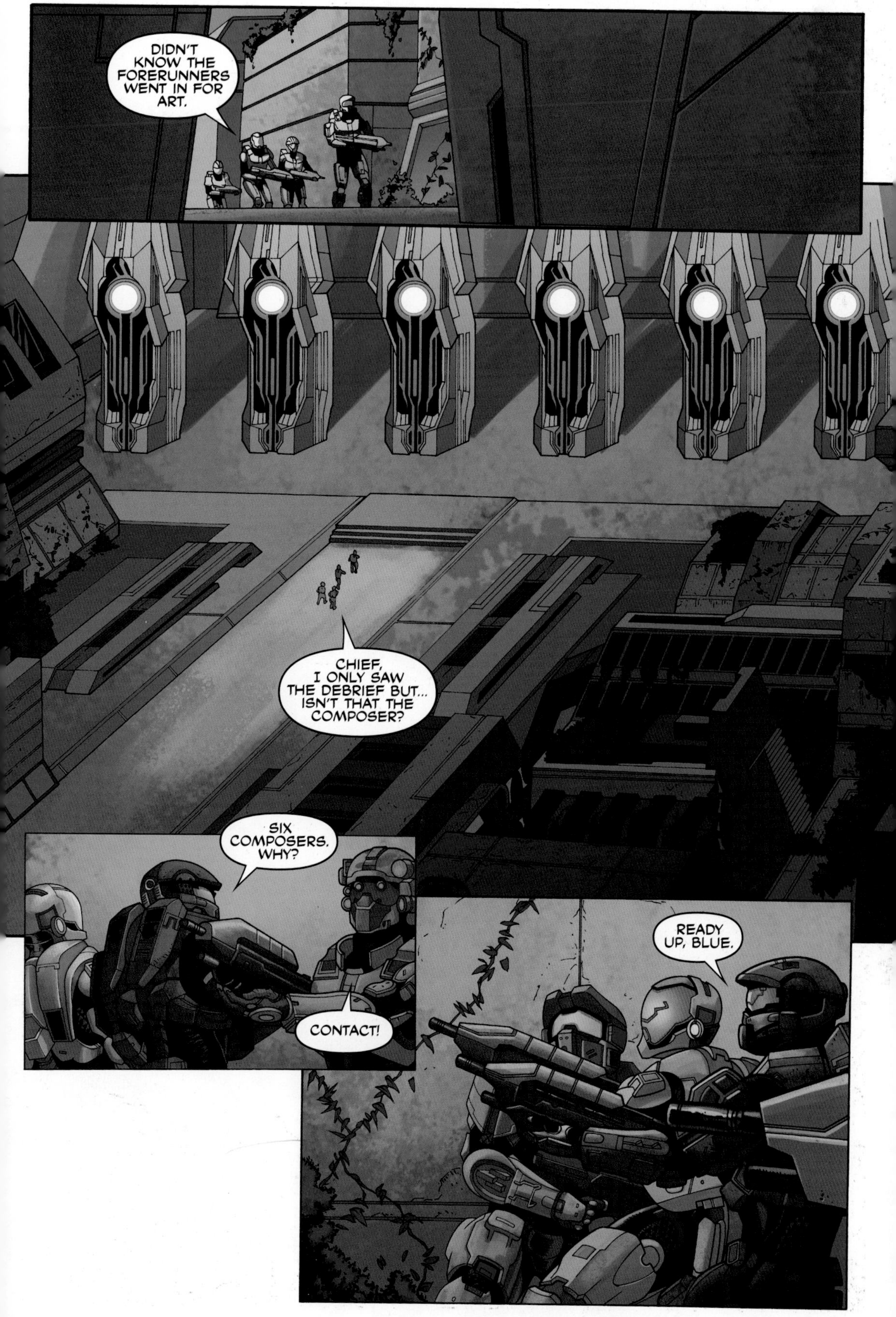
DIDN'T KNOW THE FORERUNNERS WENT IN FOR ART.
CHIEF, I ONLY SAW THE DEBRIEF BUT... ISN'T THAT THE COMPOSER?
SIX COMPOSERS. WHY?
CONTACT!
READY UP, BLUE.

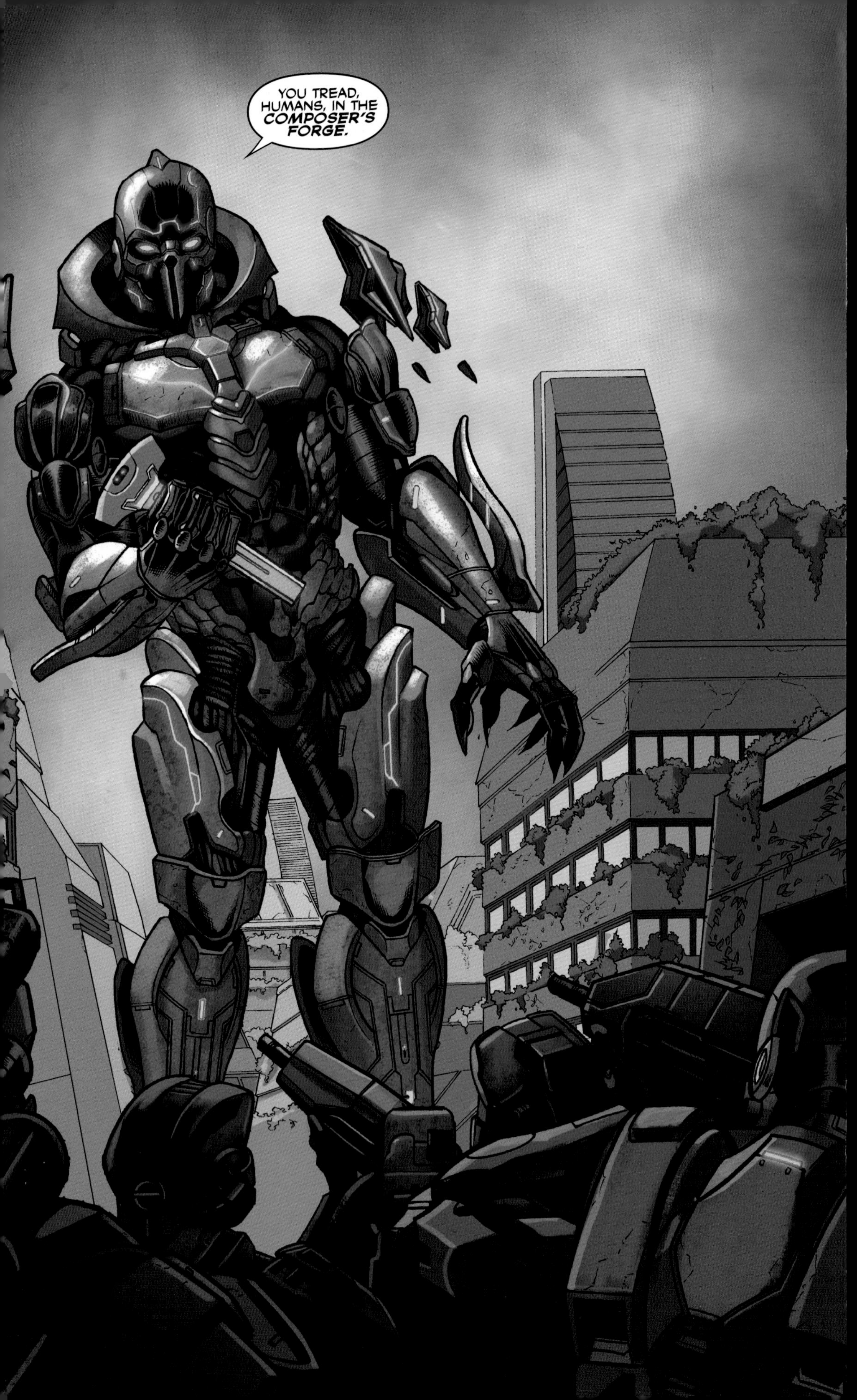
YOU TREAD, HUMANS, IN THE *COMPOSER'S FORGE.*

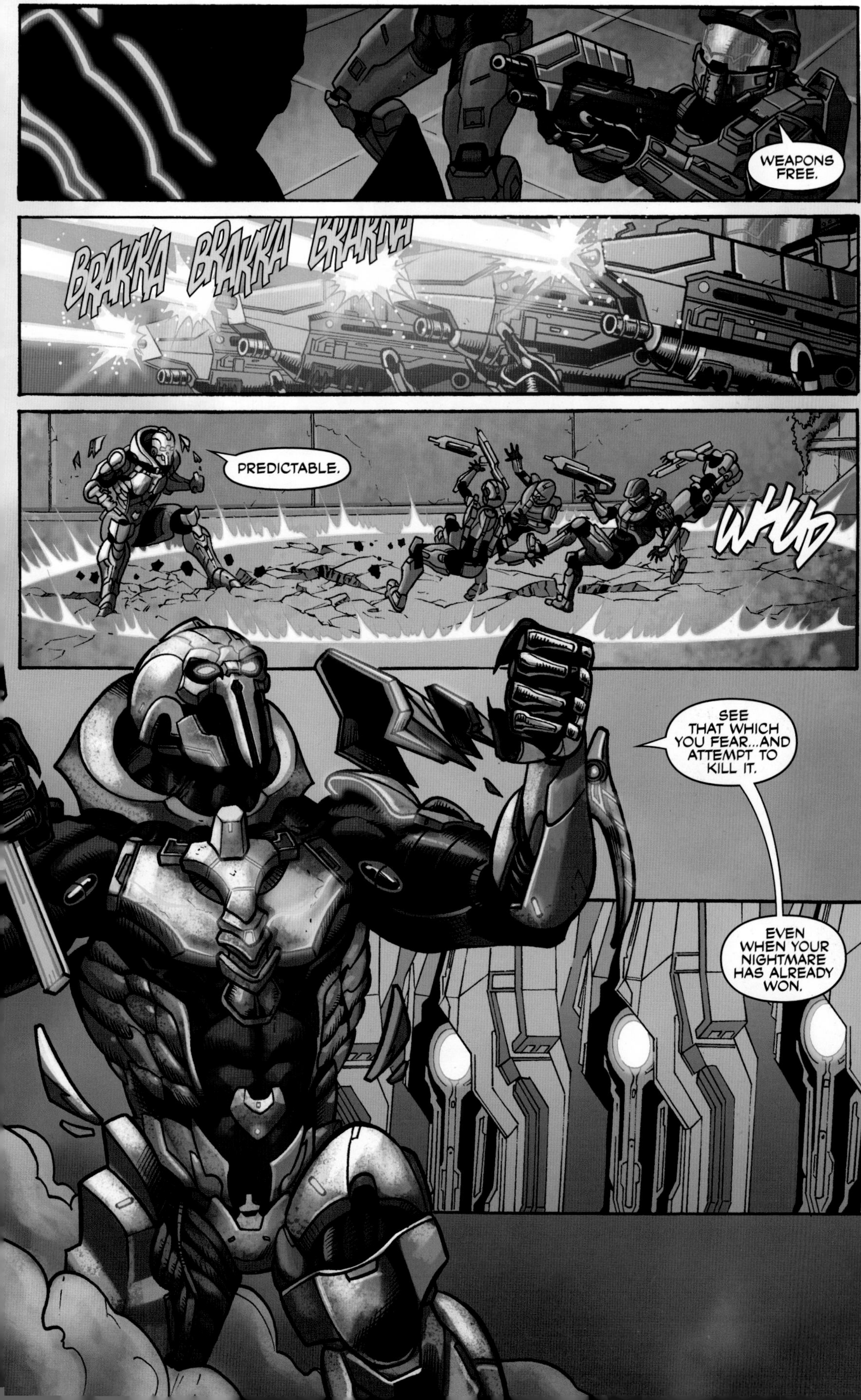
WEAPONS FREE.
BRAKKA BRAKKA BRAKKA
PREDICTABLE.
WHUD
SEE THAT WHICH YOU FEAR...AND ATTEMPT TO KILL IT.
EVEN WHEN YOUR NIGHTMARE HAS ALREADY WON.

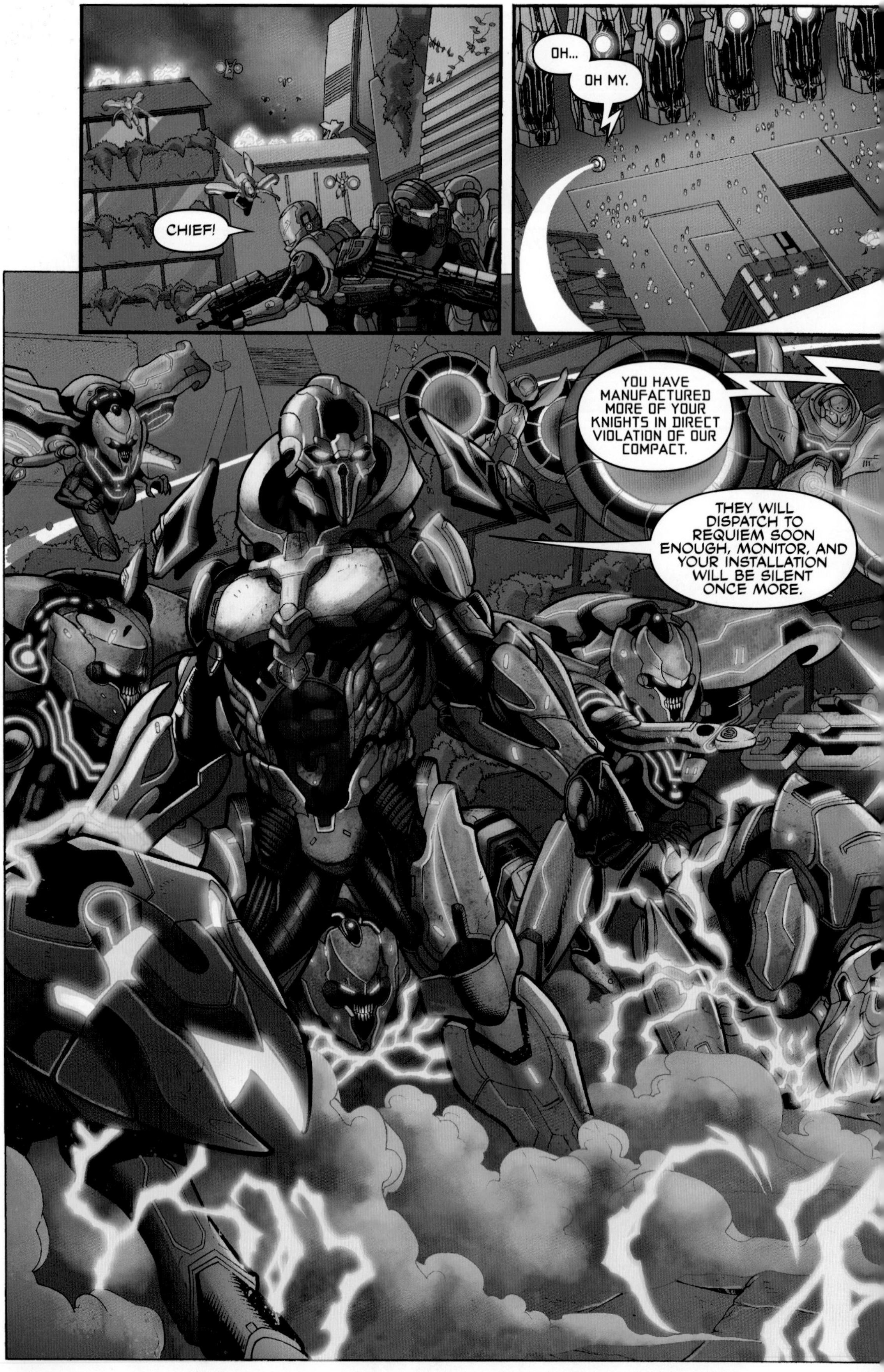
CHIEF!
OH...
OH MY.
YOU HAVE MANUFACTURED MORE OF YOUR KNIGHTS IN DIRECT VIOLATION OF OUR COMPACT.
THEY WILL DISPATCH TO REQUIEM SOON ENOUGH, MONITOR, AND YOUR INSTALLATION WILL BE SILENT ONCE MORE.

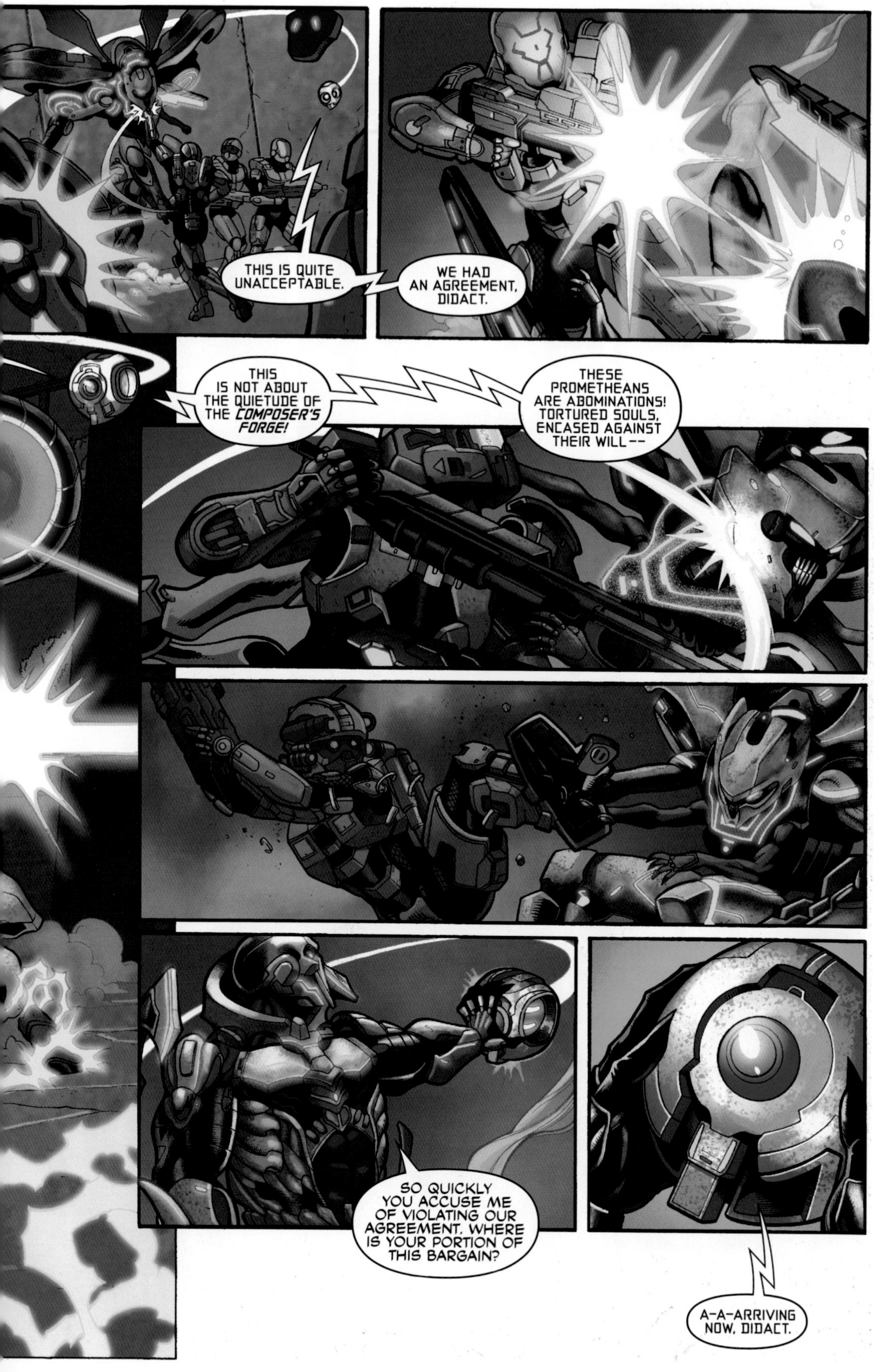
THIS IS QUITE UNACCEPTABLE.
WE HAD AN AGREEMENT, DIDACT.
THIS IS NOT ABOUT THE QUIETUDE OF THE *COMPOSER'S FORGE!*
THESE PROMETHEANS ARE ABOMINATIONS! TORTURED SOULS, ENCASED AGAINST THEIR WILL--
SO QUICKLY YOU ACCUSE ME OF VIOLATING OUR AGREEMENT. WHERE IS YOUR PORTION OF THIS BARGAIN?
A-A-ARRIVING NOW, DIDACT.

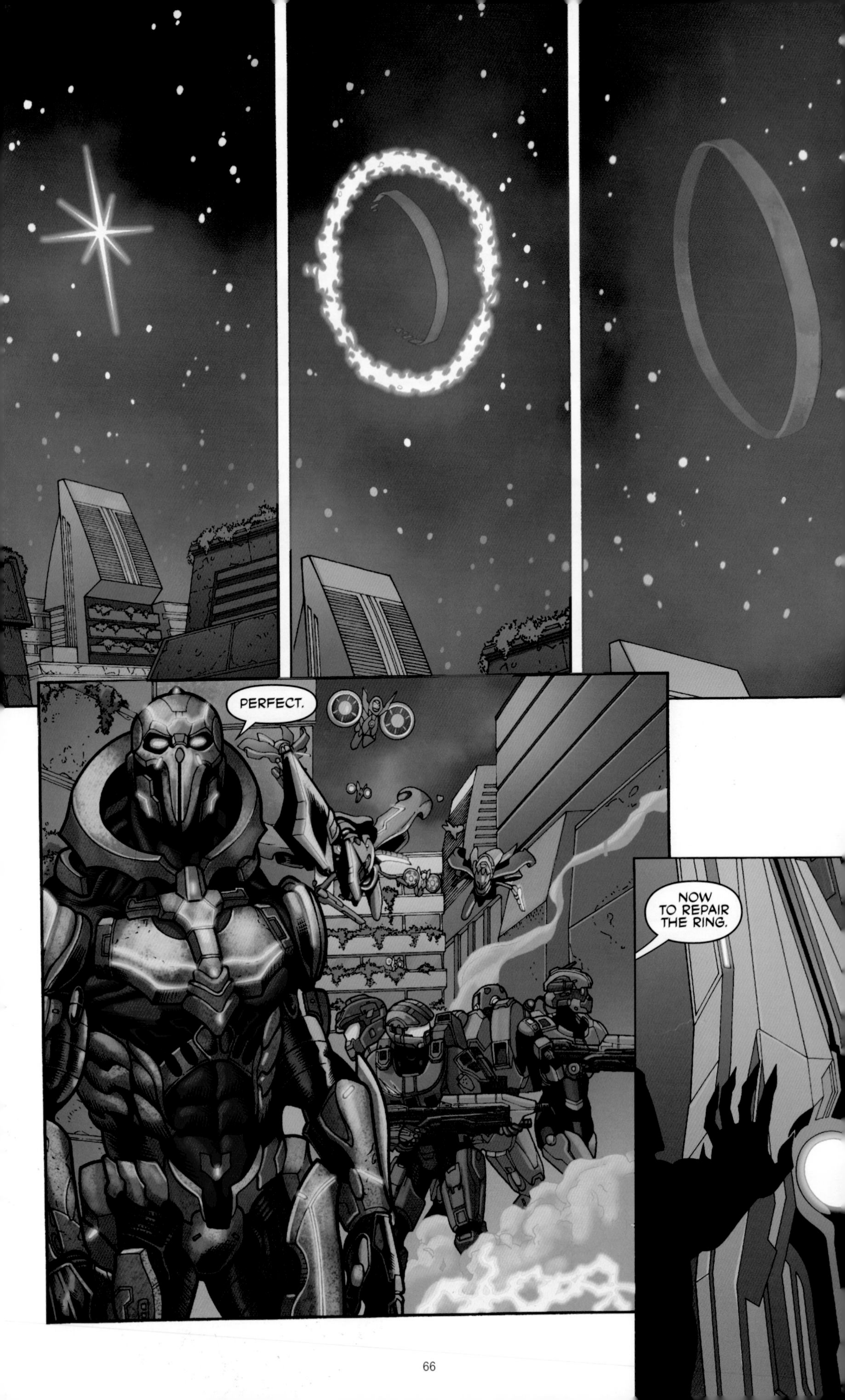
PERFECT.
NOW TO REPAIR THE RING.

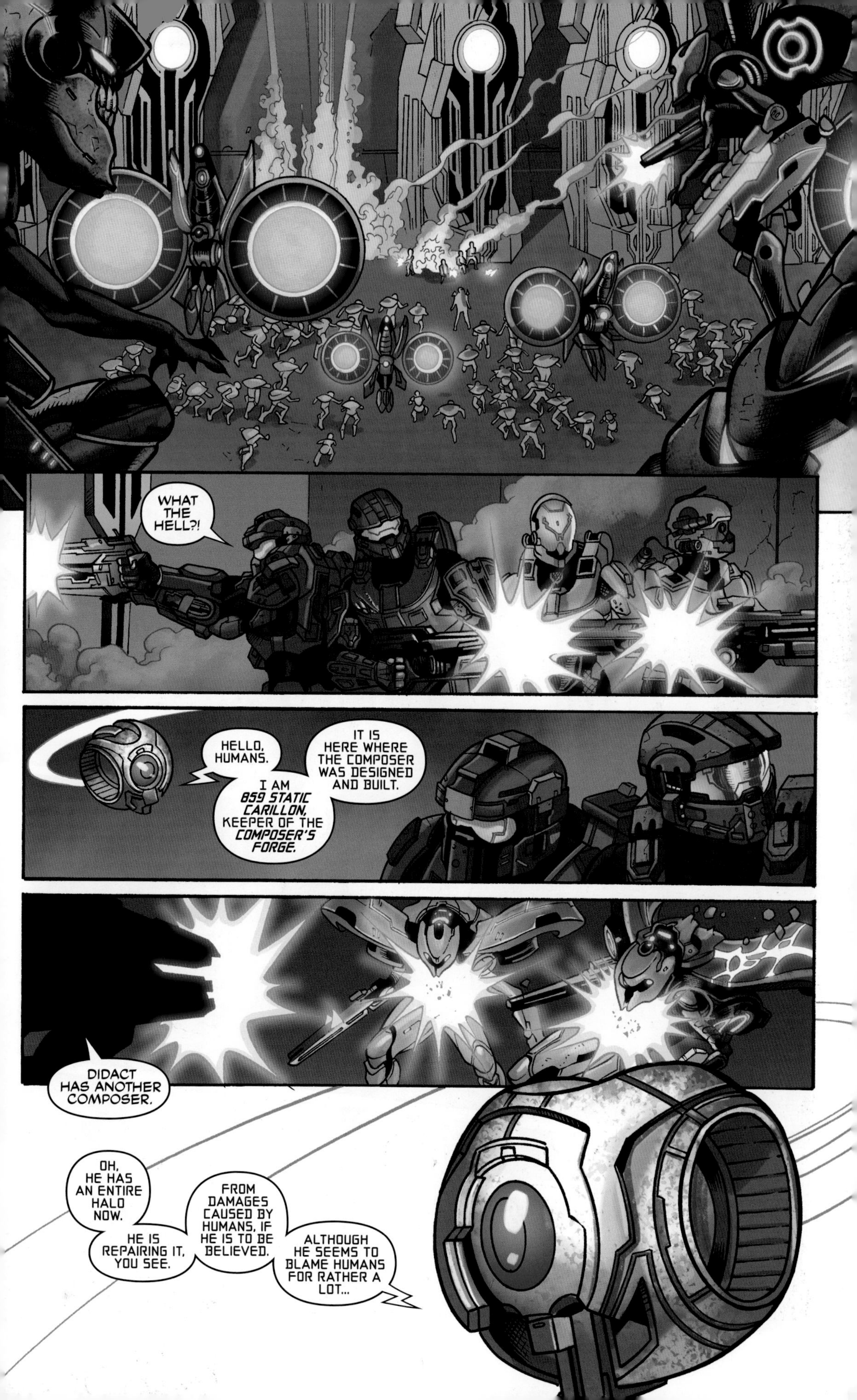
WHAT THE HELL?!
HELLO, HUMANS.
I AM 859 STATIC CARILLON, KEEPER OF THE COMPOSER'S FORGE.
IT IS HERE WHERE THE COMPOSER WAS DESIGNED AND BUILT.
DIDACT HAS ANOTHER COMPOSER.
OH, HE HAS AN ENTIRE HALO NOW.
HE IS REPAIRING IT, YOU SEE.
FROM DAMAGES CAUSED BY HUMANS, IF HE IS TO BE BELIEVED.
ALTHOUGH HE SEEMS TO BLAME HUMANS FOR RATHER A LOT...

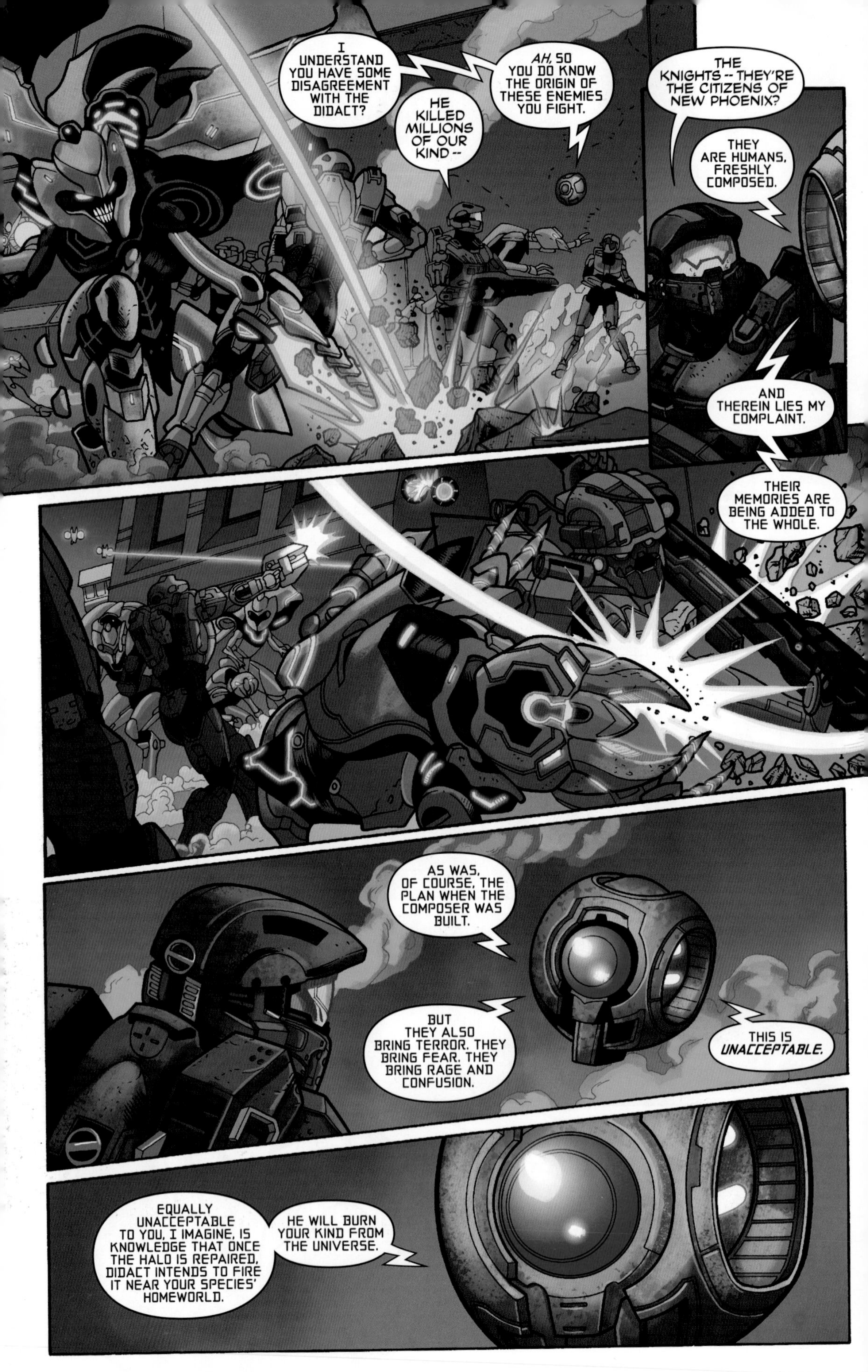
I UNDERSTAND YOU HAVE SOME DISAGREEMENT WITH THE DIDACT?
HE KILLED MILLIONS OF OUR KIND --
AH, SO YOU DO KNOW THE ORIGIN OF THESE ENEMIES YOU FIGHT.
THE KNIGHTS -- THEY'RE THE CITIZENS OF NEW PHOENIX?
THEY ARE HUMANS, FRESHLY COMPOSED.
AND THEREIN LIES MY COMPLAINT.
THEIR MEMORIES ARE BEING ADDED TO THE WHOLE.
AS WAS, OF COURSE, THE PLAN WHEN THE COMPOSER WAS BUILT.
BUT THEY ALSO BRING TERROR. THEY BRING FEAR. THEY BRING RAGE AND CONFUSION.
THIS IS *UNACCEPTABLE.*
EQUALLY UNACCEPTABLE TO YOU, I IMAGINE, IS KNOWLEDGE THAT ONCE THE HALO IS REPAIRED, DIDACT INTENDS TO FIRE IT NEAR YOUR SPECIES' HOMEWORLD.
HE WILL BURN YOUR KIND FROM THE UNIVERSE.

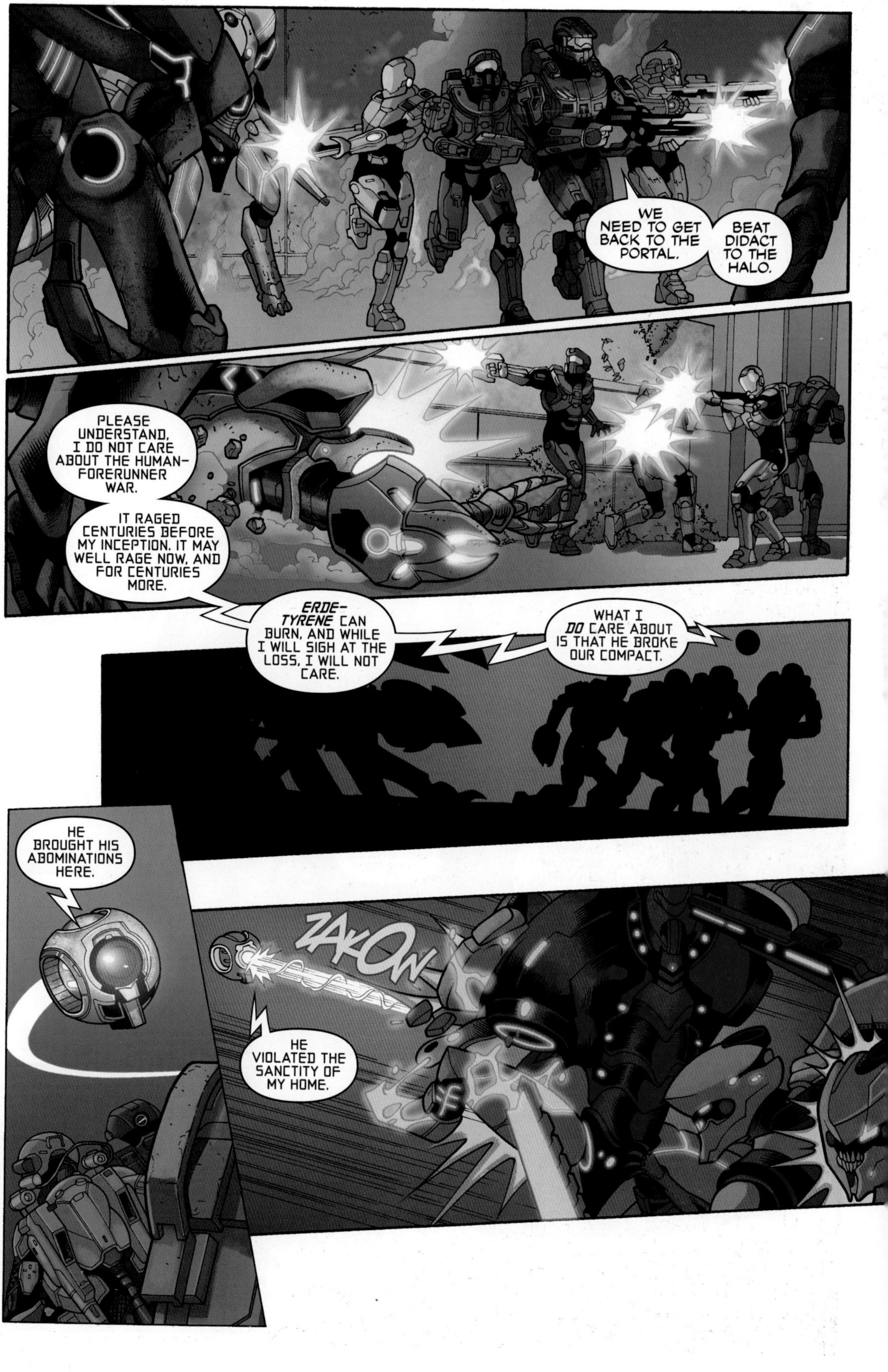
WE NEED TO GET BACK TO THE PORTAL.
BEAT DIDACT TO THE HALO.
PLEASE UNDERSTAND, I DO NOT CARE ABOUT THE HUMAN-FORERUNNER WAR.
IT RAGED CENTURIES BEFORE MY INCEPTION. IT MAY WELL RAGE NOW, AND FOR CENTURIES MORE.
ERDE-TYRENE CAN BURN, AND WHILE I WILL SIGH AT THE LOSS, I WILL NOT CARE.
WHAT I DO CARE ABOUT IS THAT HE BROKE OUR COMPACT.
HE BROUGHT HIS ABOMINATIONS HERE.
ZAKOW
HE VIOLATED THE SANCTITY OF MY HOME.

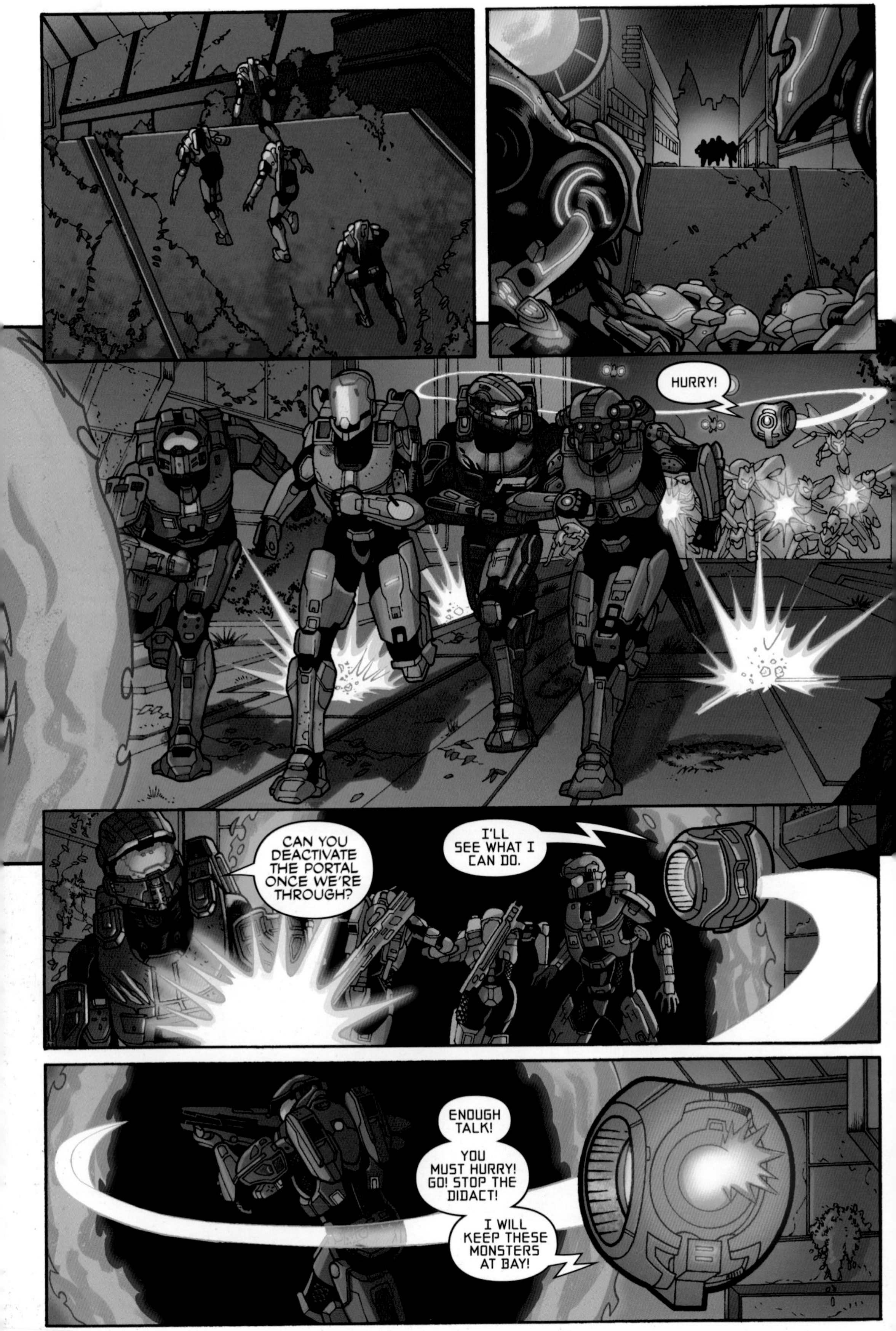
HURRY!
CAN YOU DEACTIVATE THE PORTAL ONCE WE'RE THROUGH?
I'LL SEE WHAT I CAN DO.
ENOUGH TALK!
YOU MUST HURRY! GO! STOP THE DIDACT!
I WILL KEEP THESE MONSTERS AT BAY!

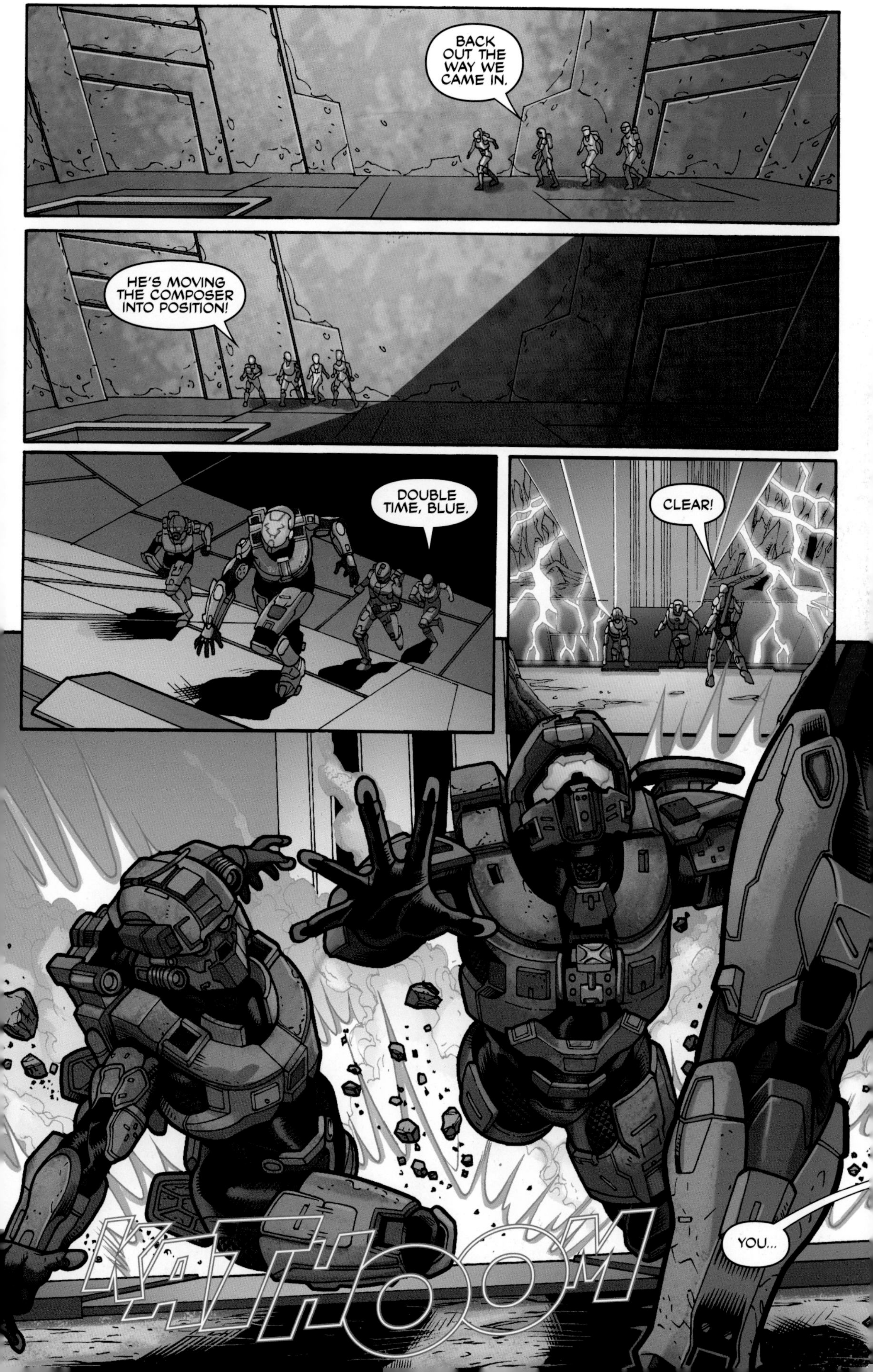
BACK OUT THE WAY WE CAME IN.
HE'S MOVING THE COMPOSER INTO POSITION!
DOUBLE TIME, BLUE.
CLEAR!
KATHOOM
YOU...

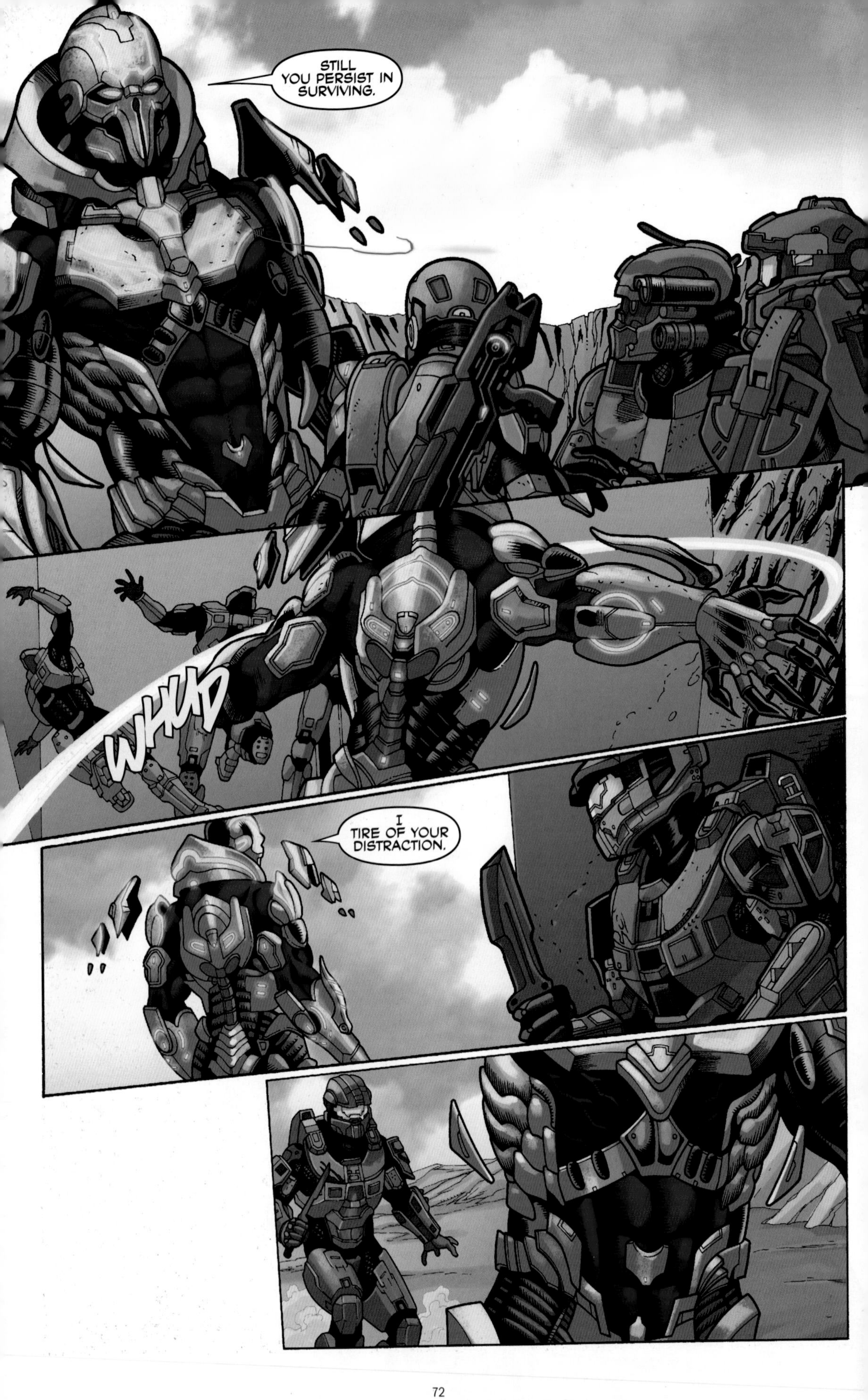
STILL YOU PERSIST IN SURVIVING.
WHUD
I TIRE OF YOUR DISTRACTION.

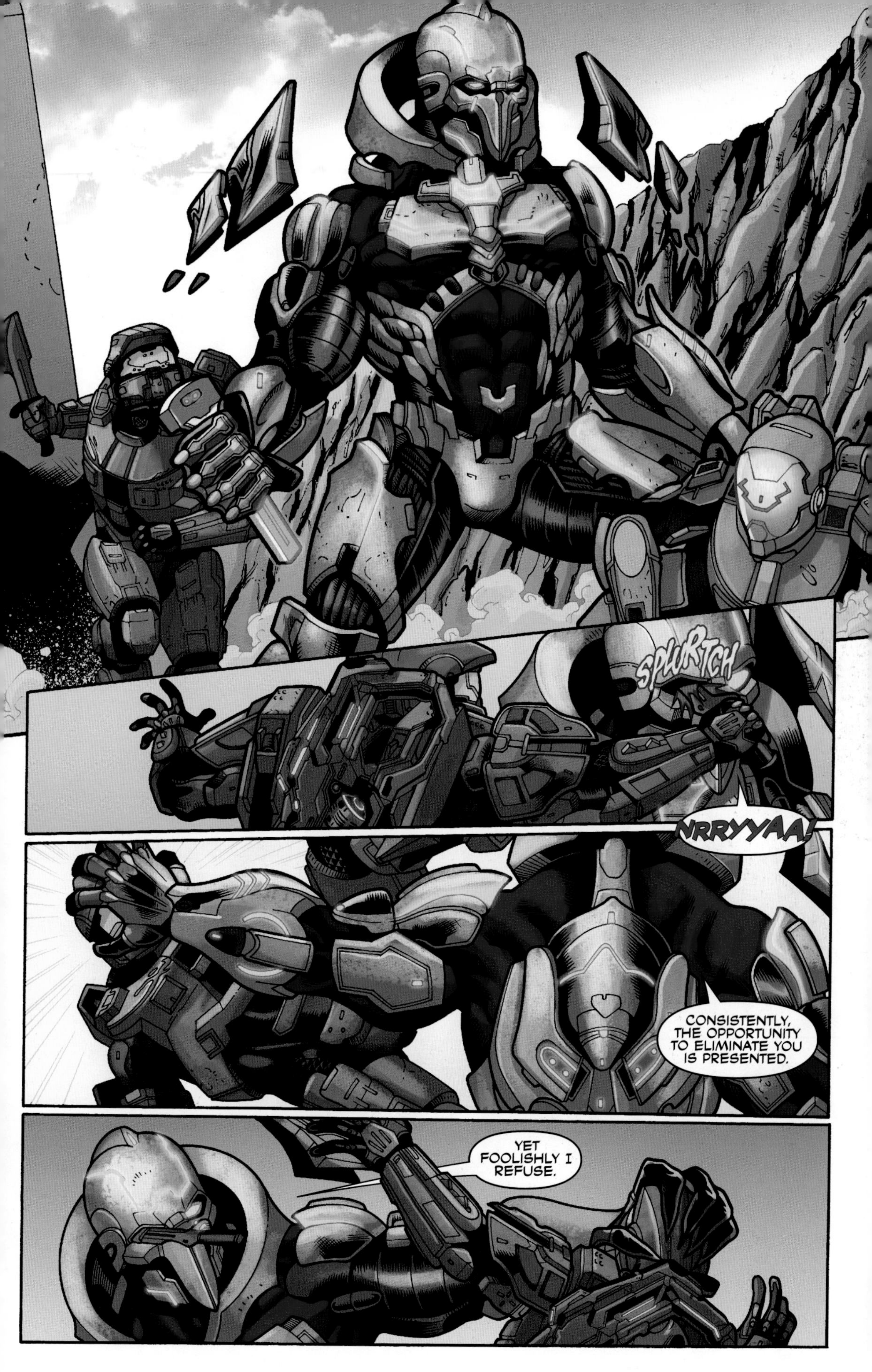
SPLURTCH
NRRYYAA!
CONSISTENTLY, THE OPPORTUNITY TO ELIMINATE YOU IS PRESENTED.
YET FOOLISHLY I REFUSE.

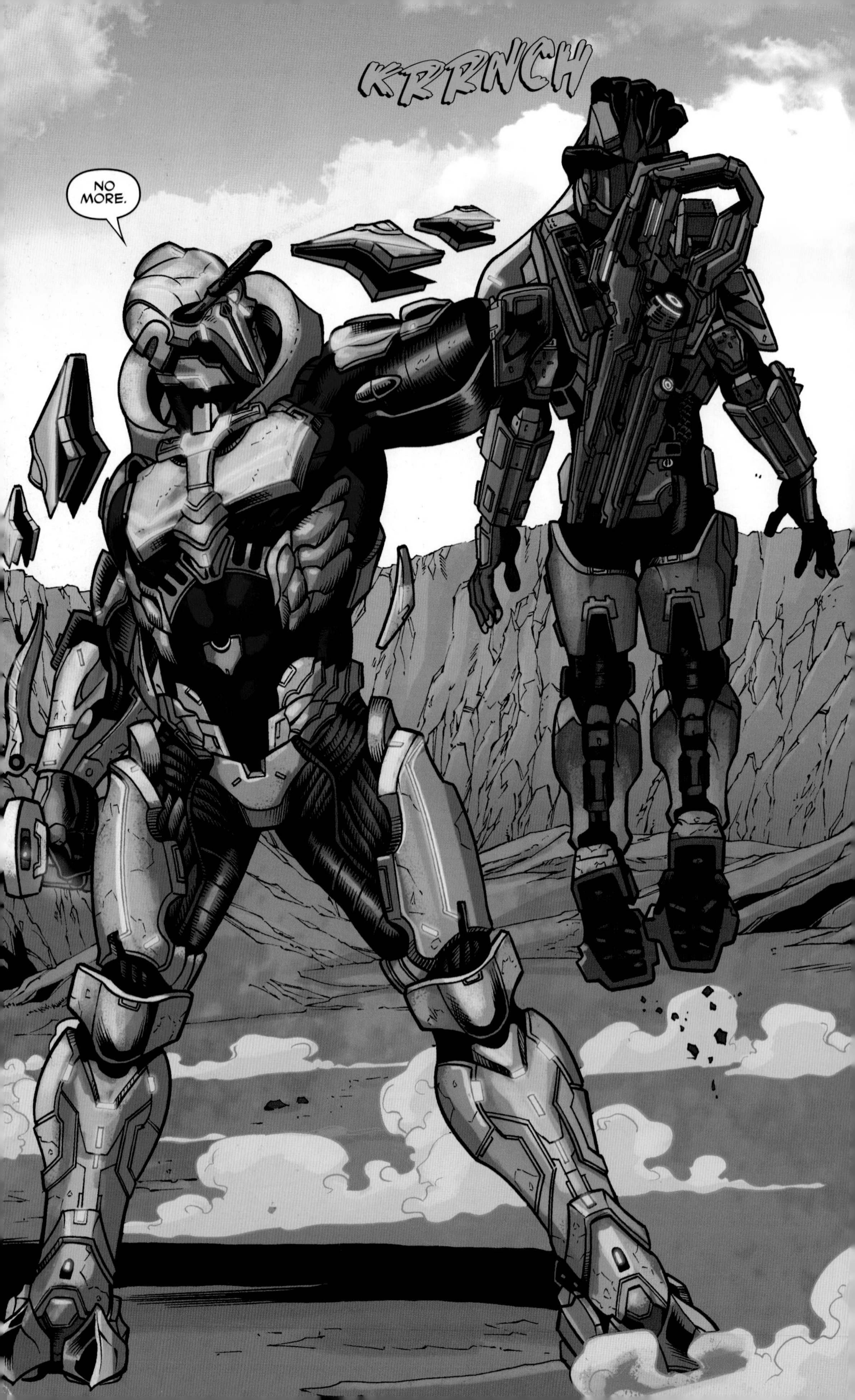
KRRNCH
NO MORE.

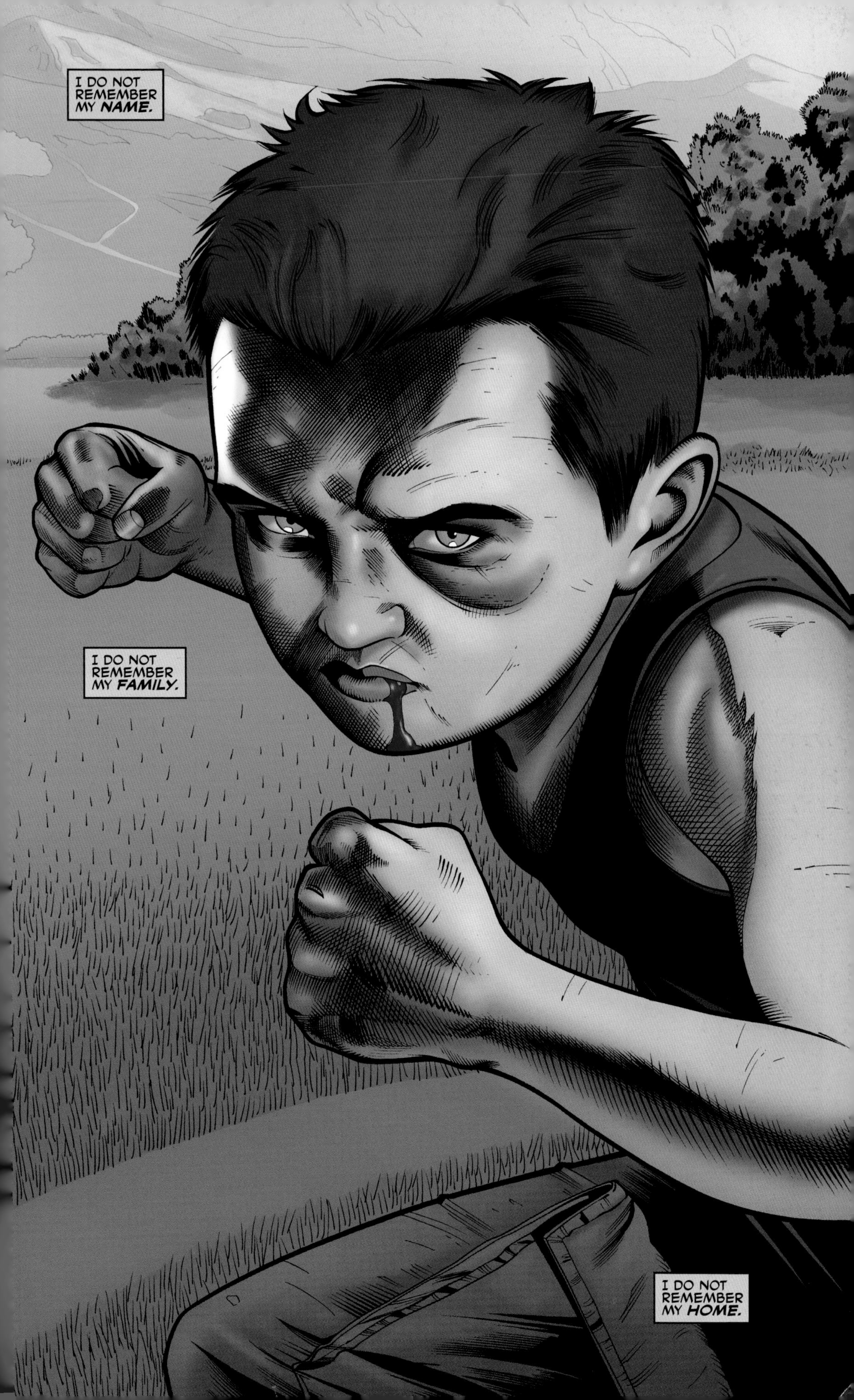
I DO NOT REMEMBER MY NAME.
I DO NOT REMEMBER MY FAMILY.
I DO NOT REMEMBER MY HOME.

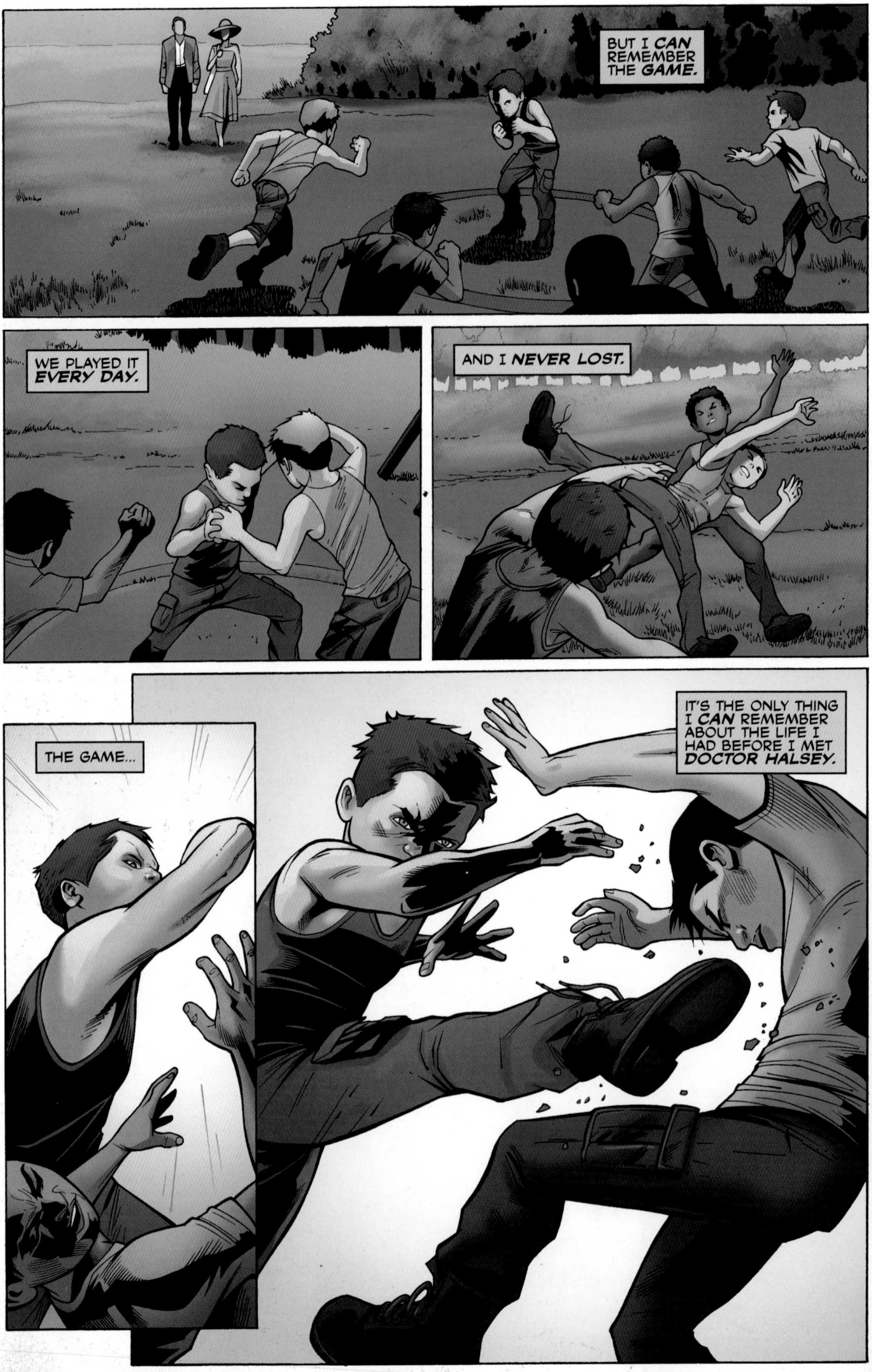
BUT I CAN REMEMBER THE GAME.
WE PLAYED IT EVERY DAY.
AND I NEVER LOST.
THE GAME...
IT'S THE ONLY THING I CAN REMEMBER ABOUT THE LIFE I HAD BEFORE I MET DOCTOR HALSEY.

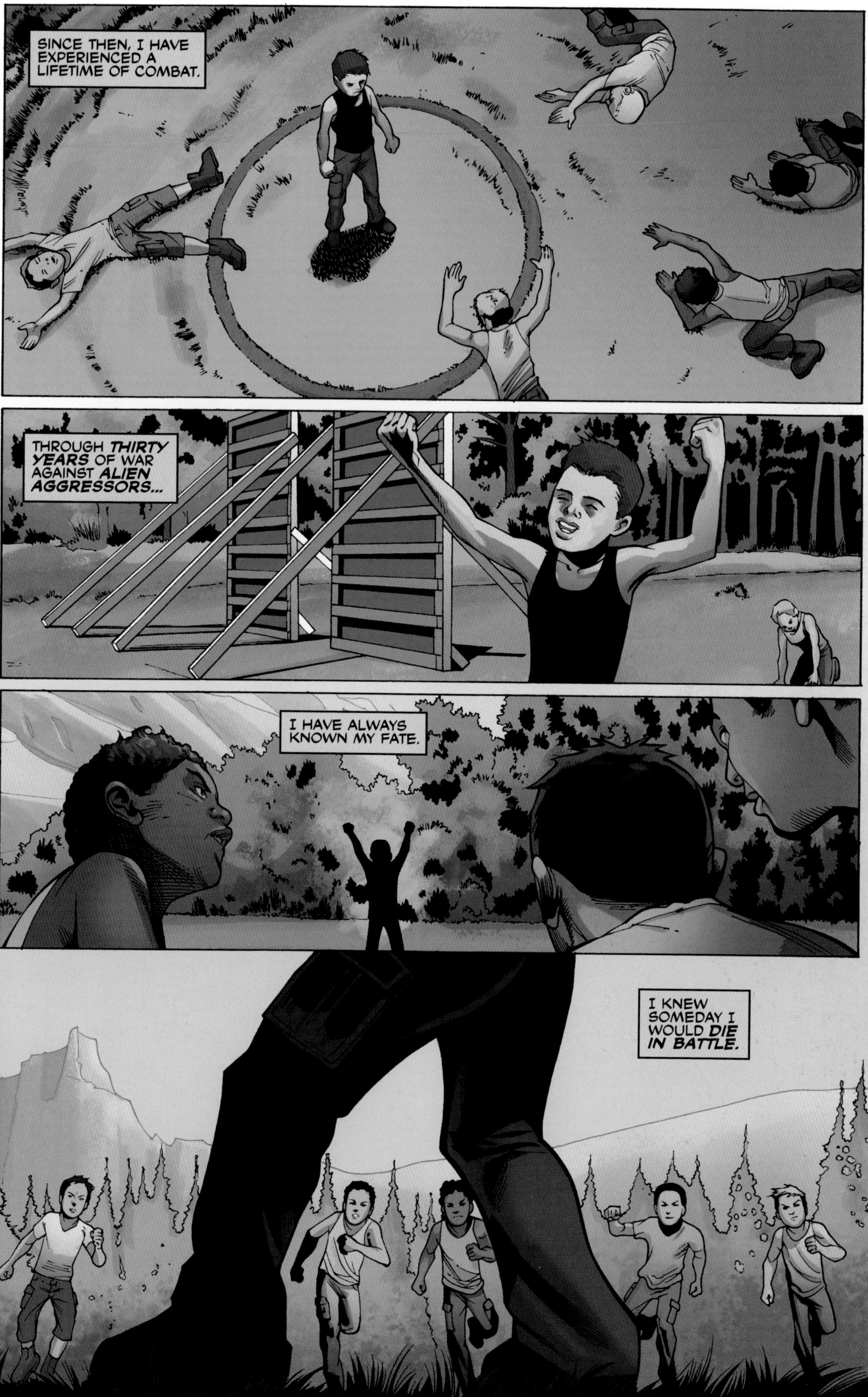
SINCE THEN, I HAVE EXPERIENCED A LIFETIME OF COMBAT.
THROUGH THIRTY YEARS OF WAR AGAINST ALIEN AGGRESSORS...
I HAVE ALWAYS KNOWN MY FATE.
I KNEW SOMEDAY I WOULD DIE IN BATTLE.

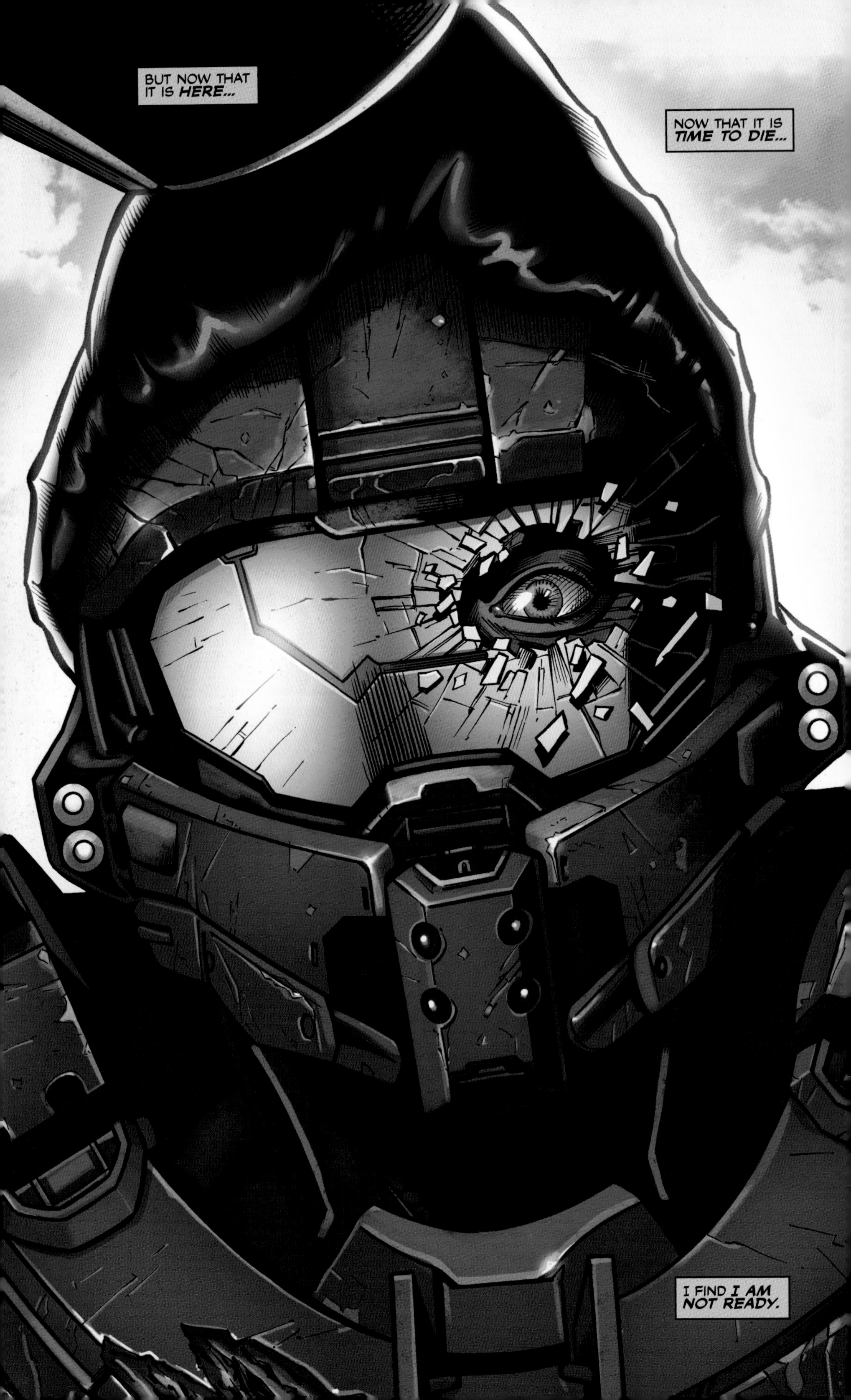
BUT NOW THAT IT IS HERE...
NOW THAT IT IS TIME TO DIE...
I FIND I AM NOT READY.

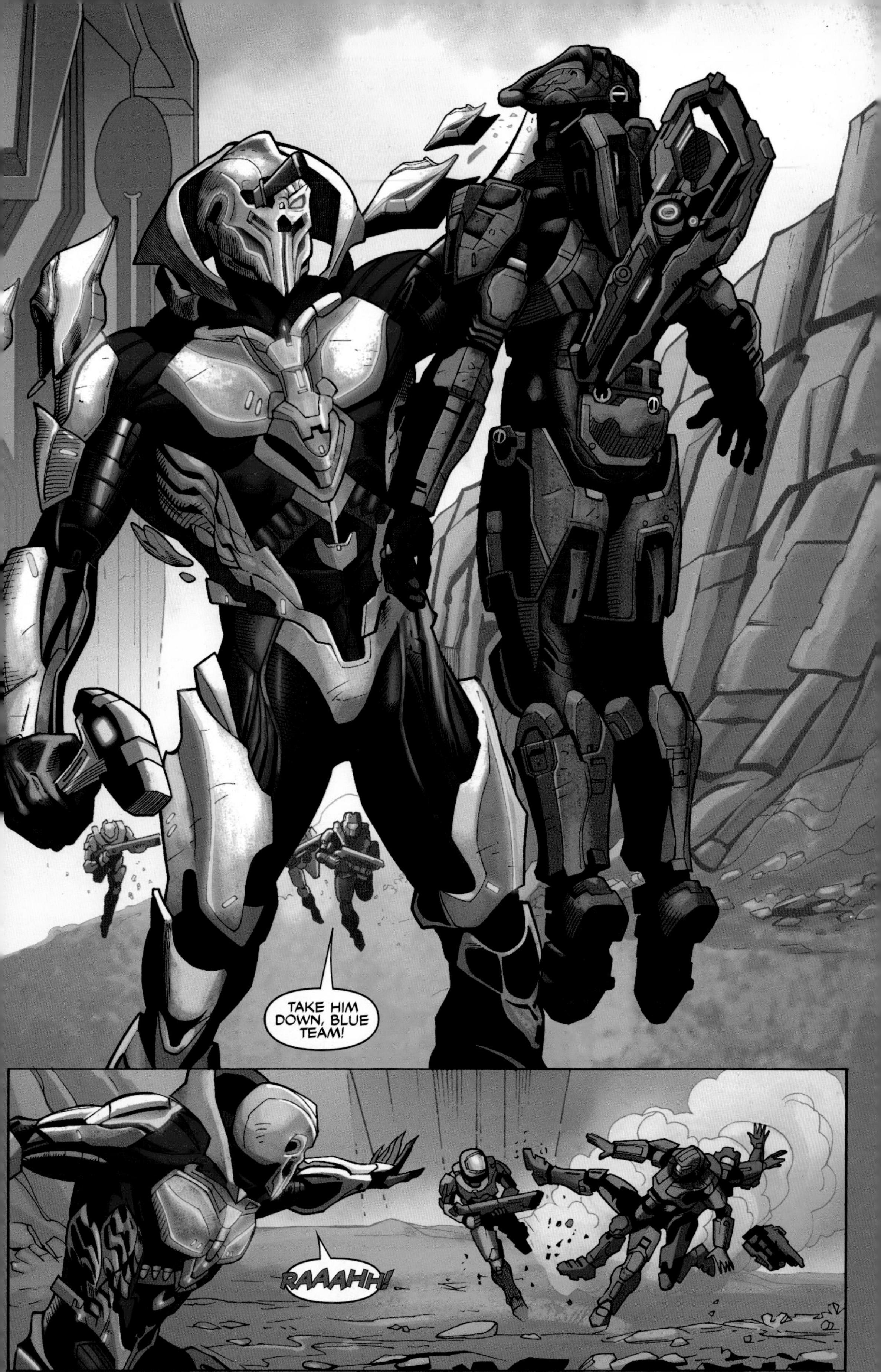
TAKE HIM DOWN, BLUE TEAM!
RAAAHH!

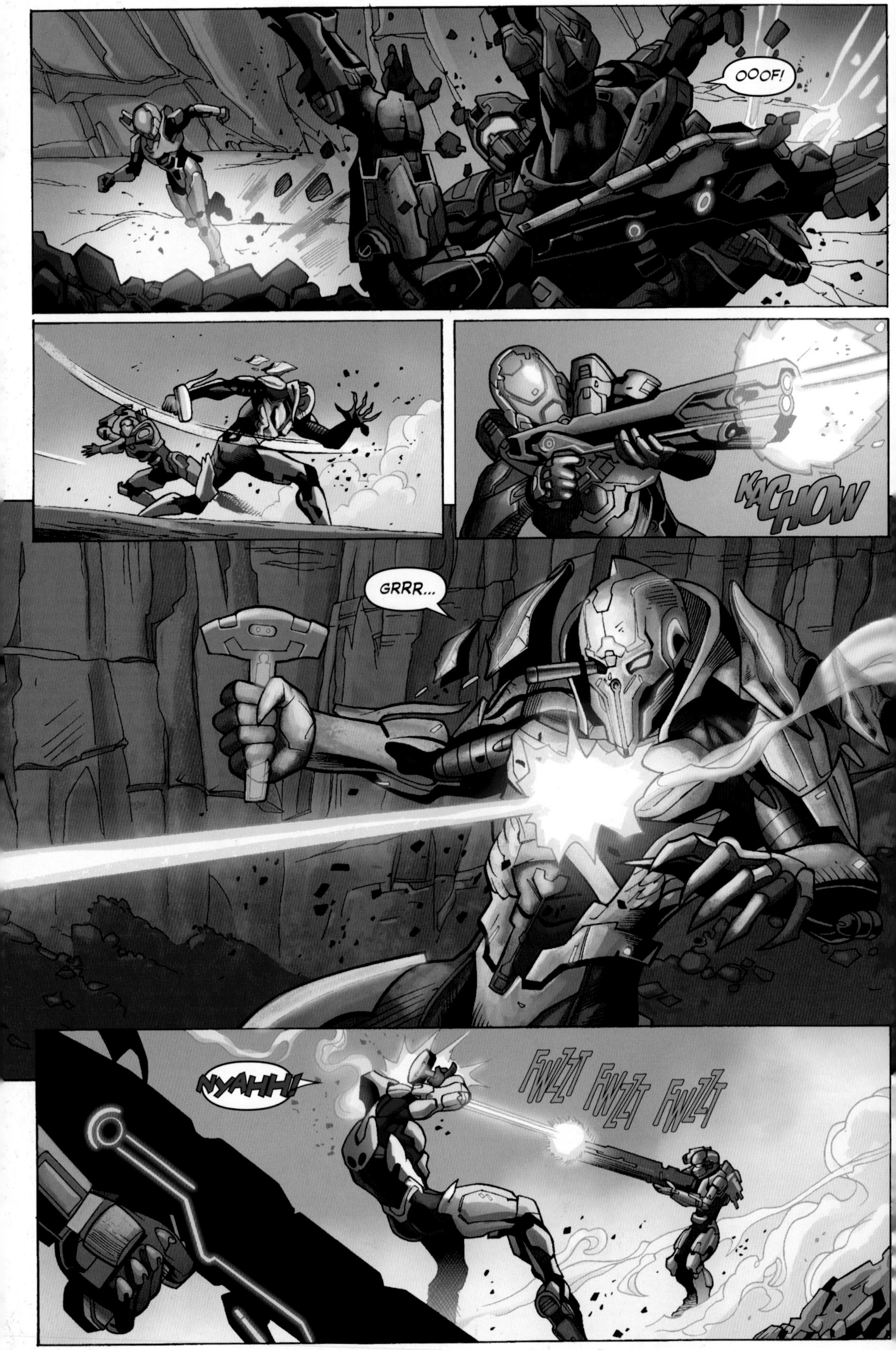
OOOF!
KACHOW
GRRR...
NYAHH!
FWZZT FWZZT FWZZT

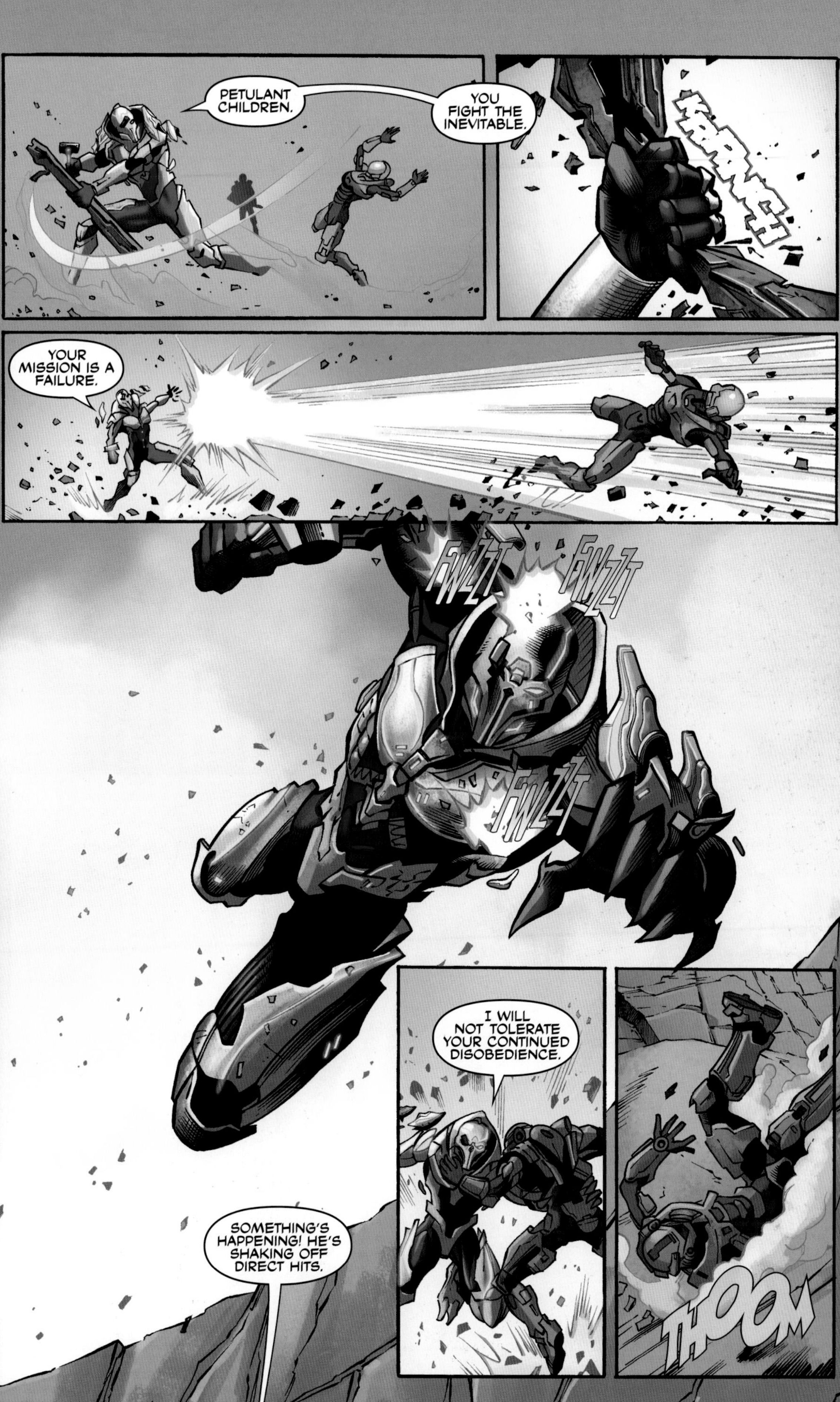

PETULANT CHILDREN.
YOU FIGHT THE INEVITABLE.
KRRNCH
YOUR MISSION IS A FAILURE.
FWZZT
FWZZT
FWZZT
SOMETHING'S HAPPENING! HE'S SHAKING OFF DIRECT HITS.
I WILL NOT TOLERATE YOUR CONTINUED DISOBEDIENCE.
THOOM

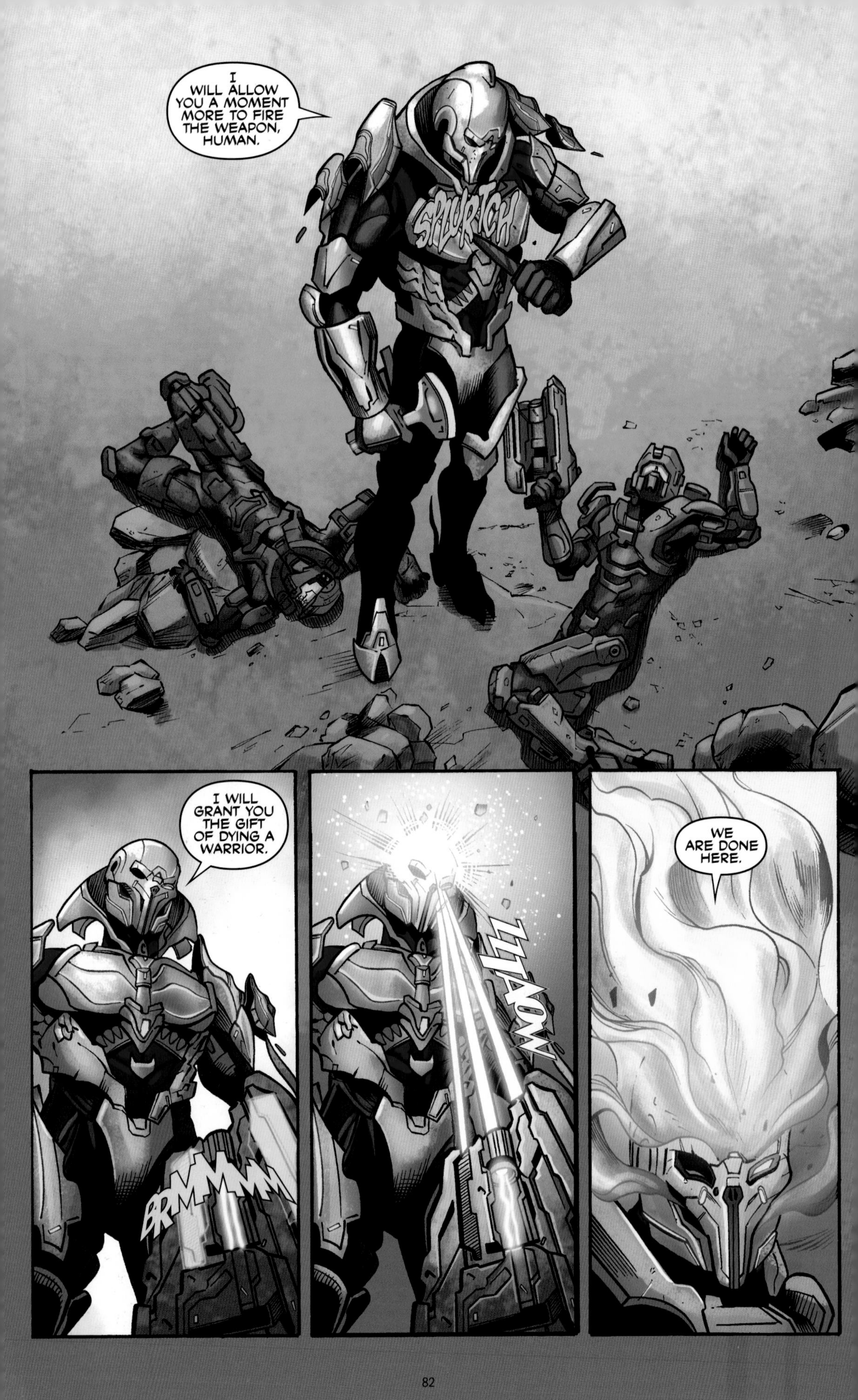
I WILL ALLOW YOU A MOMENT MORE TO FIRE THE WEAPON, HUMAN.
SPLURTCH
I WILL GRANT YOU THE GIFT OF DYING A WARRIOR.
BRMMMMM
ZZZAOW
WE ARE DONE HERE.

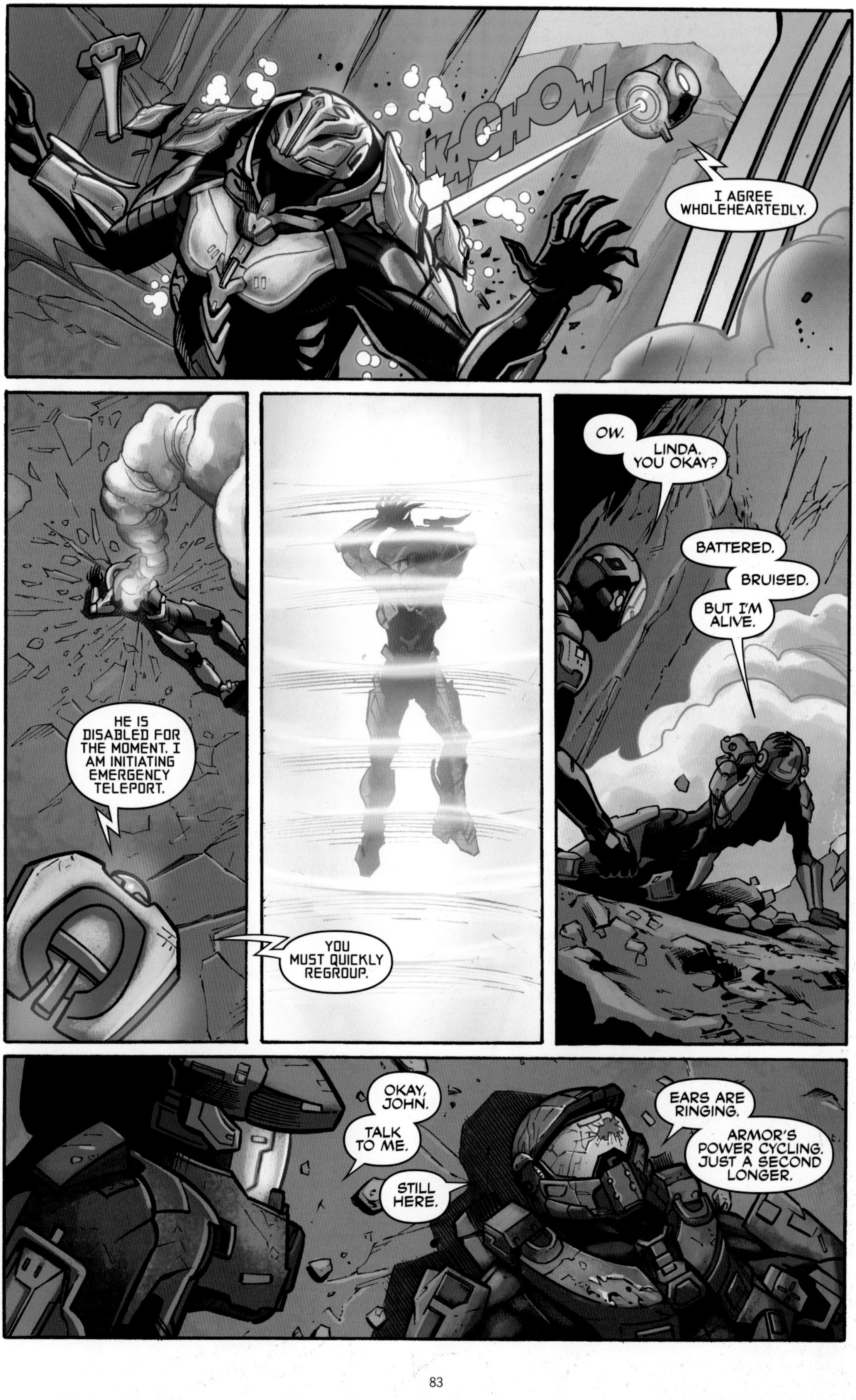
KACHOW
I AGREE WHOLEHEARTEDLY.
HE IS DISABLED FOR THE MOMENT. I AM INITIATING EMERGENCY TELEPORT.
YOU MUST QUICKLY REGROUP.
OW.
LINDA. YOU OKAY?
BATTERED.
BRUISED.
BUT I'M ALIVE.
OKAY, JOHN.
TALK TO ME.
STILL HERE.
EARS ARE RINGING.
ARMOR'S POWER CYCLING. JUST A SECOND LONGER.

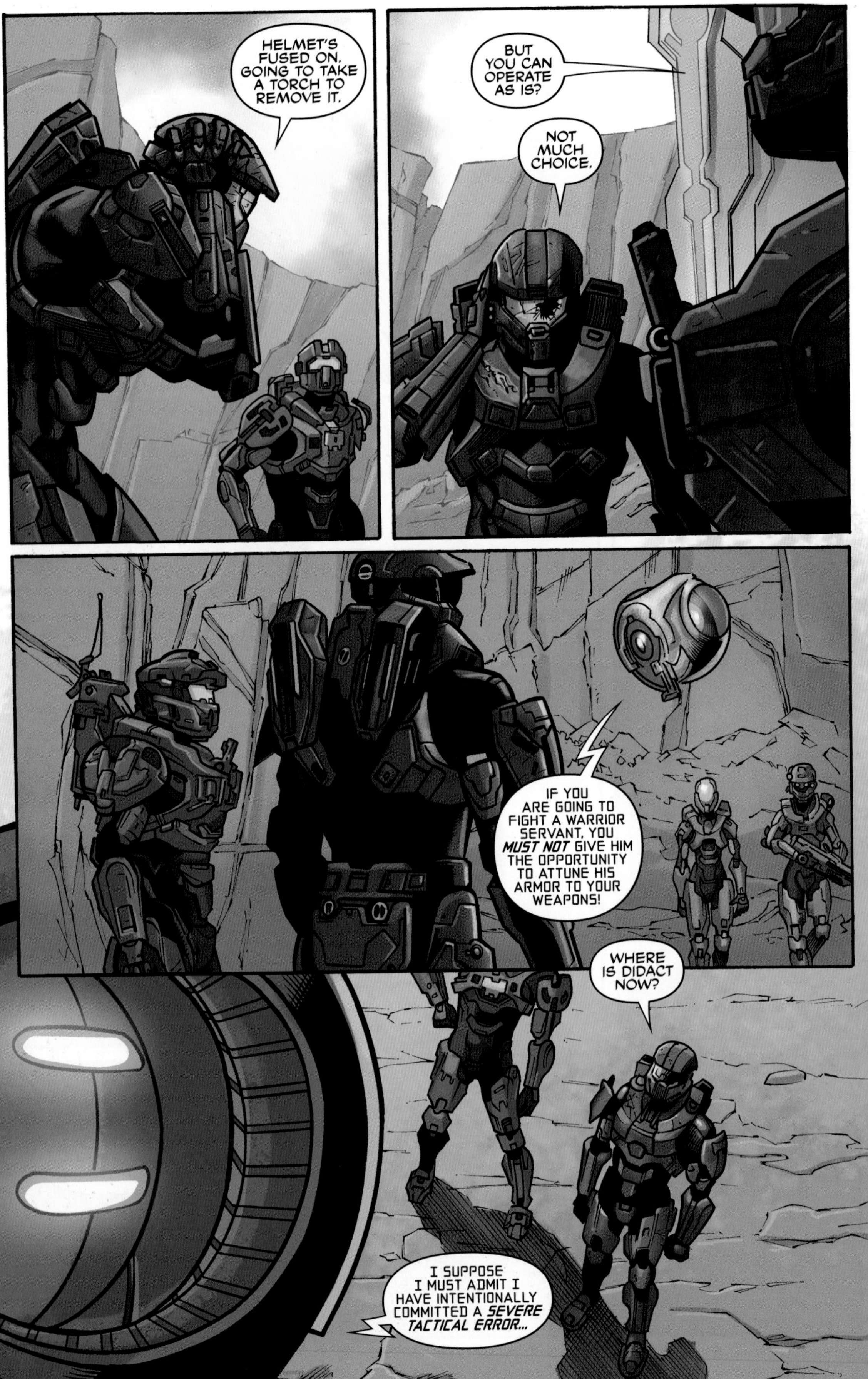
HELMET'S FUSED ON, GOING TO TAKE A TORCH TO REMOVE IT.
BUT YOU CAN OPERATE AS IS?
NOT MUCH CHOICE.
IF YOU ARE GOING TO FIGHT A WARRIOR SERVANT, YOU *MUST NOT* GIVE HIM THE OPPORTUNITY TO ATTUNE HIS ARMOR TO YOUR WEAPONS!
WHERE IS DIDACT NOW?
I SUPPOSE I MUST ADMIT I HAVE INTENTIONALLY COMMITTED A *SEVERE TACTICAL ERROR...*

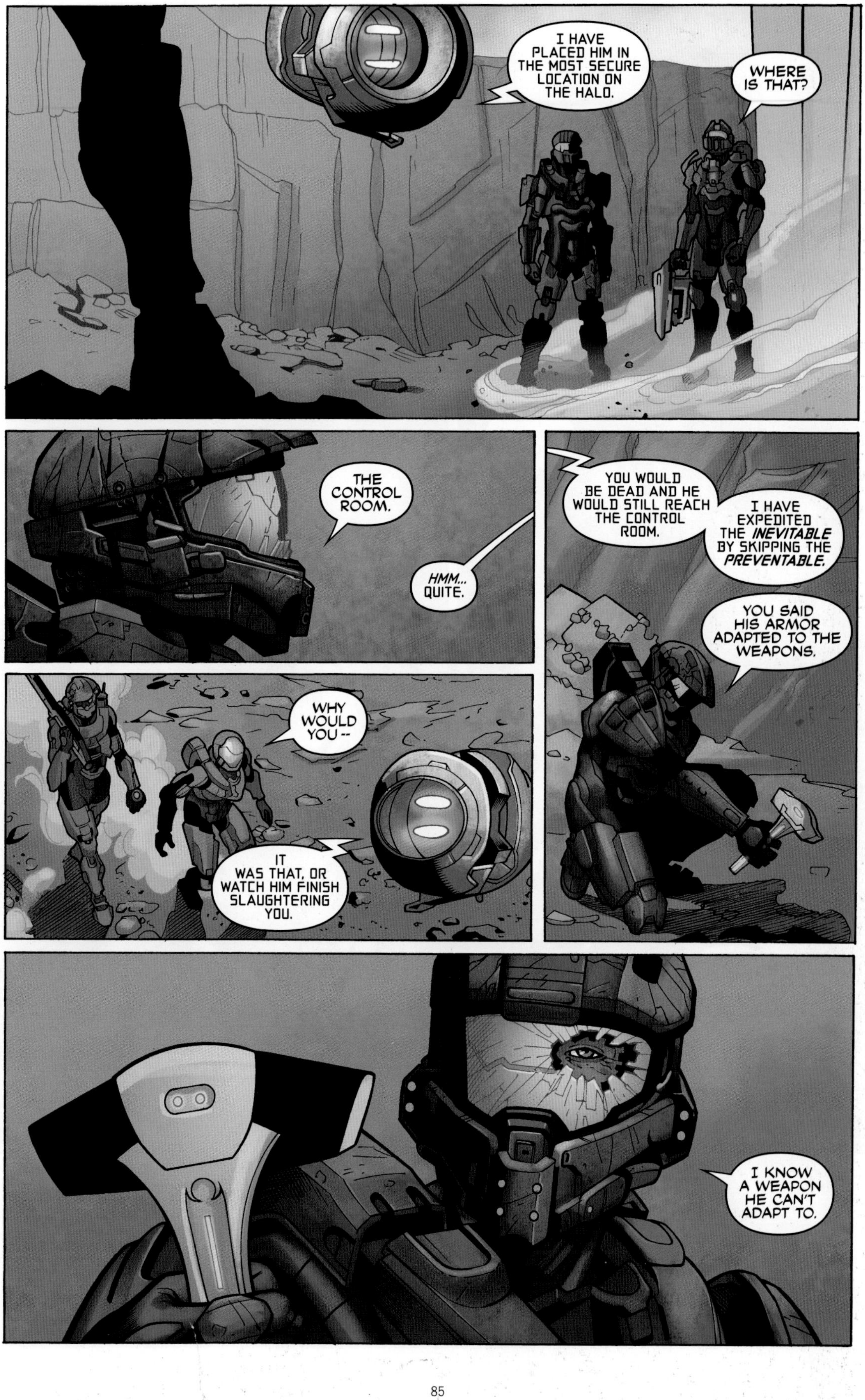
I HAVE PLACED HIM IN THE MOST SECURE LOCATION ON THE HALO.
WHERE IS THAT?
THE CONTROL ROOM.
HMM... QUITE.
YOU WOULD BE DEAD AND HE WOULD STILL REACH THE CONTROL ROOM.
I HAVE EXPEDITED THE *INEVITABLE* BY SKIPPING THE *PREVENTABLE.*
WHY WOULD YOU --
IT WAS THAT, OR WATCH HIM FINISH SLAUGHTERING YOU.
YOU SAID HIS ARMOR ADAPTED TO THE WEAPONS.
I KNOW A WEAPON HE CAN'T ADAPT TO.

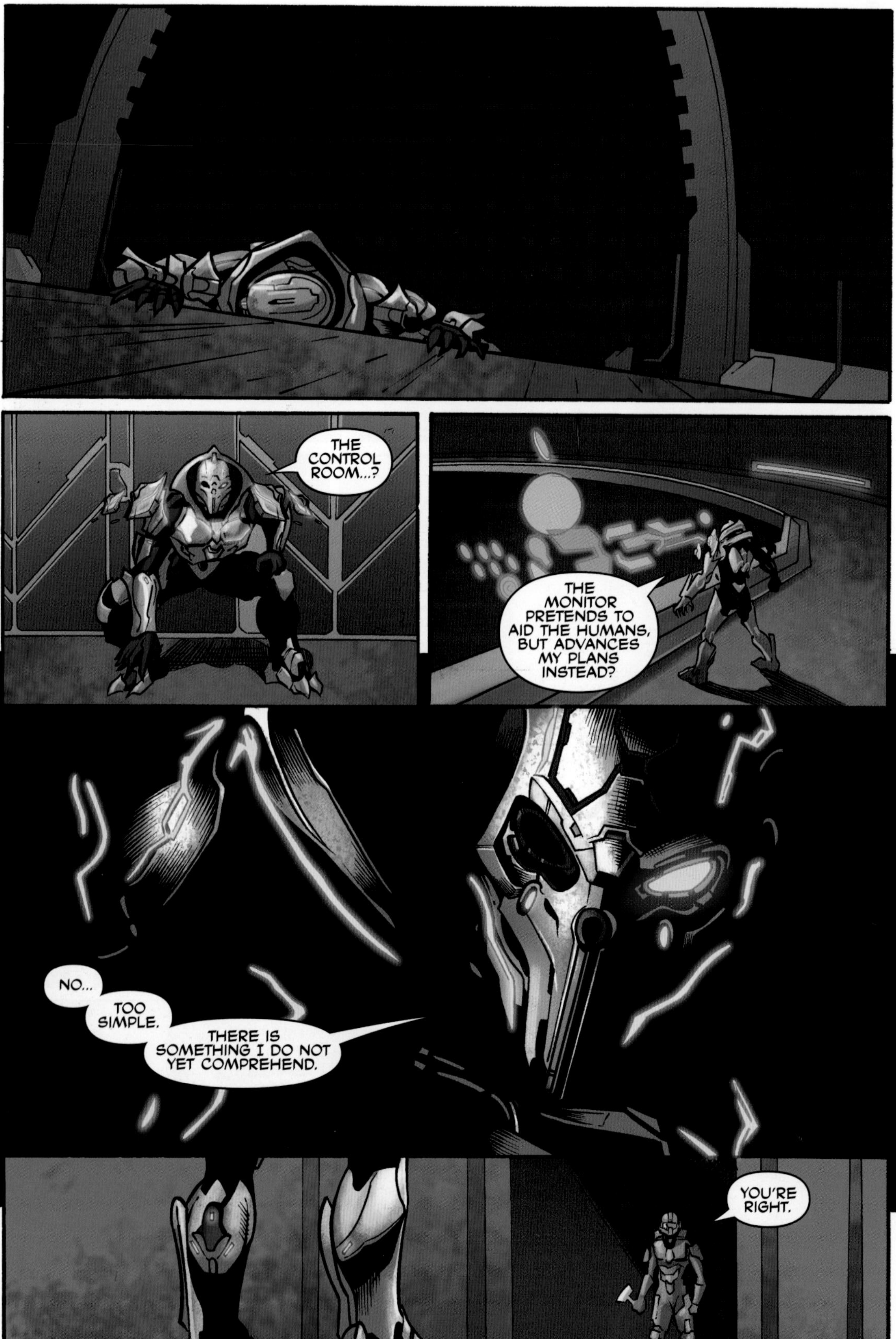
THE CONTROL ROOM...?
THE MONITOR PRETENDS TO AID THE HUMANS, BUT ADVANCES MY PLANS INSTEAD?
NO...
TOO SIMPLE.
THERE IS SOMETHING I DO NOT YET COMPREHEND.
YOU'RE RIGHT.

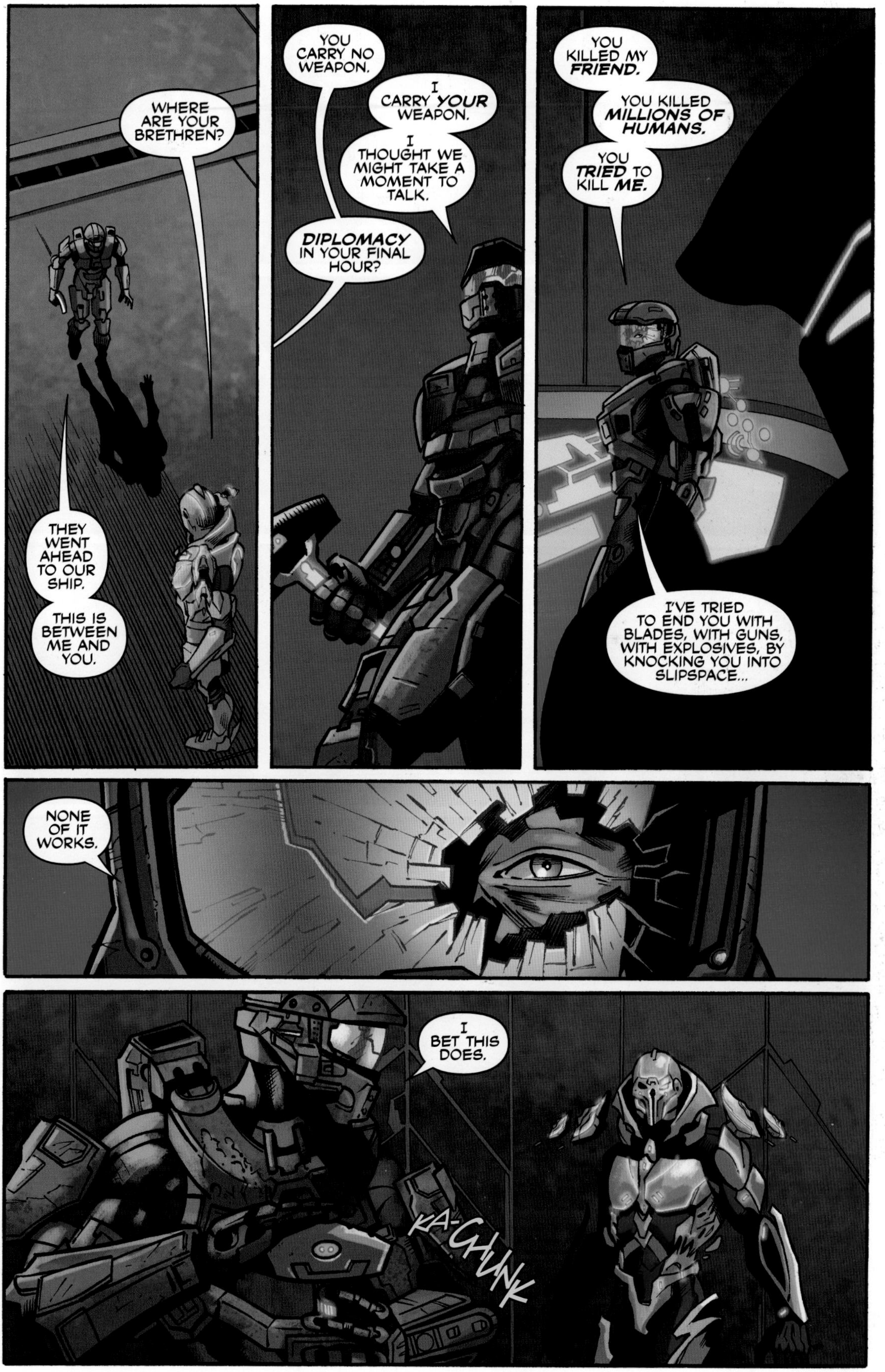
WHERE ARE YOUR BRETHREN?
THEY WENT AHEAD TO OUR SHIP.
THIS IS BETWEEN ME AND YOU.
YOU CARRY NO WEAPON.
I CARRY *YOUR* WEAPON.
I THOUGHT WE MIGHT TAKE A MOMENT TO TALK.
DIPLOMACY IN YOUR FINAL HOUR?
YOU KILLED MY *FRIEND.*
YOU KILLED *MILLIONS OF HUMANS.*
YOU *TRIED* TO KILL *ME.*
I'VE TRIED TO END YOU WITH BLADES, WITH GUNS, WITH EXPLOSIVES, BY KNOCKING YOU INTO SLIPSPACE...
NONE OF IT WORKS.
I BET THIS DOES.
KA-CHUNK

YOU WOULD FIRE THE HALO.

JUST TO ELIMINATE ME?

YES.

BUT THEN THE MONITOR REMINDED ME THAT WOULD ALSO KILL ALL LIFE WITHIN *TWENTY-FIVE LIGHT YEARS*...

SO HE SUGGESTED A BETTER PLAN.

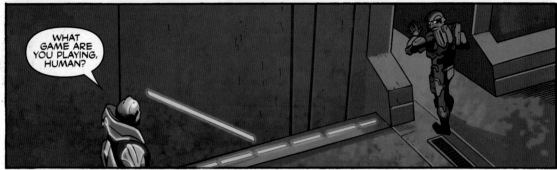

WHAT GAME ARE YOU PLAYING, HUMAN?

TWO-STEP PROCESS.

FIRST, I MANUALLY DEACTIVATE THE SAFETY PROTOCOLS.

SECOND... MONITOR EJECTS US, RIGHT INTO THE PLANET.

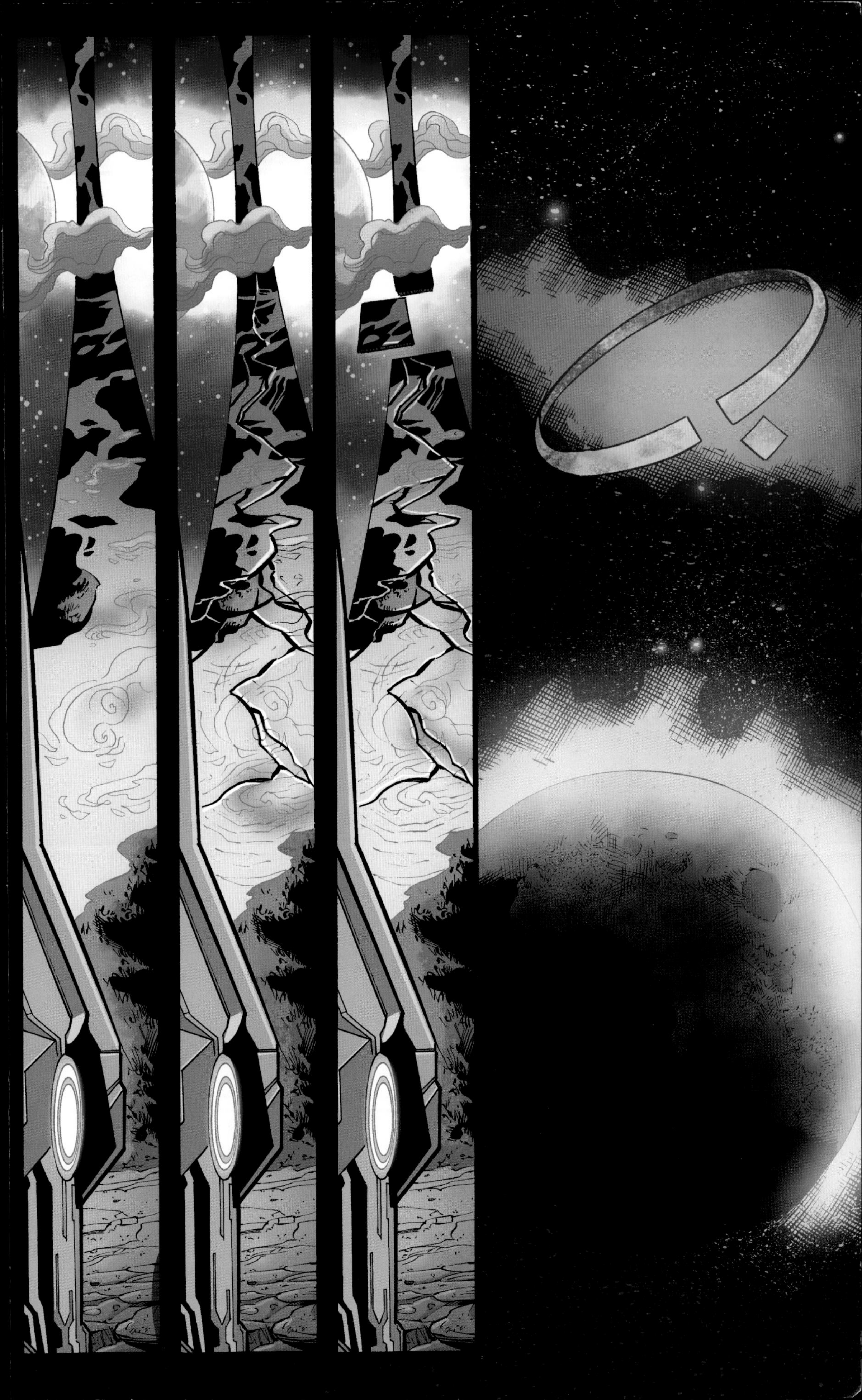

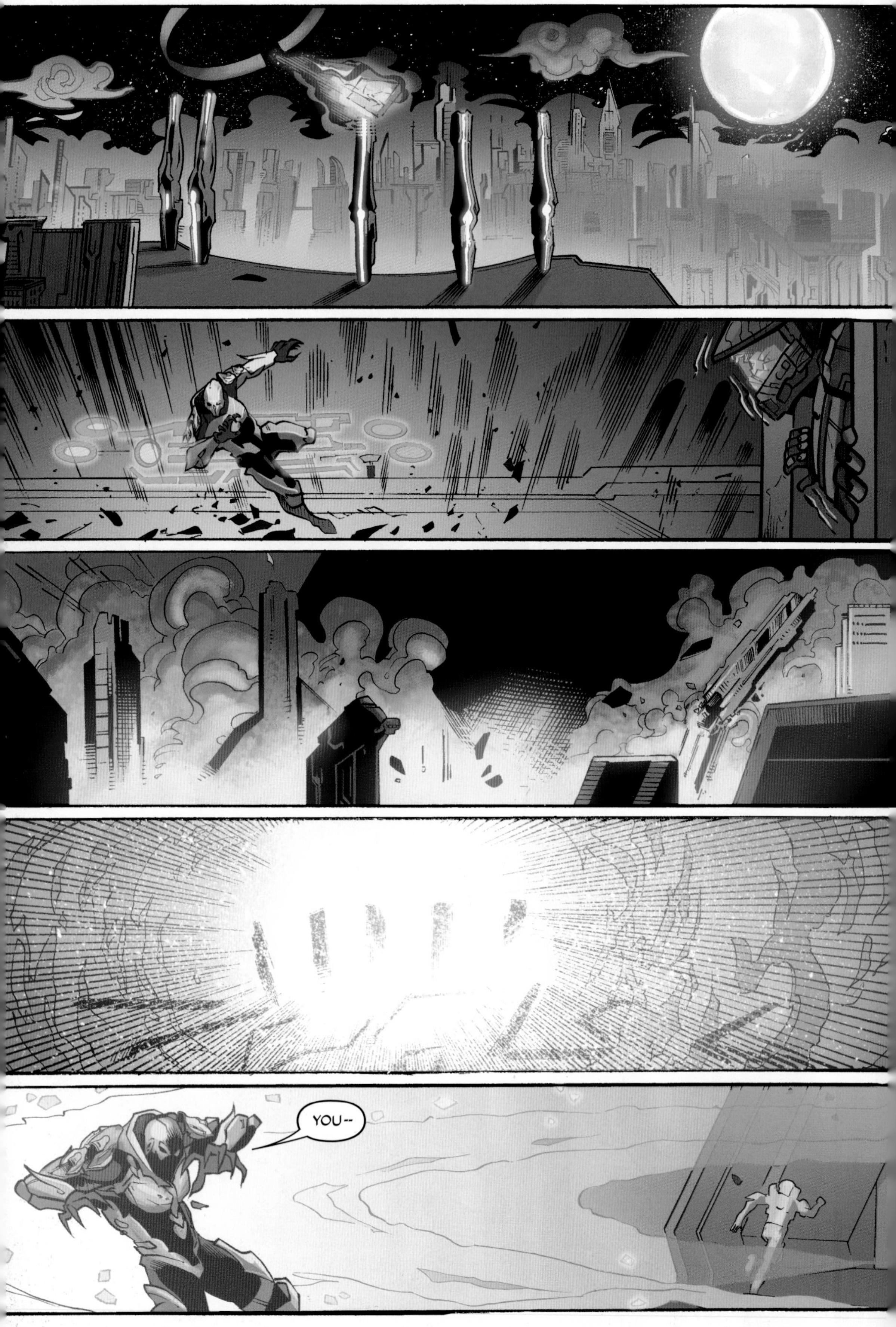
YOU--

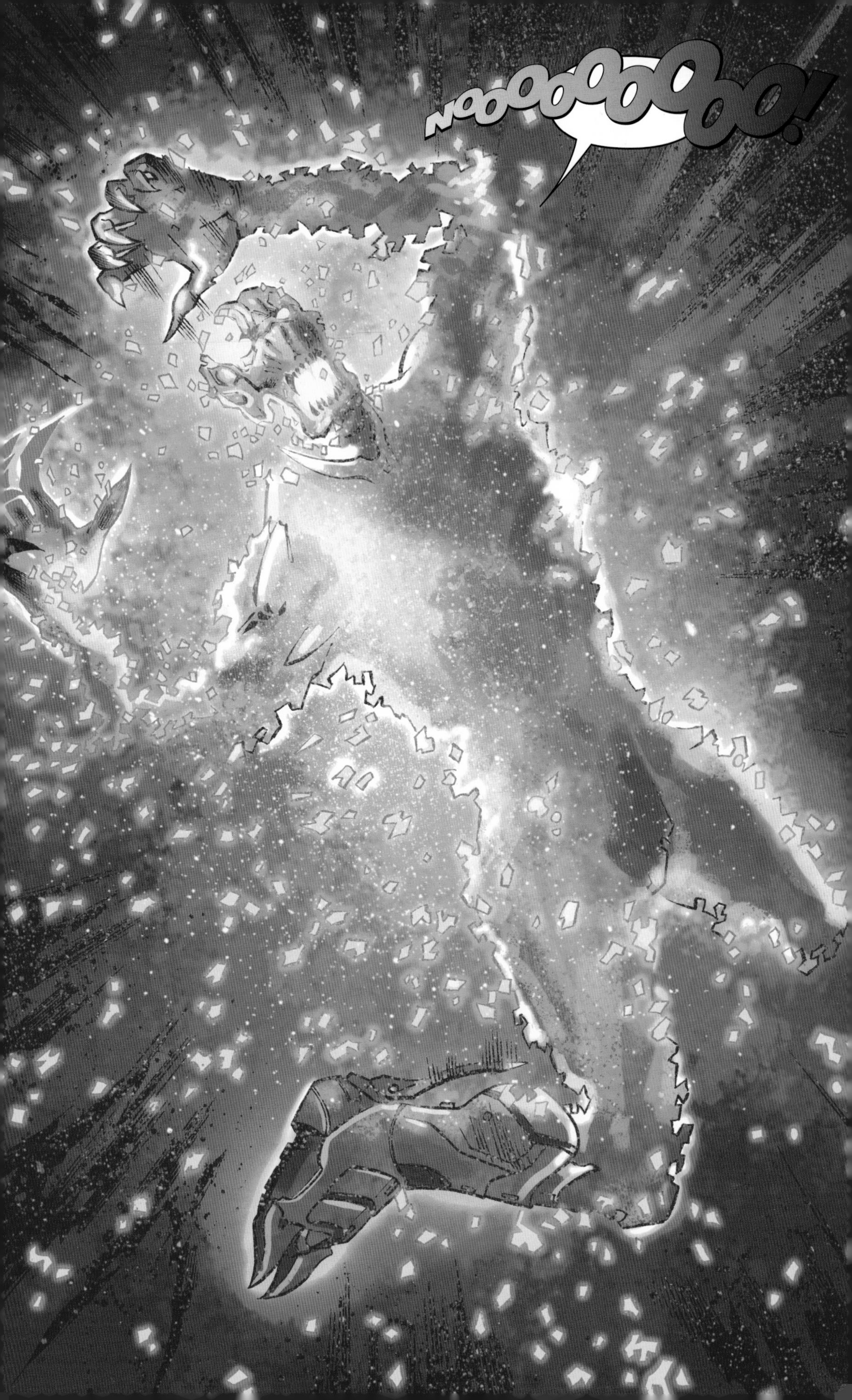
NOOOOOOOOOO!

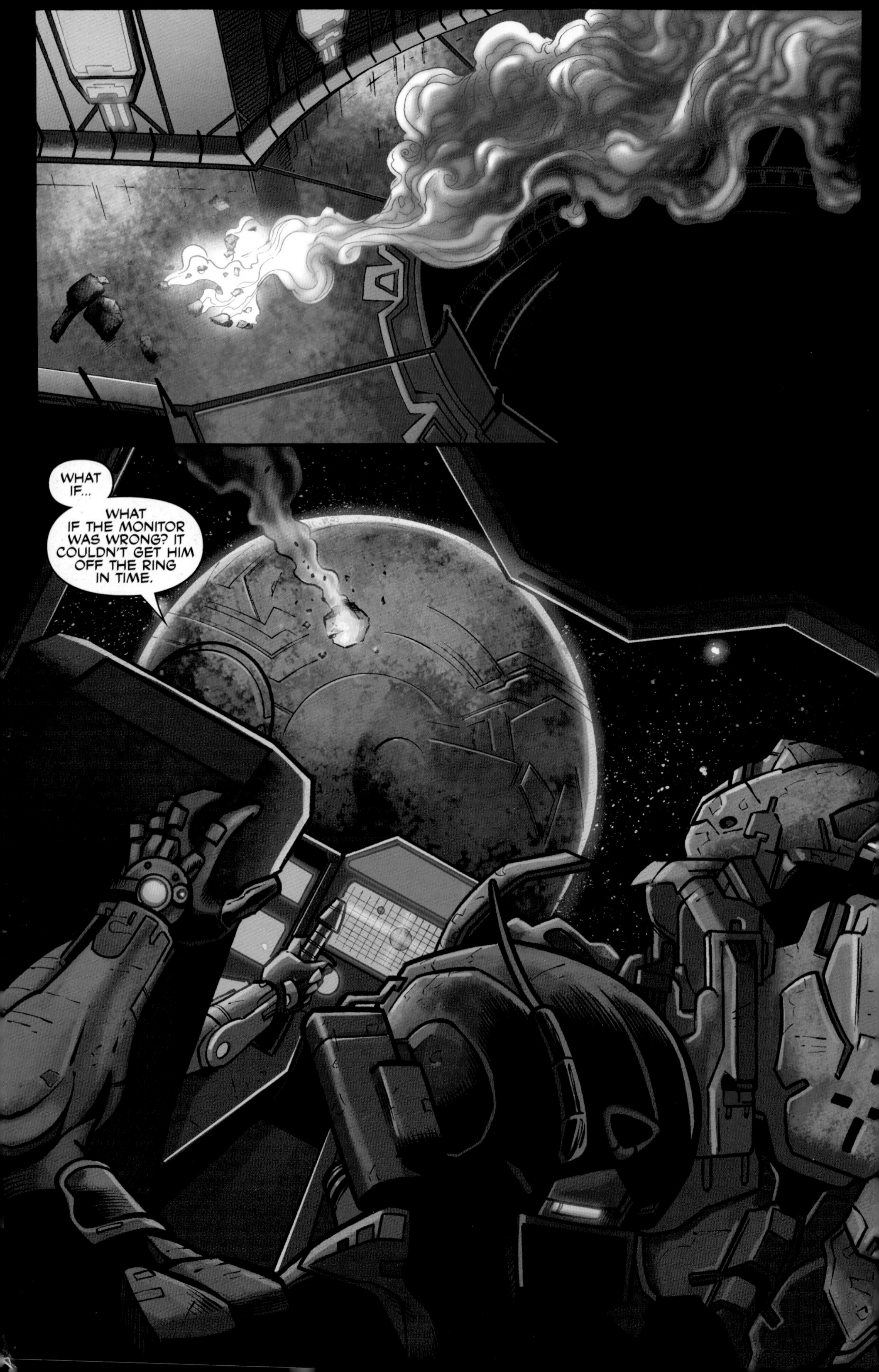
WHAT IF...
WHAT IF THE MONITOR WAS WRONG? IT COULDN'T GET HIM OFF THE RING IN TIME.

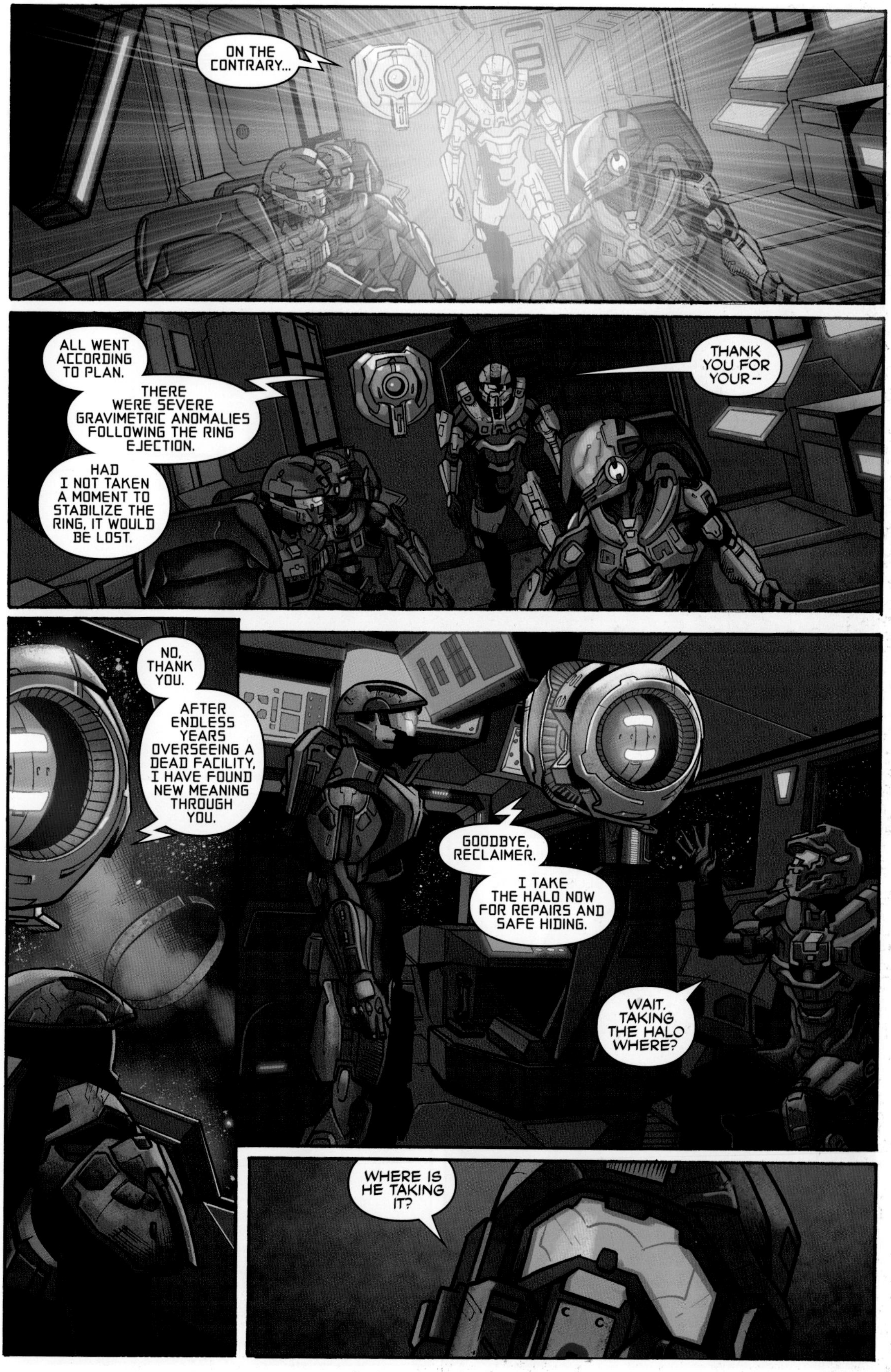
ON THE CONTRARY...
ALL WENT ACCORDING TO PLAN.
THERE WERE SEVERE GRAVIMETRIC ANOMALIES FOLLOWING THE RING EJECTION.
HAD I NOT TAKEN A MOMENT TO STABILIZE THE RING, IT WOULD BE LOST.
THANK YOU FOR YOUR--
NO, THANK YOU.
AFTER ENDLESS YEARS OVERSEEING A DEAD FACILITY, I HAVE FOUND NEW MEANING THROUGH YOU.
GOODBYE, RECLAIMER.
I TAKE THE HALO NOW FOR REPAIRS AND SAFE HIDING.
WAIT. TAKING THE HALO WHERE?
WHERE IS HE TAKING IT?

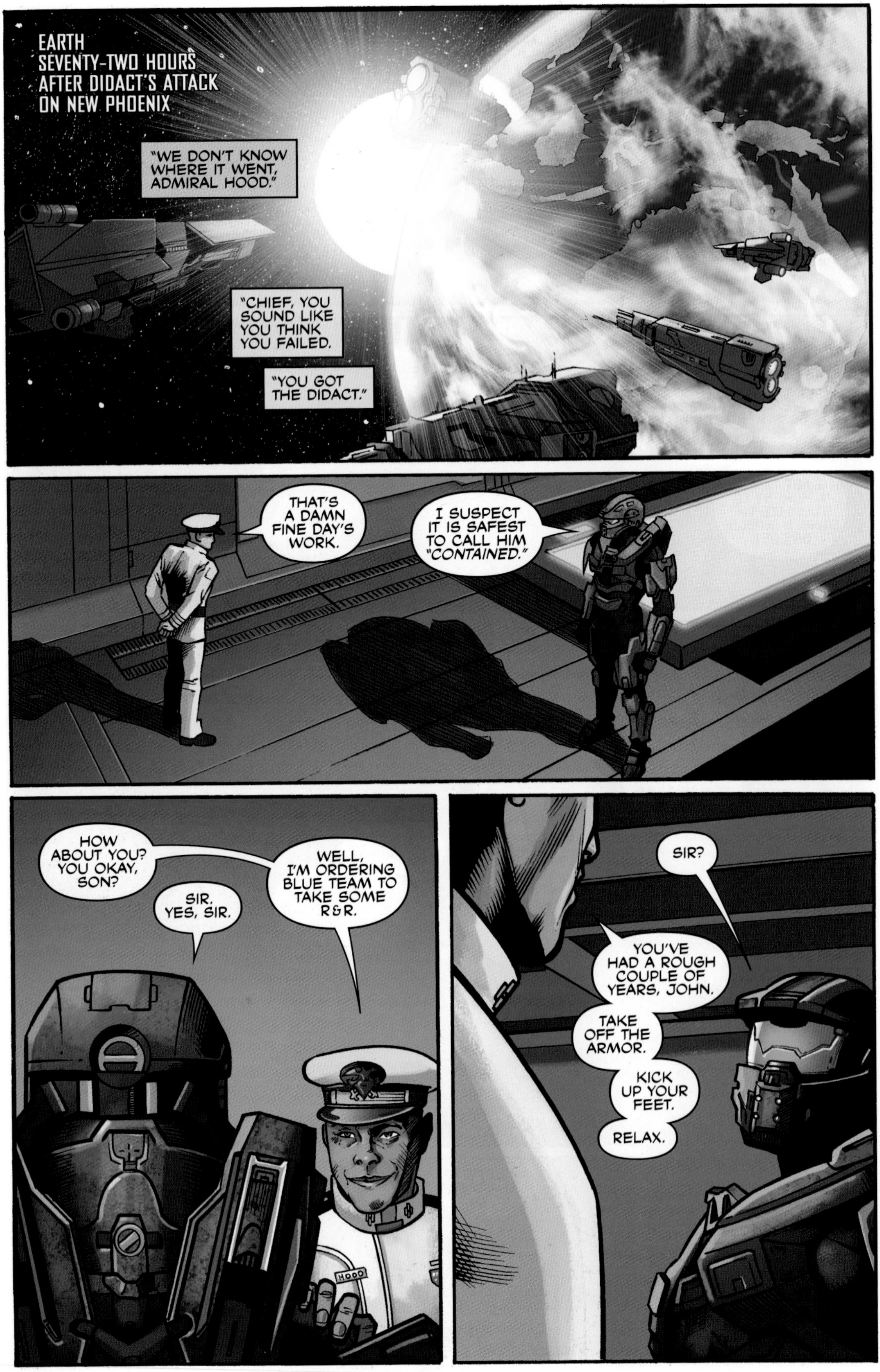
EARTH
SEVENTY-TWO HOURS AFTER DIDACT'S ATTACK ON NEW PHOENIX
"WE DON'T KNOW WHERE IT WENT, ADMIRAL HOOD."
"CHIEF, YOU SOUND LIKE YOU THINK YOU FAILED.
"YOU GOT THE DIDACT."
THAT'S A DAMN FINE DAY'S WORK.
I SUSPECT IT IS SAFEST TO CALL HIM "CONTAINED."
HOW ABOUT YOU? YOU OKAY, SON?
SIR. YES, SIR.
WELL, I'M ORDERING BLUE TEAM TO TAKE SOME R&R.
HOOD
SIR?
YOU'VE HAD A ROUGH COUPLE OF YEARS, JOHN.
TAKE OFF THE ARMOR.
KICK UP YOUR FEET.
RELAX.

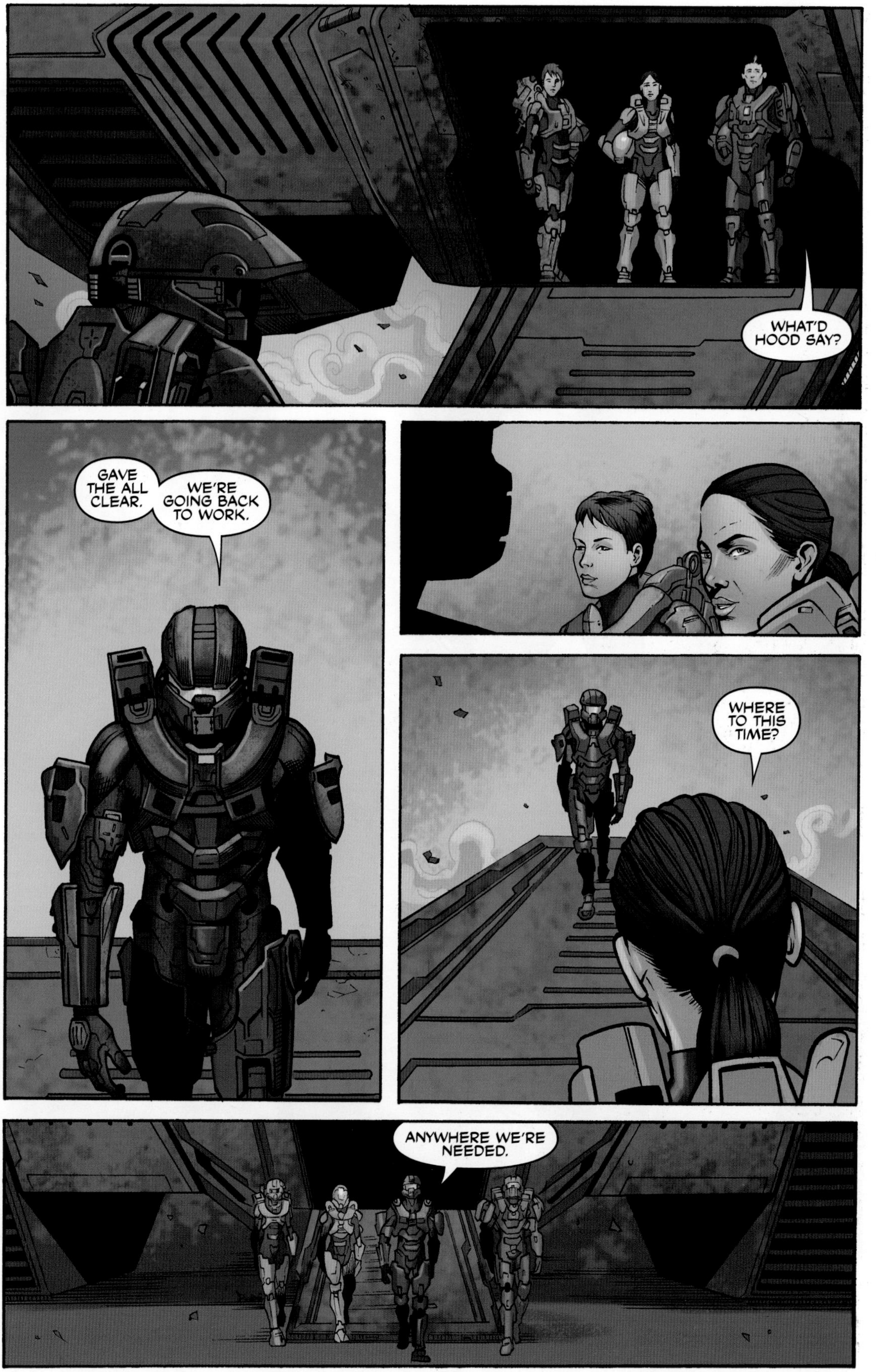
WHAT'D HOOD SAY?
GAVE THE ALL CLEAR.
WE'RE GOING BACK TO WORK.
WHERE TO THIS TIME?
ANYWHERE WE'RE NEEDED.

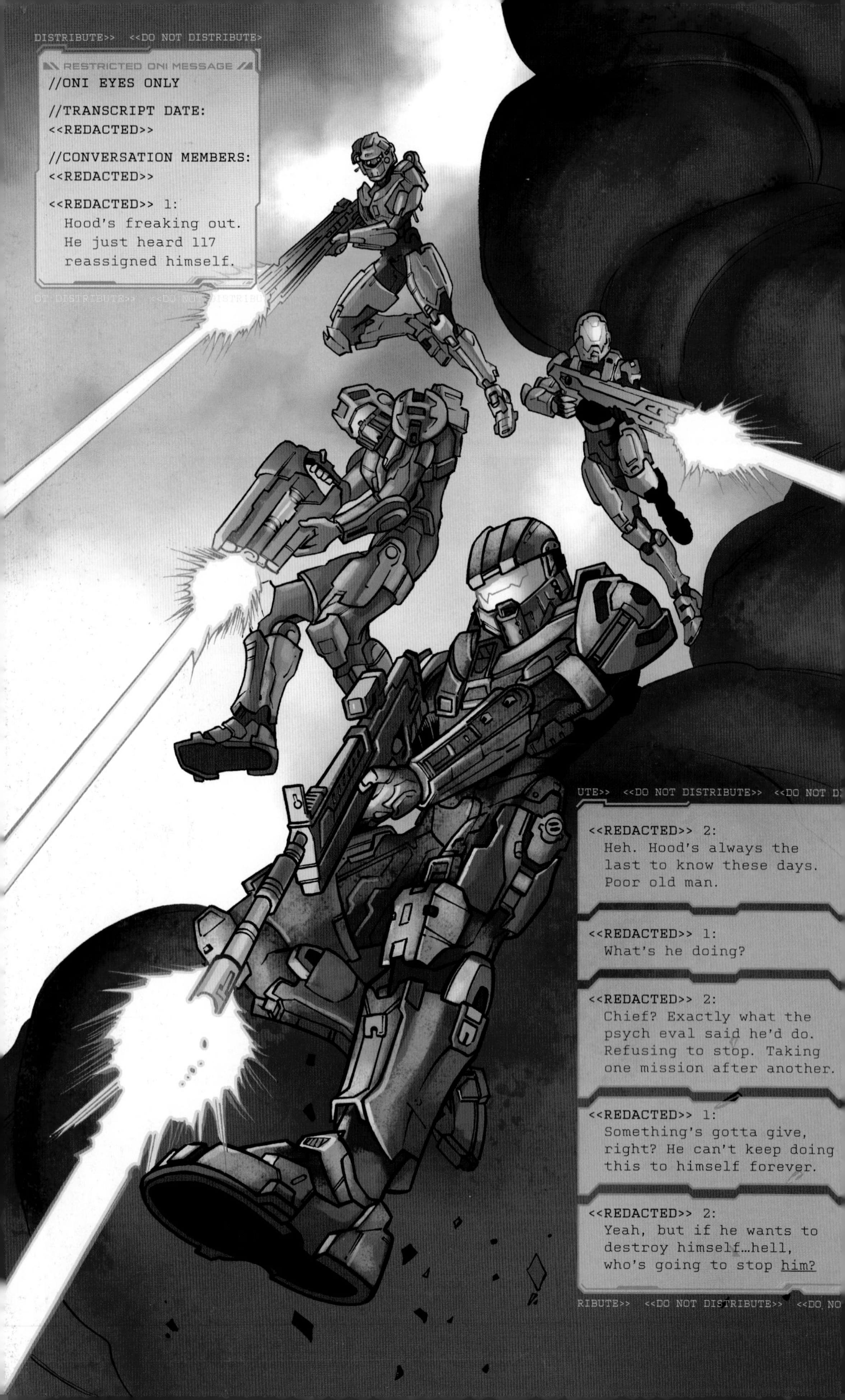

DISTRIBUTE>> <<DO NOT DISTRIBUTE>
RESTRICTED ONI MESSAGE
//ONI EYES ONLY
//TRANSCRIPT DATE: <<REDACTED>>
//CONVERSATION MEMBERS: <<REDACTED>>
<<REDACTED>> 1: Hood's freaking out. He just heard 117 reassigned himself.
UTE>> <<DO NOT DISTRIBUTE>> <<DO NOT D
<<REDACTED>> 2: Heh. Hood's always the last to know these days. Poor old man.
<<REDACTED>> 1: What's he doing?
<<REDACTED>> 2: Chief? Exactly what the psych eval said he'd do. Refusing to stop. Taking one mission after another.
<<REDACTED>> 1: Something's gotta give, right? He can't keep doing this to himself forever.
<<REDACTED>> 2: Yeah, but if he wants to destroy himself…hell, who's going to stop him?
RIBUTE>> <<DO NOT DISTRIBUTE>> <<DO NO

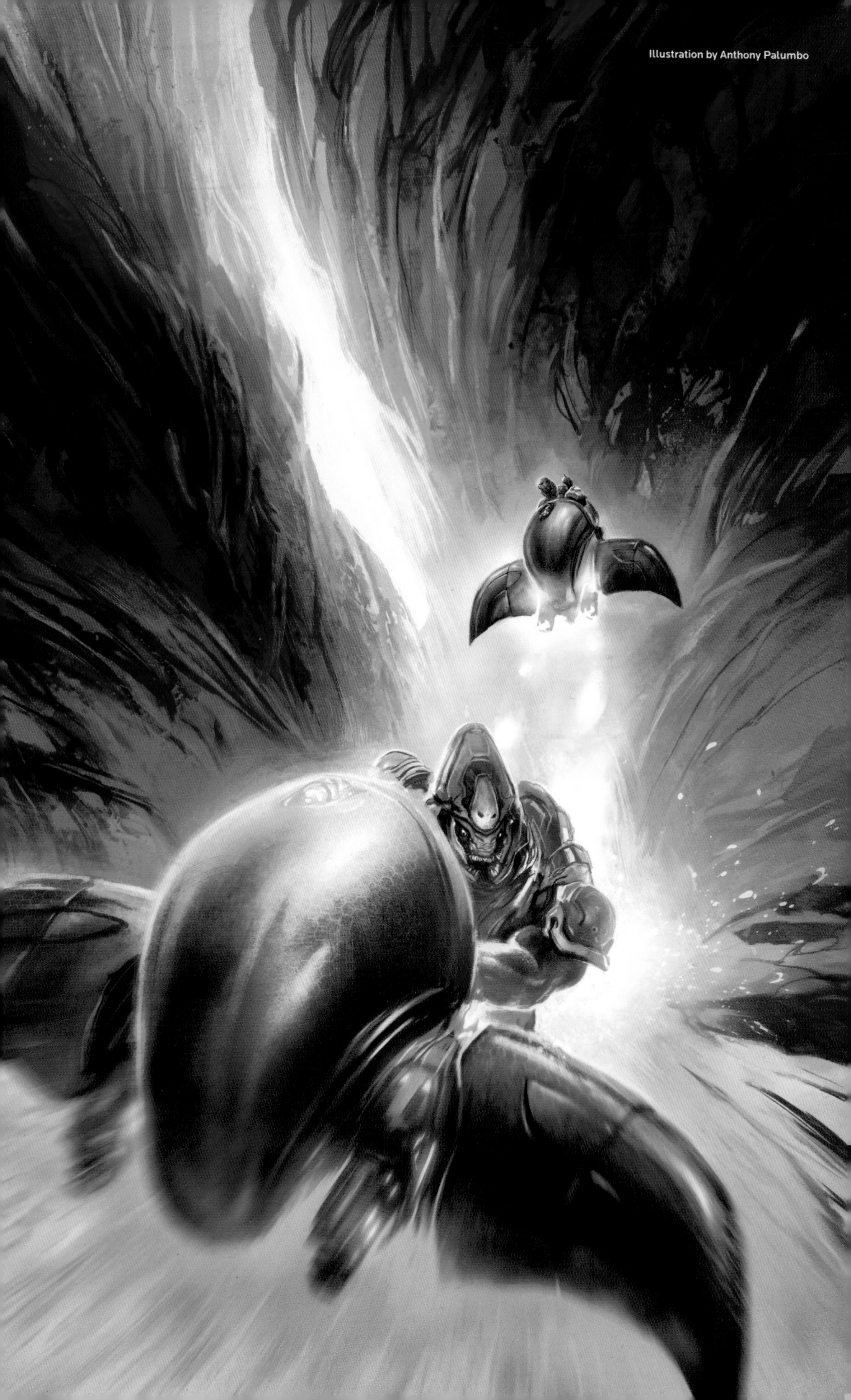

Illustration by Anthony Palumbo

It is a time of great instability in the postwar galaxy. As the UNSC *Infinity* conducts its continuing mission of research and exploration, it must also act as the first line of defense against the bizarre new threats emerging from the chaos . . .

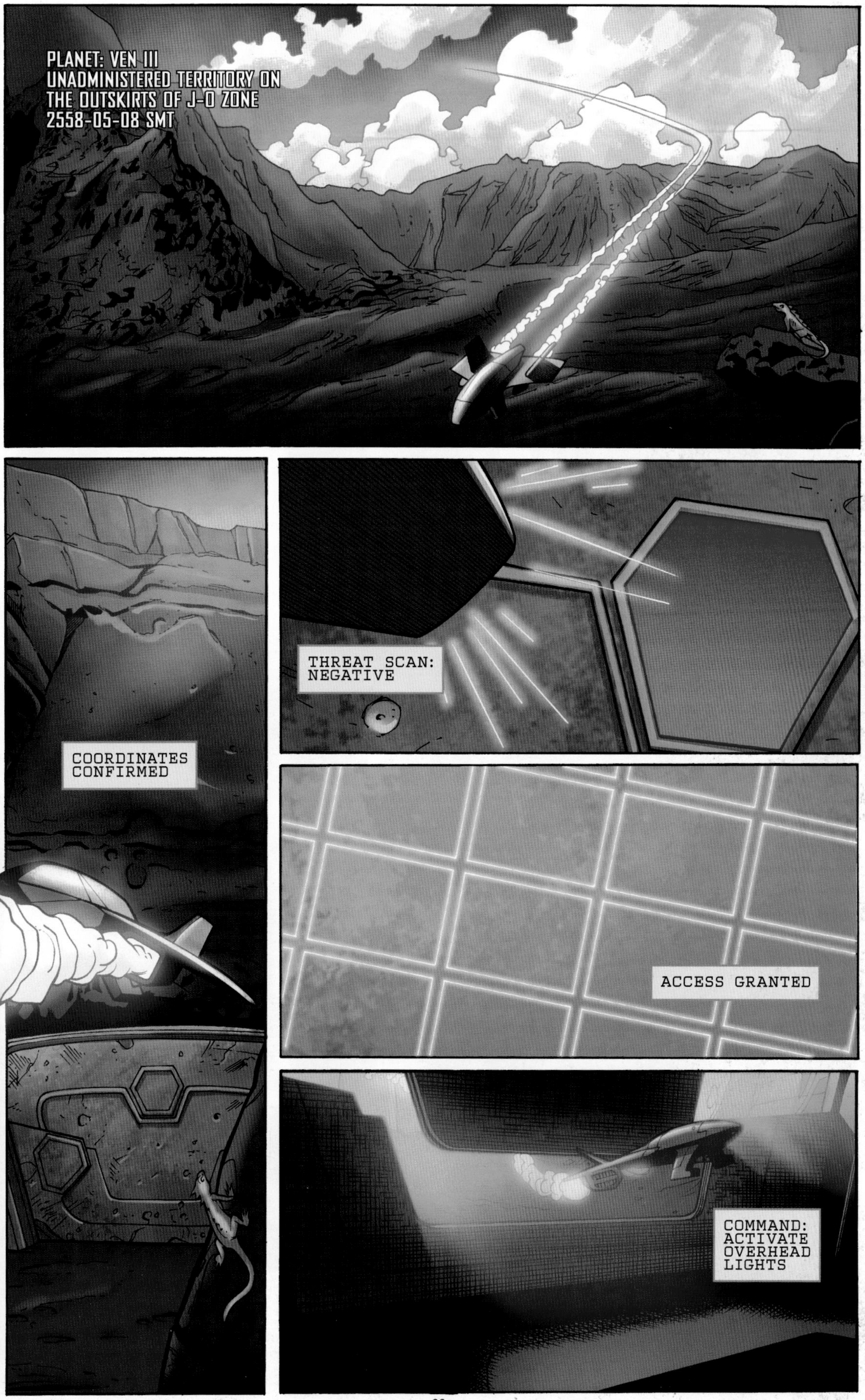
PLANET: VEN III
UNADMINISTERED TERRITORY ON THE OUTSKIRTS OF J-O ZONE
2558-05-08 SMT
COORDINATES CONFIRMED
THREAT SCAN: NEGATIVE
ACCESS GRANTED
COMMAND: ACTIVATE OVERHEAD LIGHTS

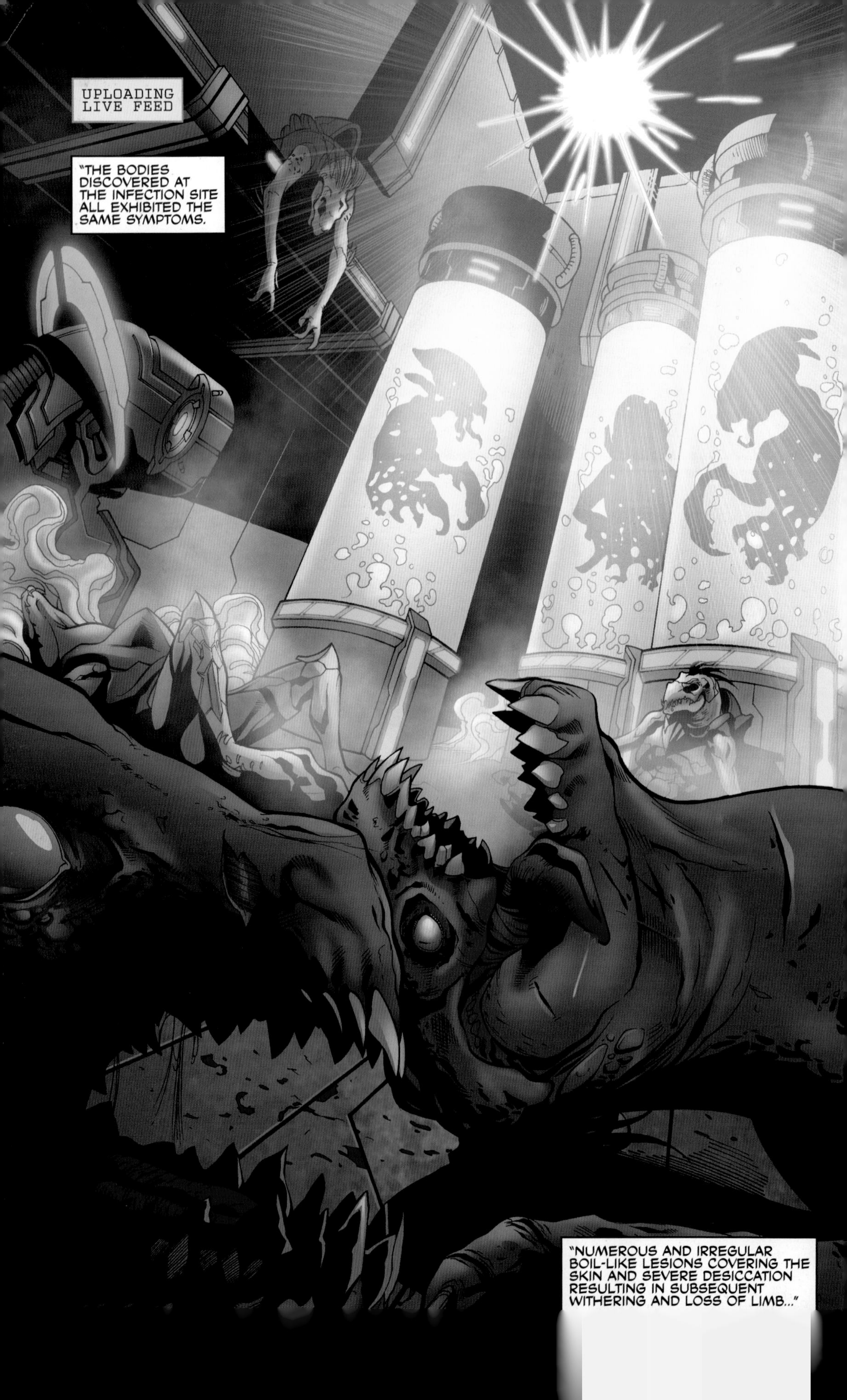
UPLOADING LIVE FEED
"THE BODIES DISCOVERED AT THE INFECTION SITE ALL EXHIBITED THE SAME SYMPTOMS.
"NUMEROUS AND IRREGULAR BOIL-LIKE LESIONS COVERING THE SKIN AND SEVERE DESICCATION RESULTING IN SUBSEQUENT WITHERING AND LOSS OF LIMB..."

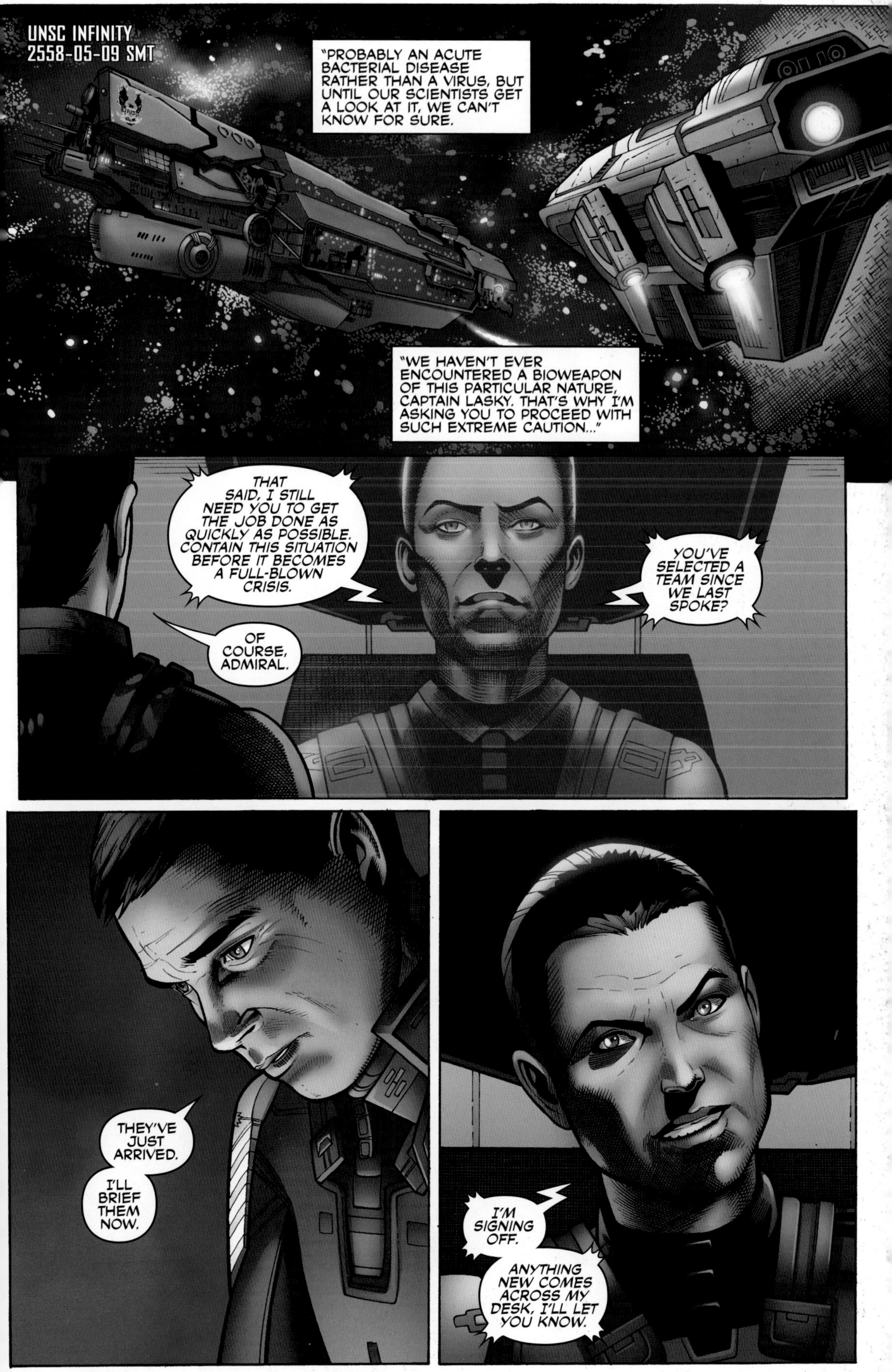
UNSC INFINITY
2558-05-09 SMT
"PROBABLY AN ACUTE BACTERIAL DISEASE RATHER THAN A VIRUS, BUT UNTIL OUR SCIENTISTS GET A LOOK AT IT, WE CAN'T KNOW FOR SURE.
"WE HAVEN'T EVER ENCOUNTERED A BIOWEAPON OF THIS PARTICULAR NATURE, CAPTAIN LASKY. THAT'S WHY I'M ASKING YOU TO PROCEED WITH SUCH EXTREME CAUTION..."
THAT SAID, I STILL NEED YOU TO GET THE JOB DONE AS QUICKLY AS POSSIBLE. CONTAIN THIS SITUATION BEFORE IT BECOMES A FULL-BLOWN CRISIS.
OF COURSE, ADMIRAL.
YOU'VE SELECTED A TEAM SINCE WE LAST SPOKE?
THEY'VE JUST ARRIVED.
I'LL BRIEF THEM NOW.
I'M SIGNING OFF.
ANYTHING NEW COMES ACROSS MY DESK, I'LL LET YOU KNOW.

CAPTAIN.

RAY. THORNE. COME ON IN...

WE'VE GOT AN URGENT SITUATION UNFOLDING ON THE PLANET *VEN III*. A LITTLE ROCK OUT ON THE EDGE OF THE J-O ZONE.

IT'S ALMOST UNINHABITABLE. COVENANT USED IT ON AND OFF OVER THE YEARS AS A STAGING AREA FOR BIG OFFENSIVES.

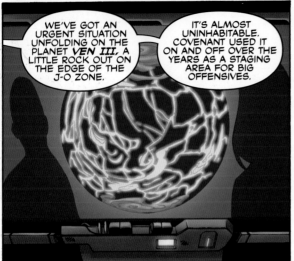

AFTER THE REALIGNMENT, IT WAS LEFT *UNCLAIMED.*

IN THE MEANTIME, A SMALL POPULATION OF *JACKALS* HAVE SQUATTED THERE.

APPARENTLY A FEW OF THEM DISCOVERED AN OLD COVENANT *RESEARCH LAB.* THEY DUSTED OFF THE EQUIPMENT, TRIED TO GET IT UP AND RUNNING AGAIN...

...AS YOU CAN SEE FROM IMAGES CAPTURED BY ONE OF OUR SPY DRONES, IT DIDN'T GO SO WELL...

UGGGHHH...

OH GOD...

BUT HERE'S WHERE IT GETS REALLY STRANGE...

WE SPOTTED THIS *YET-TO-BE-IDENTIFIED ELITE* EXITING THE LAB A MERE TWELVE HOURS BEFORE WE FOUND THE BODIES. HE WAS THE LAST ONE TO LEAVE THERE ALIVE.

AND HE TOOK A LITTLE SOMETHING WITH HIM...

OUR GUESS IS WHATEVER'S IN THAT *CANISTER* IS THE SAME SPECIAL CONCOCTION THAT LED TO THE DEMISE OF OUR BURGEONING BIOCHEMISTS...

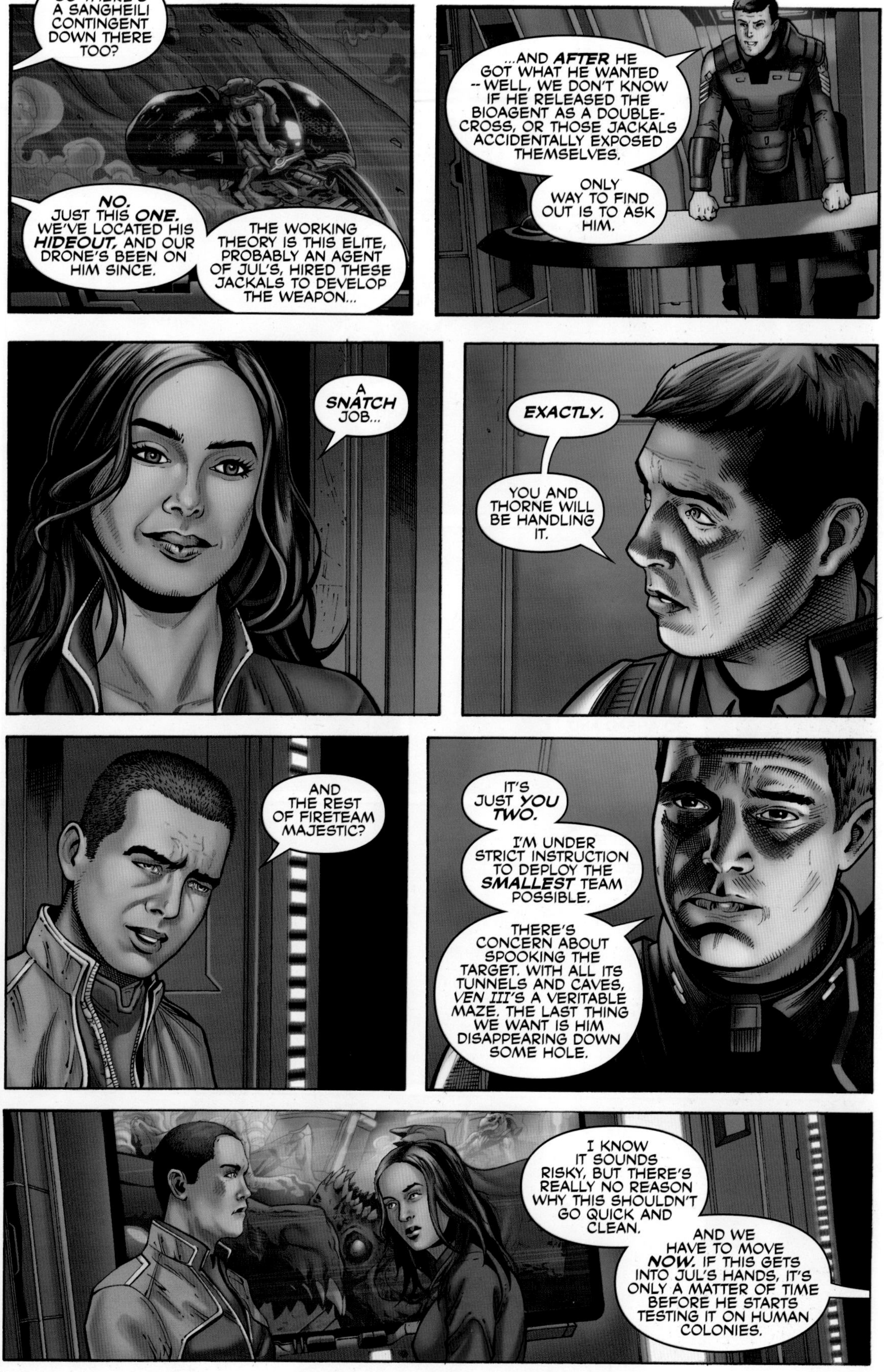
SO THERE'S A SANGHEILI CONTINGENT DOWN THERE TOO?
NO. JUST THIS ONE. WE'VE LOCATED HIS HIDEOUT, AND OUR DRONE'S BEEN ON HIM SINCE.
THE WORKING THEORY IS THIS ELITE, PROBABLY AN AGENT OF JUL'S, HIRED THESE JACKALS TO DEVELOP THE WEAPON...
...AND AFTER HE GOT WHAT HE WANTED -- WELL, WE DON'T KNOW IF HE RELEASED THE BIOAGENT AS A DOUBLE-CROSS, OR THOSE JACKALS ACCIDENTALLY EXPOSED THEMSELVES.
ONLY WAY TO FIND OUT IS TO ASK HIM.
A SNATCH JOB...
EXACTLY.
YOU AND THORNE WILL BE HANDLING IT.
AND THE REST OF FIRETEAM MAJESTIC?
IT'S JUST YOU TWO.
I'M UNDER STRICT INSTRUCTION TO DEPLOY THE SMALLEST TEAM POSSIBLE.
THERE'S CONCERN ABOUT SPOOKING THE TARGET. WITH ALL ITS TUNNELS AND CAVES, VEN III'S A VERITABLE MAZE. THE LAST THING WE WANT IS HIM DISAPPEARING DOWN SOME HOLE.
I KNOW IT SOUNDS RISKY, BUT THERE'S REALLY NO REASON WHY THIS SHOULDN'T GO QUICK AND CLEAN.
AND WE HAVE TO MOVE NOW. IF THIS GETS INTO JUL'S HANDS, IT'S ONLY A MATTER OF TIME BEFORE HE STARTS TESTING IT ON HUMAN COLONIES.

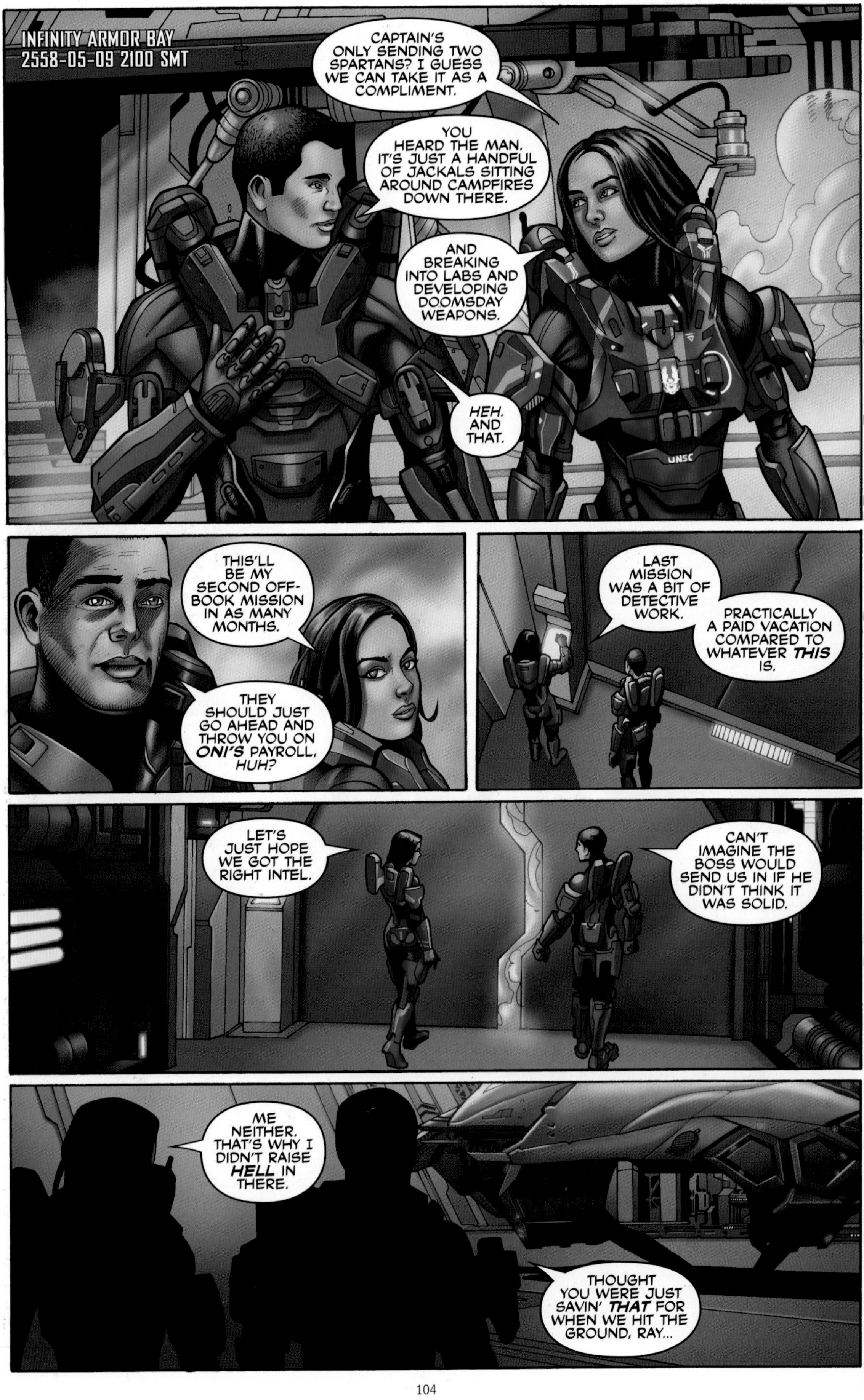
INFINITY ARMOR BAY
2558-05-09 2100 SMT
CAPTAIN'S ONLY SENDING TWO SPARTANS? I GUESS WE CAN TAKE IT AS A COMPLIMENT.
YOU HEARD THE MAN. IT'S JUST A HANDFUL OF JACKALS SITTING AROUND CAMPFIRES DOWN THERE.
AND BREAKING INTO LABS AND DEVELOPING DOOMSDAY WEAPONS.
HEH. AND THAT.
THIS'LL BE MY SECOND OFF-BOOK MISSION IN AS MANY MONTHS.
THEY SHOULD JUST GO AHEAD AND THROW YOU ON ONI'S PAYROLL, HUH?
LAST MISSION WAS A BIT OF DETECTIVE WORK.
PRACTICALLY A PAID VACATION COMPARED TO WHATEVER THIS IS.
LET'S JUST HOPE WE GOT THE RIGHT INTEL.
CAN'T IMAGINE THE BOSS WOULD SEND US IN IF HE DIDN'T THINK IT WAS SOLID.
ME NEITHER. THAT'S WHY I DIDN'T RAISE HELL IN THERE.
THOUGHT YOU WERE JUST SAVIN' THAT FOR WHEN WE HIT THE GROUND, RAY...
UNSC

HMMM...

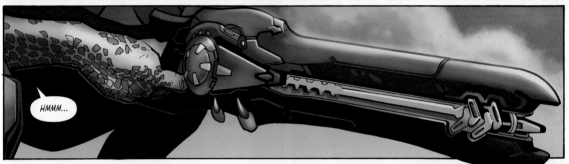

SPLAT

HEHHEHHEH

HUH?

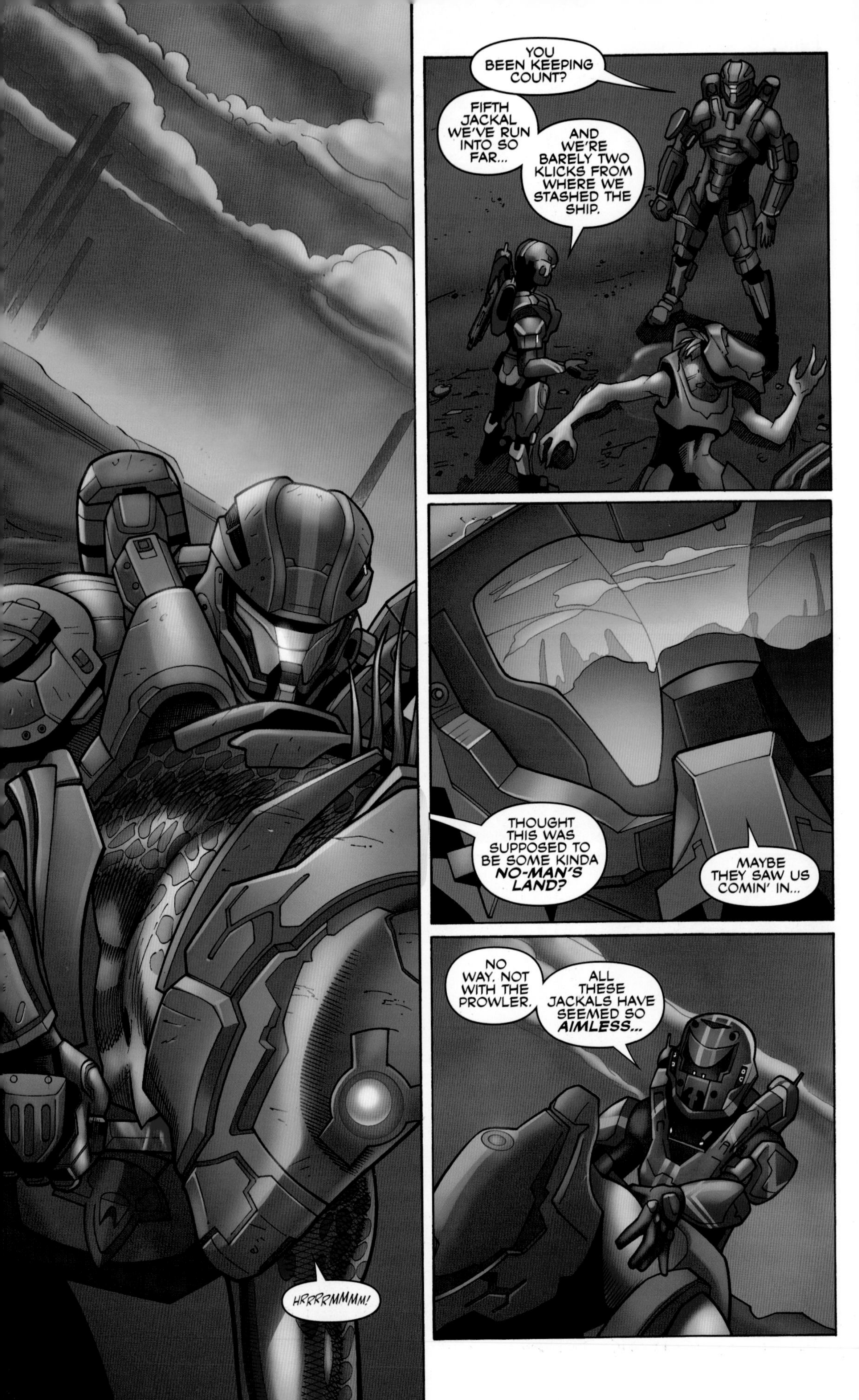
HRRRRMMMM!
YOU BEEN KEEPING COUNT?
FIFTH JACKAL WE'VE RUN INTO SO FAR...
AND WE'RE BARELY TWO KLICKS FROM WHERE WE STASHED THE SHIP.
THOUGHT THIS WAS SUPPOSED TO BE SOME KINDA NO-MAN'S LAND?
MAYBE THEY SAW US COMIN' IN...
NO WAY. NOT WITH THE PROWLER.
ALL THESE JACKALS HAVE SEEMED SO AIMLESS...

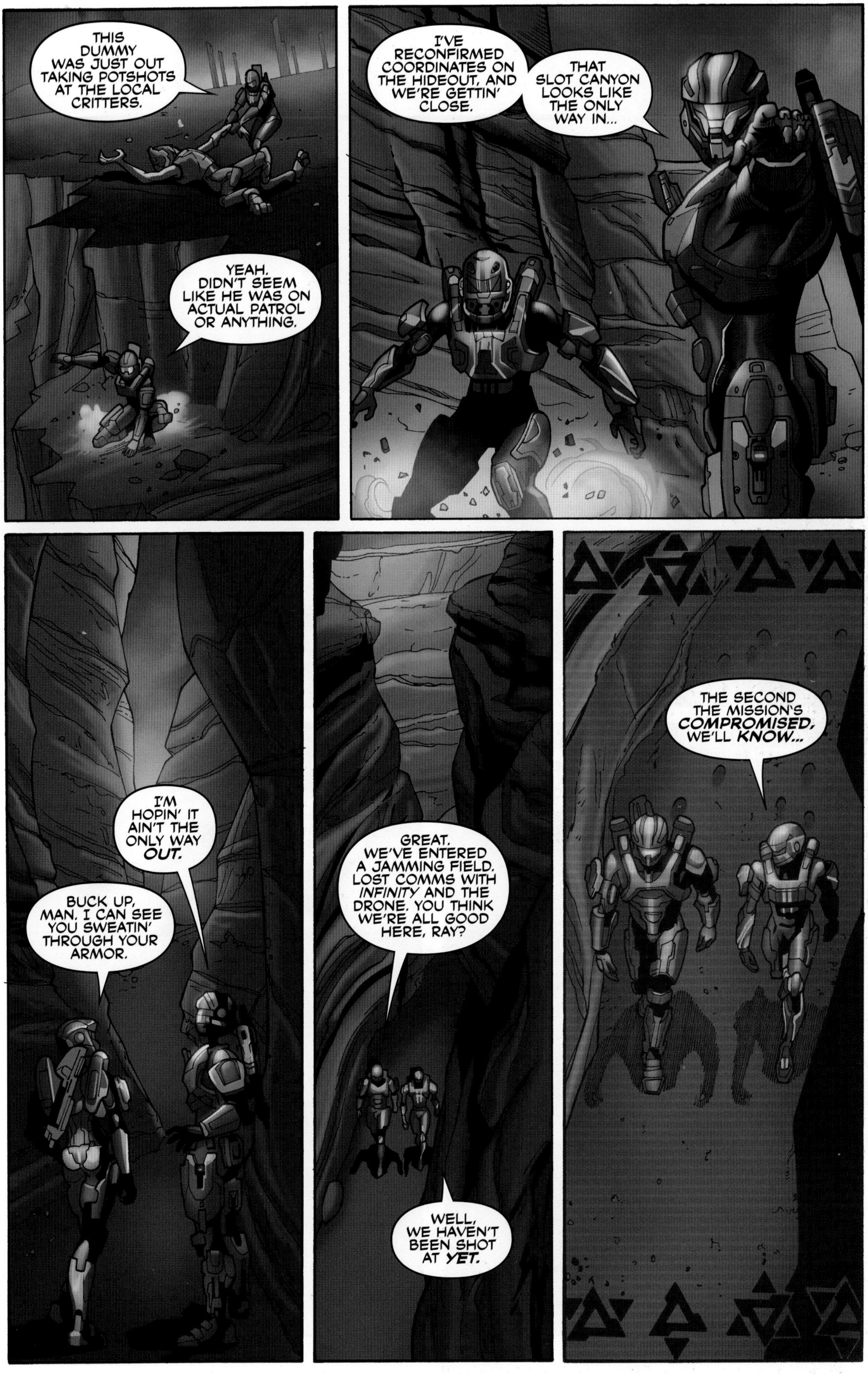
THIS DUMMY WAS JUST OUT TAKING POTSHOTS AT THE LOCAL CRITTERS.
YEAH. DIDN'T SEEM LIKE HE WAS ON ACTUAL PATROL OR ANYTHING.
I'VE RECONFIRMED COORDINATES ON THE HIDEOUT, AND WE'RE GETTIN' CLOSE.
THAT SLOT CANYON LOOKS LIKE THE ONLY WAY IN...
I'M HOPIN' IT AIN'T THE ONLY WAY OUT.
BUCK UP, MAN. I CAN SEE YOU SWEATIN' THROUGH YOUR ARMOR.
GREAT. WE'VE ENTERED A JAMMING FIELD. LOST COMMS WITH INFINITY AND THE DRONE. YOU THINK WE'RE ALL GOOD HERE, RAY?
WELL, WE HAVEN'T BEEN SHOT AT YET.
THE SECOND THE MISSION'S COMPROMISED, WE'LL KNOW...

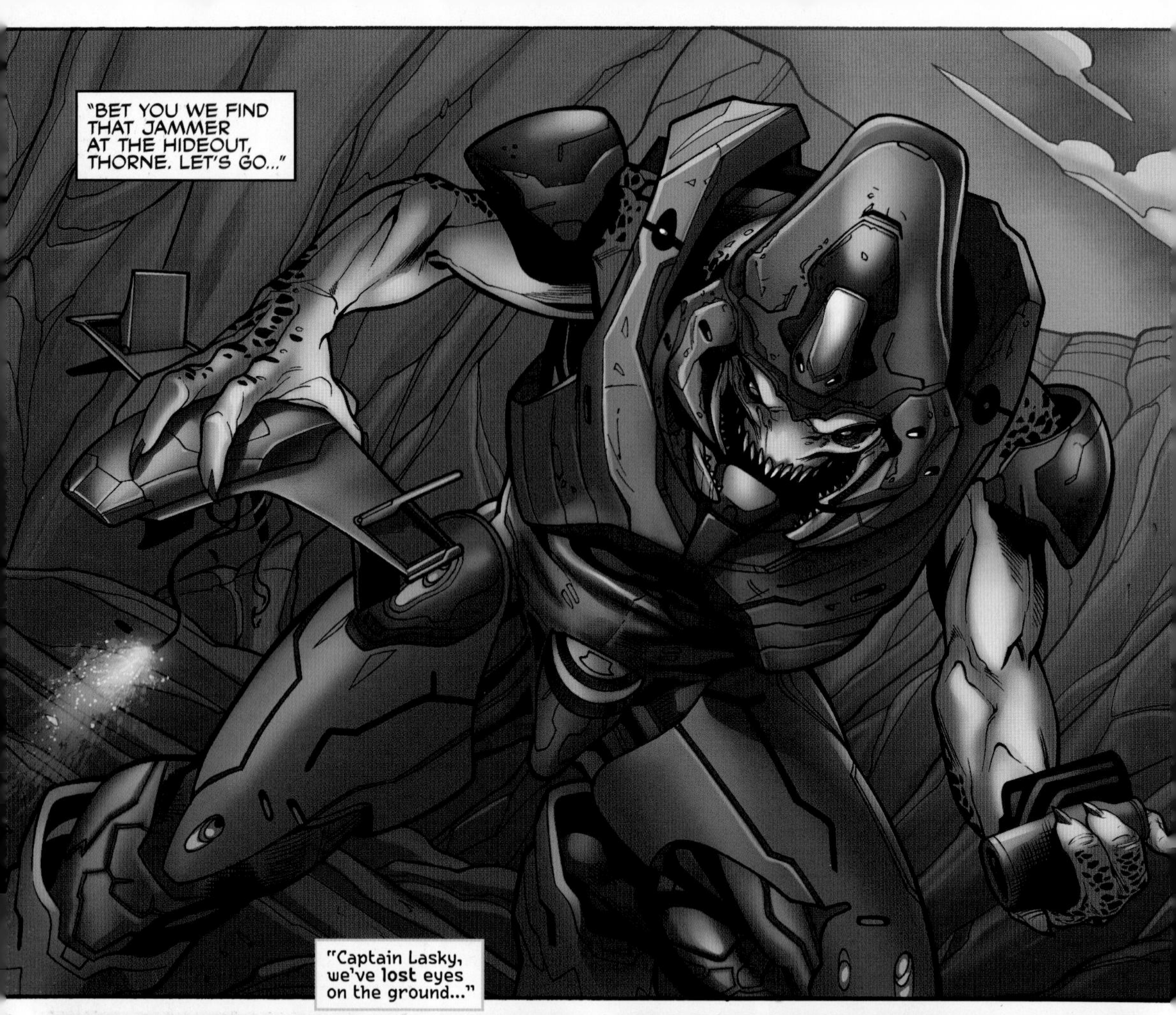
"BET YOU WE FIND THAT JAMMER AT THE HIDEOUT, THORNE. LET'S GO..."
"Captain Lasky, we've lost eyes on the ground..."

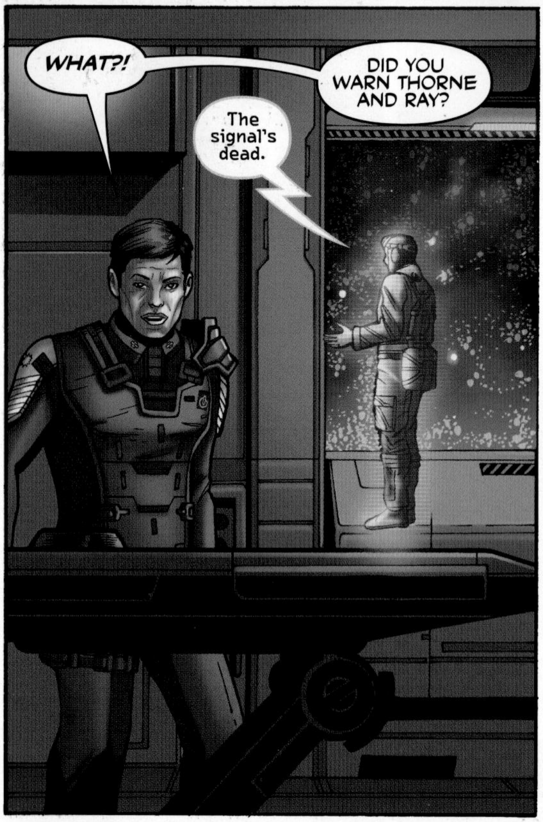
WHAT?!
DID YOU WARN THORNE AND RAY?
The signal's dead.

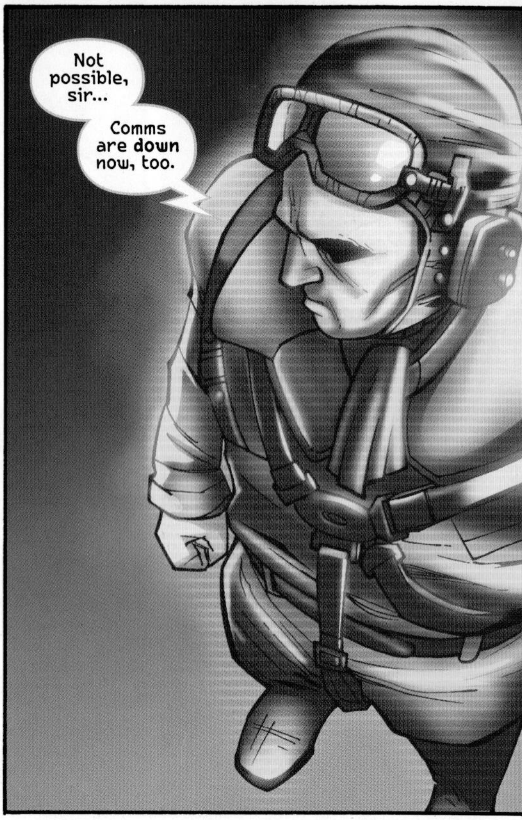
Not possible, sir...
Comms are down now, too.

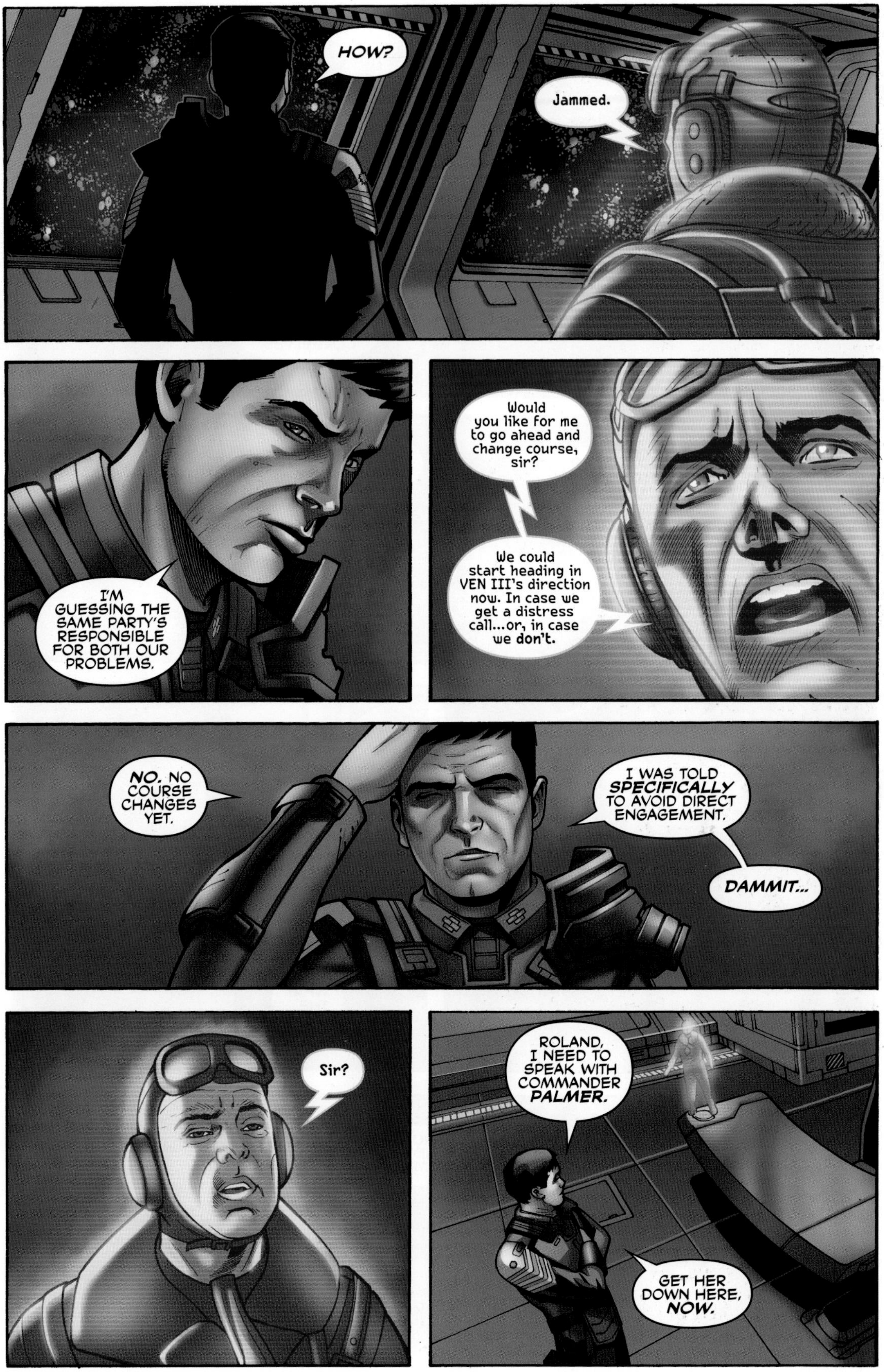
HOW?
Jammed.
I'M GUESSING THE SAME PARTY'S RESPONSIBLE FOR BOTH OUR PROBLEMS.
Would you like for me to go ahead and change course, sir?
We could start heading in VEN III's direction now. In case we get a distress call...or, in case we don't.
NO. NO COURSE CHANGES YET.
I WAS TOLD SPECIFICALLY TO AVOID DIRECT ENGAGEMENT.
DAMMIT...
Sir?
ROLAND, I NEED TO SPEAK WITH COMMANDER PALMER.
GET HER DOWN HERE, NOW.

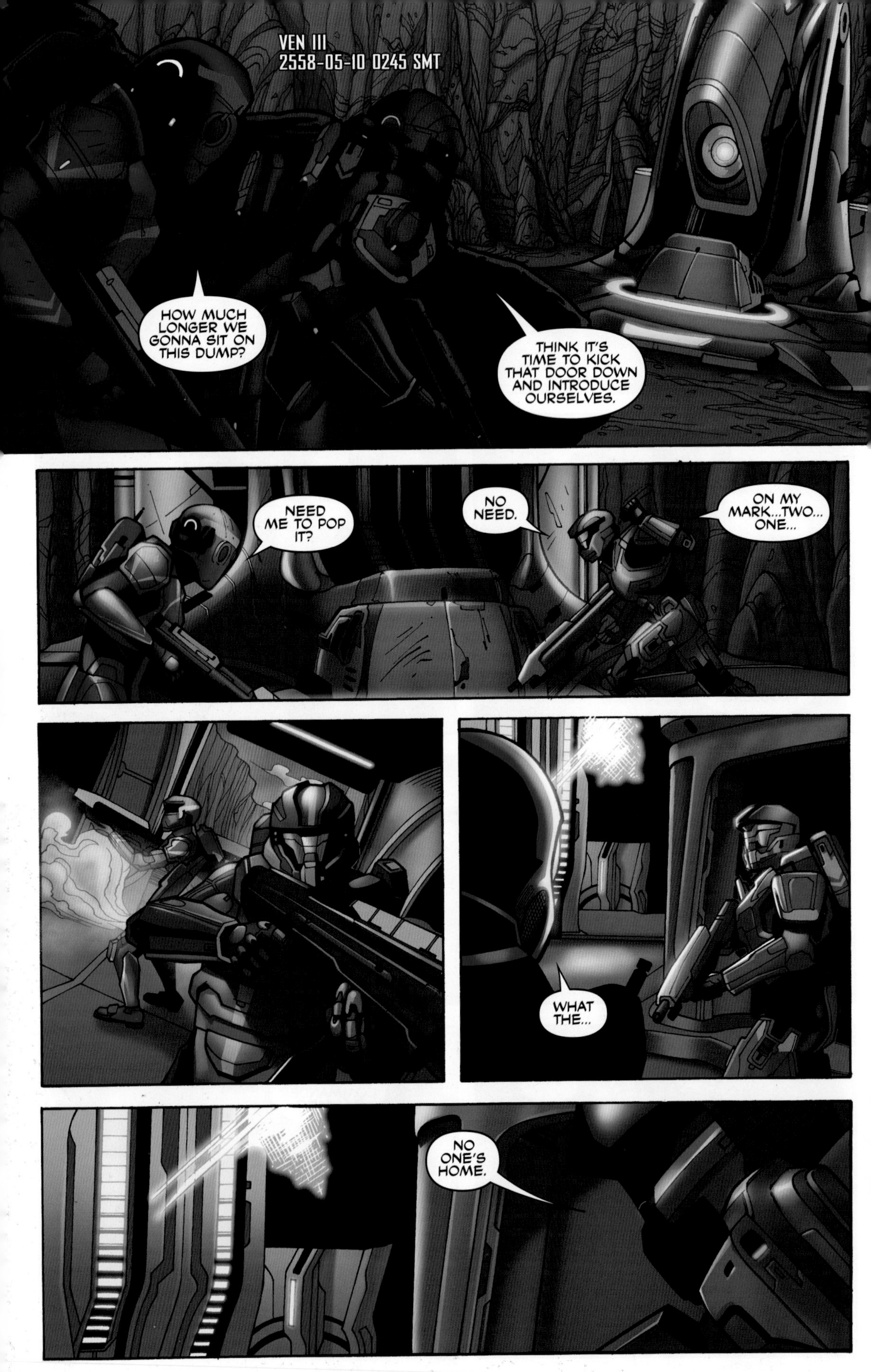
VEN III
2558-05-10 0245 SMT
HOW MUCH LONGER WE GONNA SIT ON THIS DUMP?
THINK IT'S TIME TO KICK THAT DOOR DOWN AND INTRODUCE OURSELVES.
NEED ME TO POP IT?
NO NEED.
ON MY MARK...TWO... ONE...
WHAT THE...
NO ONE'S HOME.

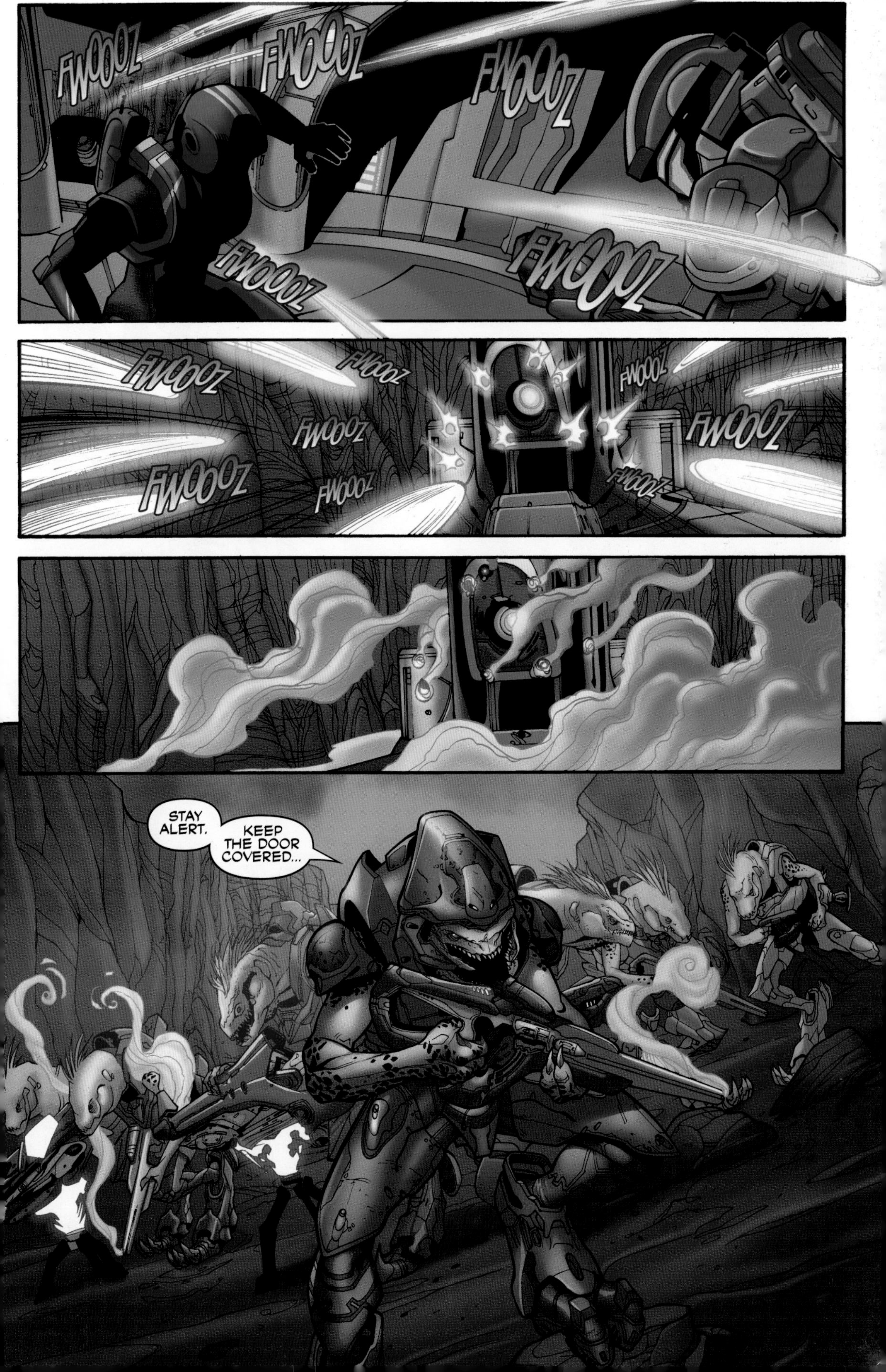
FWOOOZ
FWOOOZ
FWOOOZ
FWOOOZ
FWOOOZ
FWOOOZ
FWOOOZ
FWOOOZ
FWOOOZ
FWOOOZ
FWOOOZ
FWOOOZ
FWOOOZ
STAY ALERT.
KEEP THE DOOR COVERED...

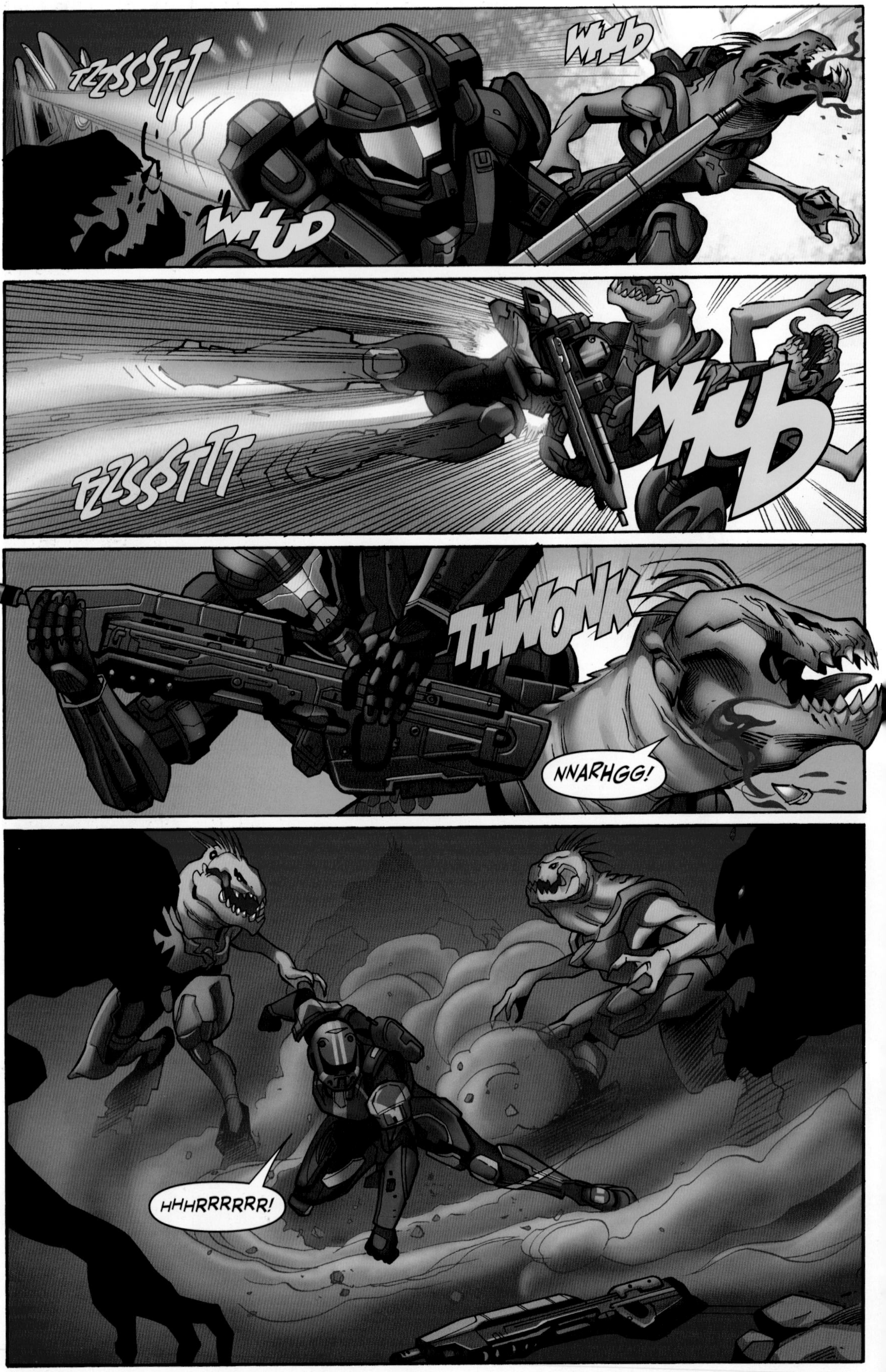
TZZSSSTTT
WHUD
WHUD
TZZSSSTTT
WHUD
THWONK
NNARHGG!
HHHRRRRRR!

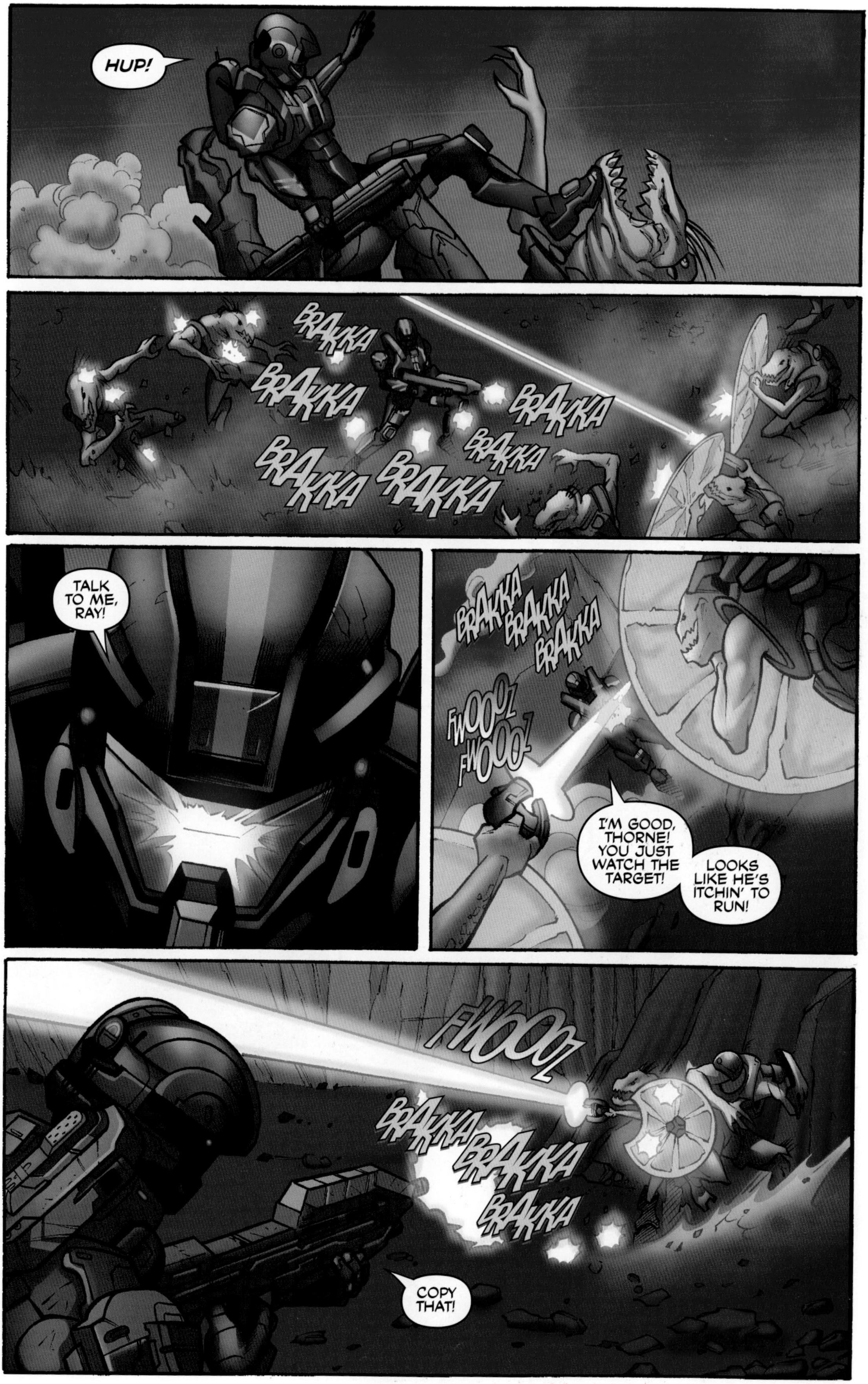
HUP!
BRAKKA
BRAKKA
BRAKKA
BRAKKA
BRAKKA
BRAKKA
TALK TO ME, RAY!
BRAKKA
BRAKKA
BRAKKA
FWOOOZ
FWOOOZ
I'M GOOD, THORNE! YOU JUST WATCH THE TARGET!
LOOKS LIKE HE'S ITCHIN' TO RUN!
FWOOOZ
BRAKKA
BRAKKA
BRAKKA
COPY THAT!

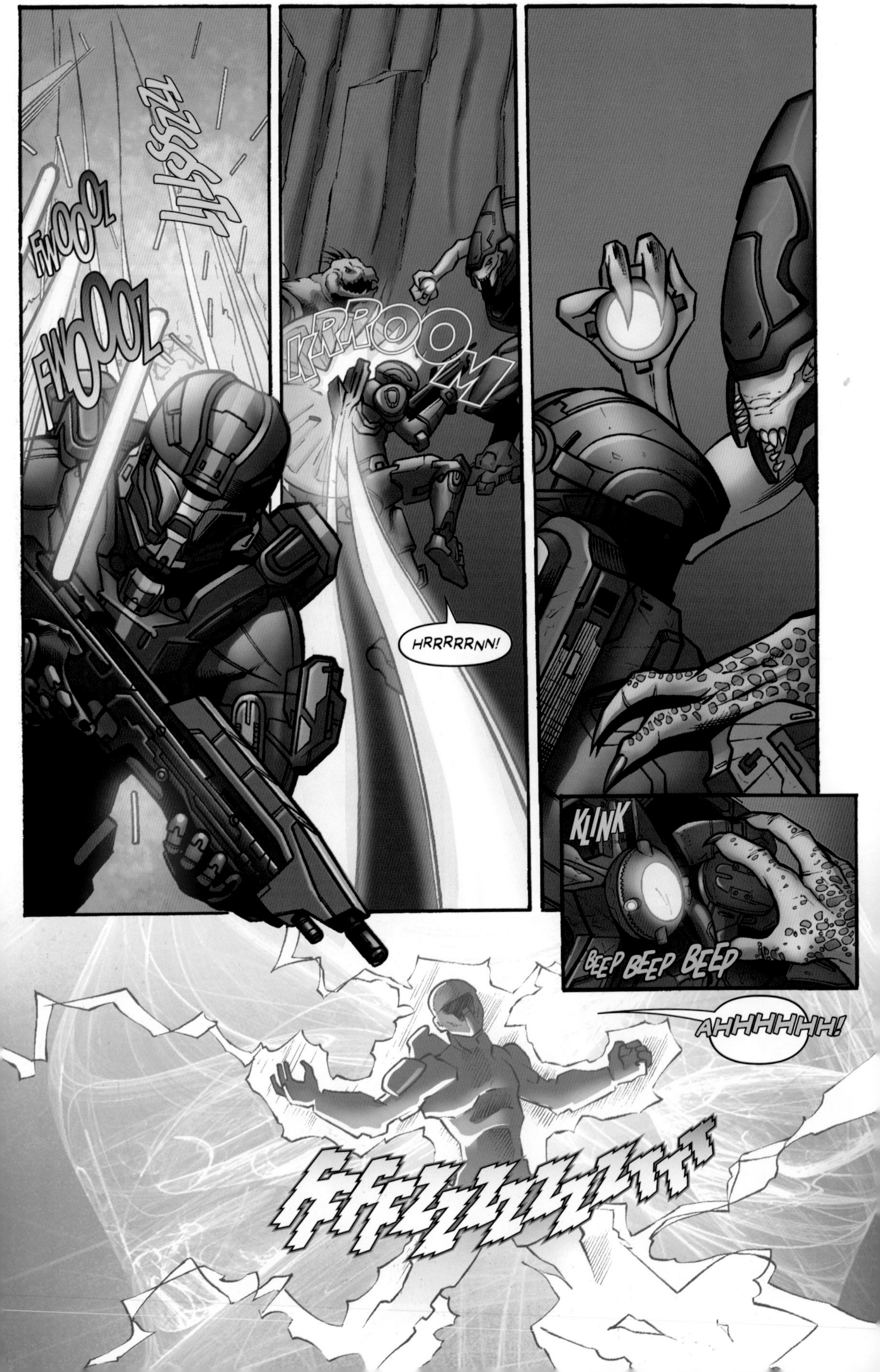
FWOOOZ
FWOOOZ
TZZSSTTT
KRROOOM
HRRRRRNN!
KLINK
BEEP BEEP BEEP
AHHHHHH!
FFFZZZZZZZTTTT

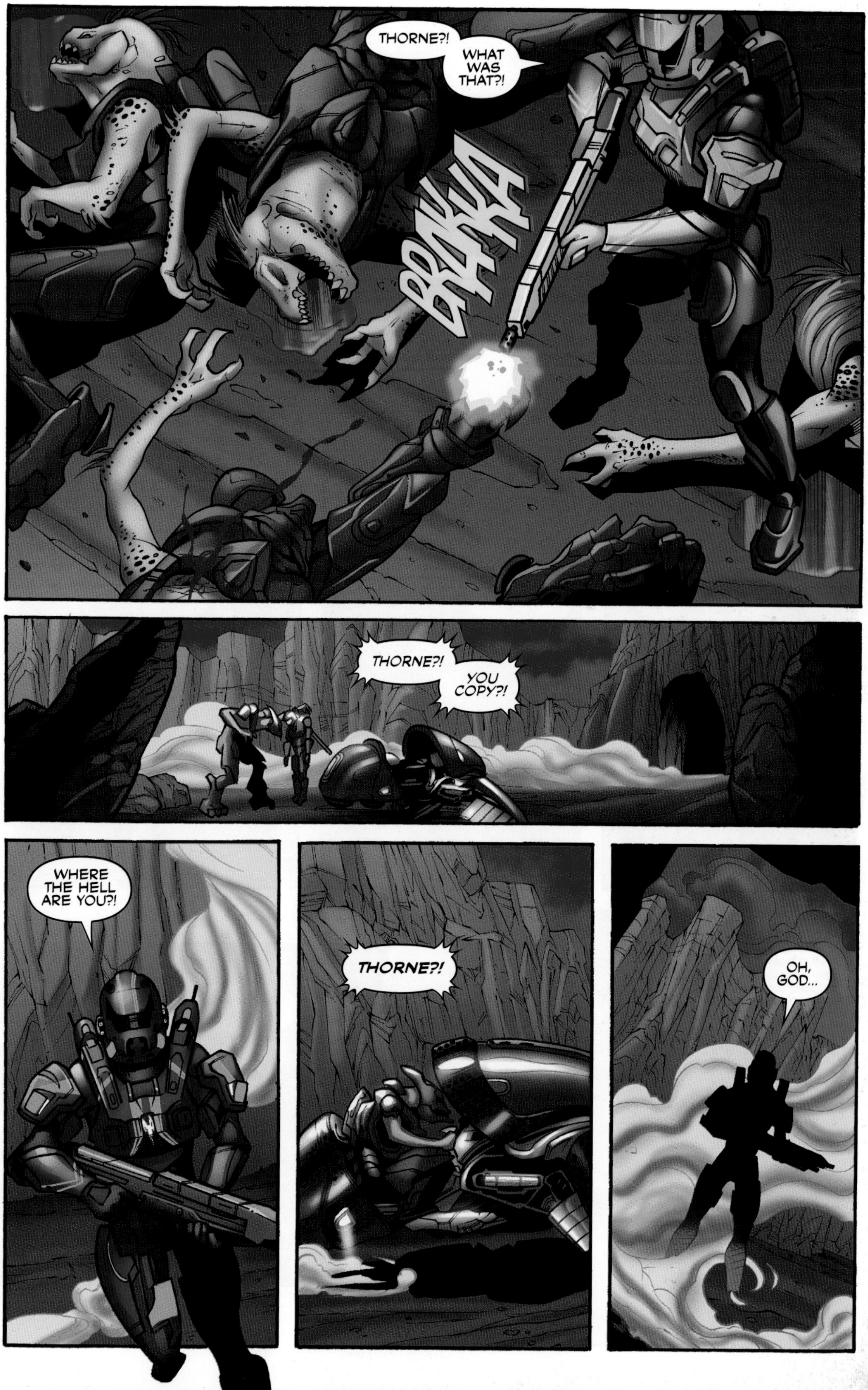
THORNE?!
WHAT WAS THAT?!
BRAKA
THORNE?!
YOU COPY?!
WHERE THE HELL ARE YOU?!
THORNE?!
OH, GOD...

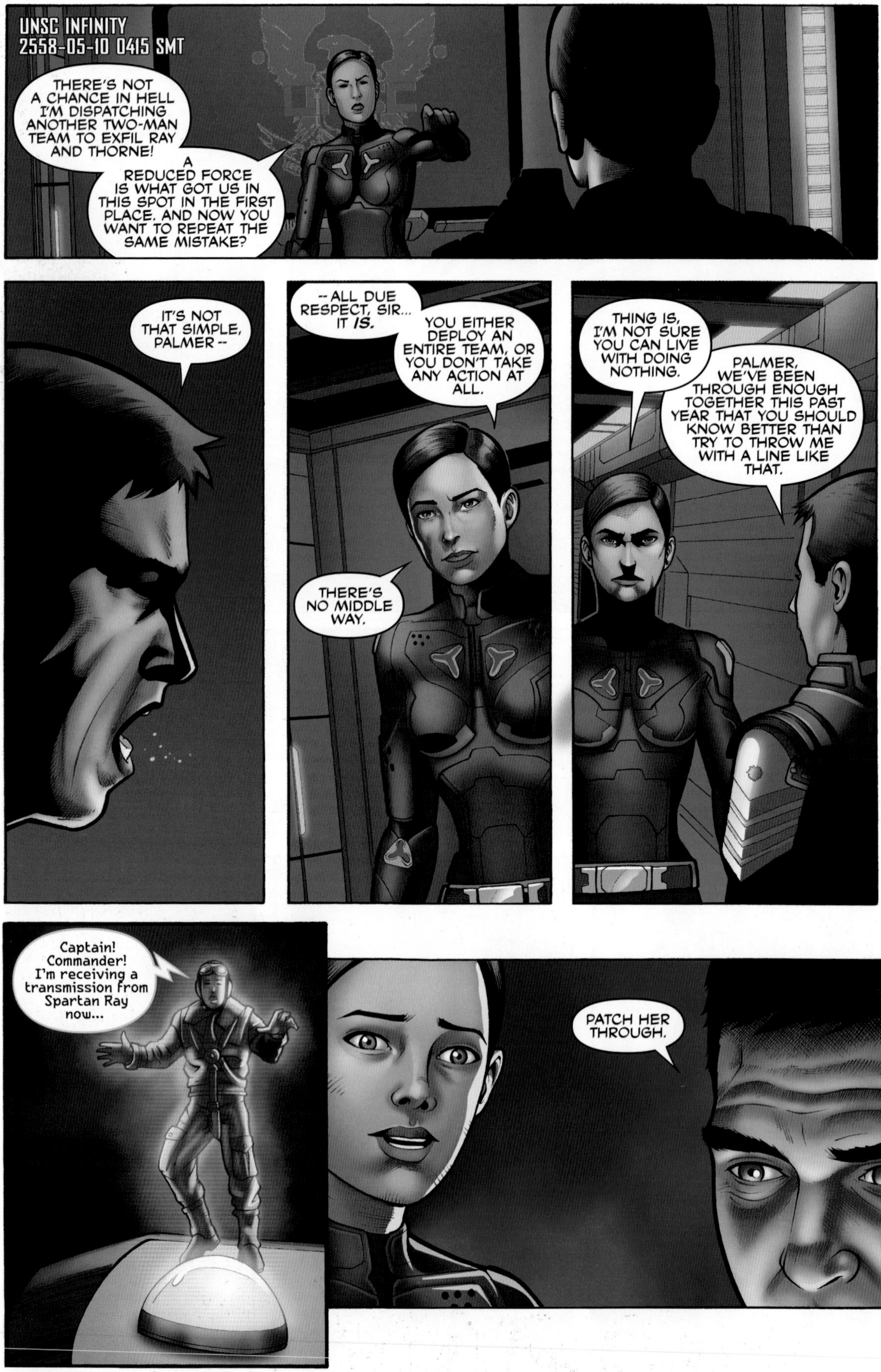
UNSC INFINITY
2558-05-10 0415 SMT
THERE'S NOT A CHANCE IN HELL I'M DISPATCHING ANOTHER TWO-MAN TEAM TO EXFIL RAY AND THORNE!
A REDUCED FORCE IS WHAT GOT US IN THIS SPOT IN THE FIRST PLACE. AND NOW YOU WANT TO REPEAT THE SAME MISTAKE?
IT'S NOT THAT SIMPLE, PALMER --
-- ALL DUE RESPECT, SIR... IT *IS*.
YOU EITHER DEPLOY AN ENTIRE TEAM, OR YOU DON'T TAKE ANY ACTION AT ALL.
THERE'S NO MIDDLE WAY.
THING IS, I'M NOT SURE YOU CAN LIVE WITH DOING NOTHING.
PALMER, WE'VE BEEN THROUGH ENOUGH TOGETHER THIS PAST YEAR THAT YOU SHOULD KNOW BETTER THAN TRY TO THROW ME WITH A LINE LIKE THAT.
Captain! Commander! I'm receiving a transmission from Spartan Ray now...
PATCH HER THROUGH.

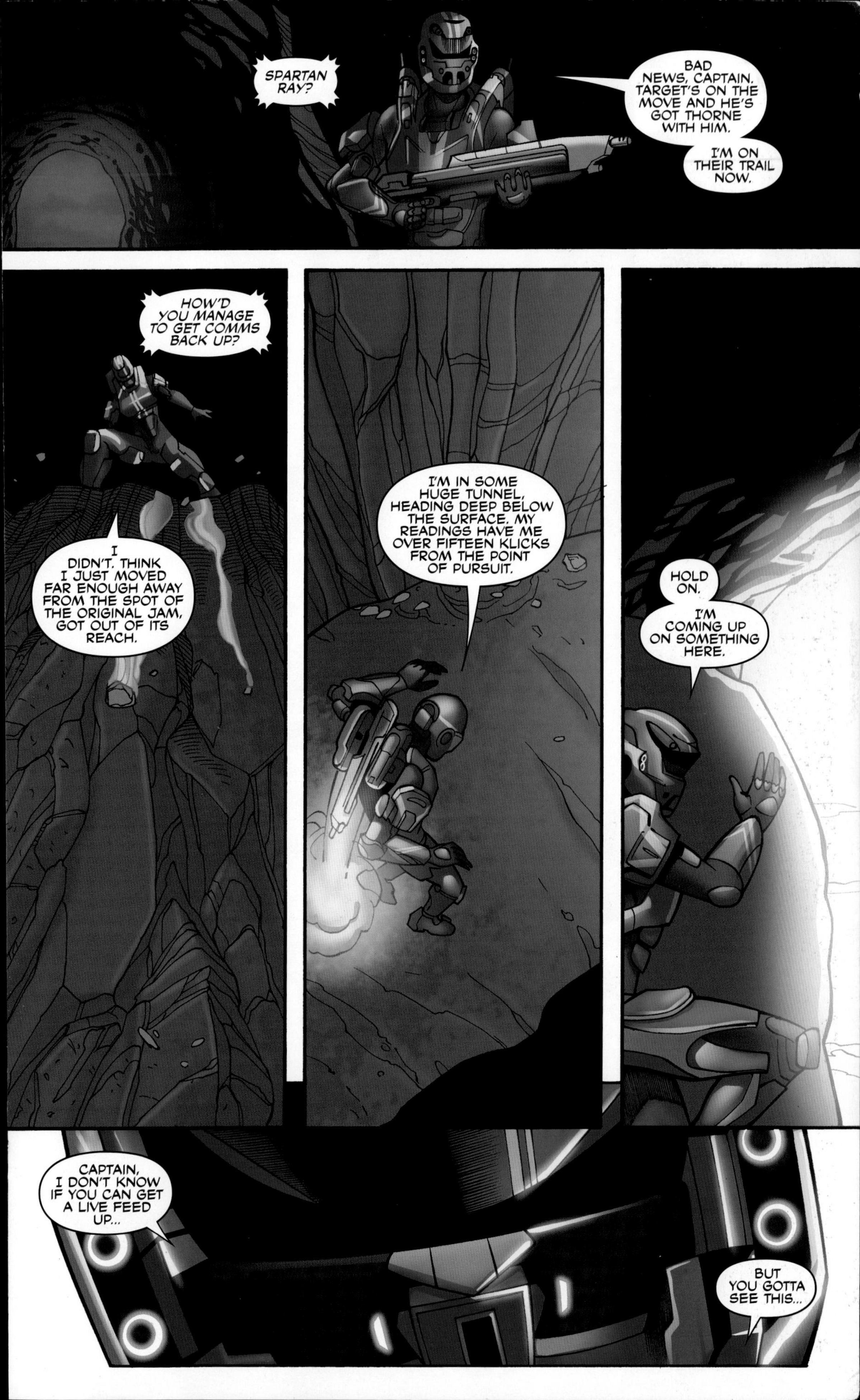
SPARTAN RAY?
BAD NEWS, CAPTAIN. TARGET'S ON THE MOVE AND HE'S GOT THORNE WITH HIM.
I'M ON THEIR TRAIL NOW.
HOW'D YOU MANAGE TO GET COMMS BACK UP?
I DIDN'T. THINK I JUST MOVED FAR ENOUGH AWAY FROM THE SPOT OF THE ORIGINAL JAM, GOT OUT OF ITS REACH.
I'M IN SOME HUGE TUNNEL, HEADING DEEP BELOW THE SURFACE. MY READINGS HAVE ME OVER FIFTEEN KLICKS FROM THE POINT OF PURSUIT.
HOLD ON.
I'M COMING UP ON SOMETHING HERE.
CAPTAIN, I DON'T KNOW IF YOU CAN GET A LIVE FEED UP...
BUT YOU GOTTA SEE THIS...

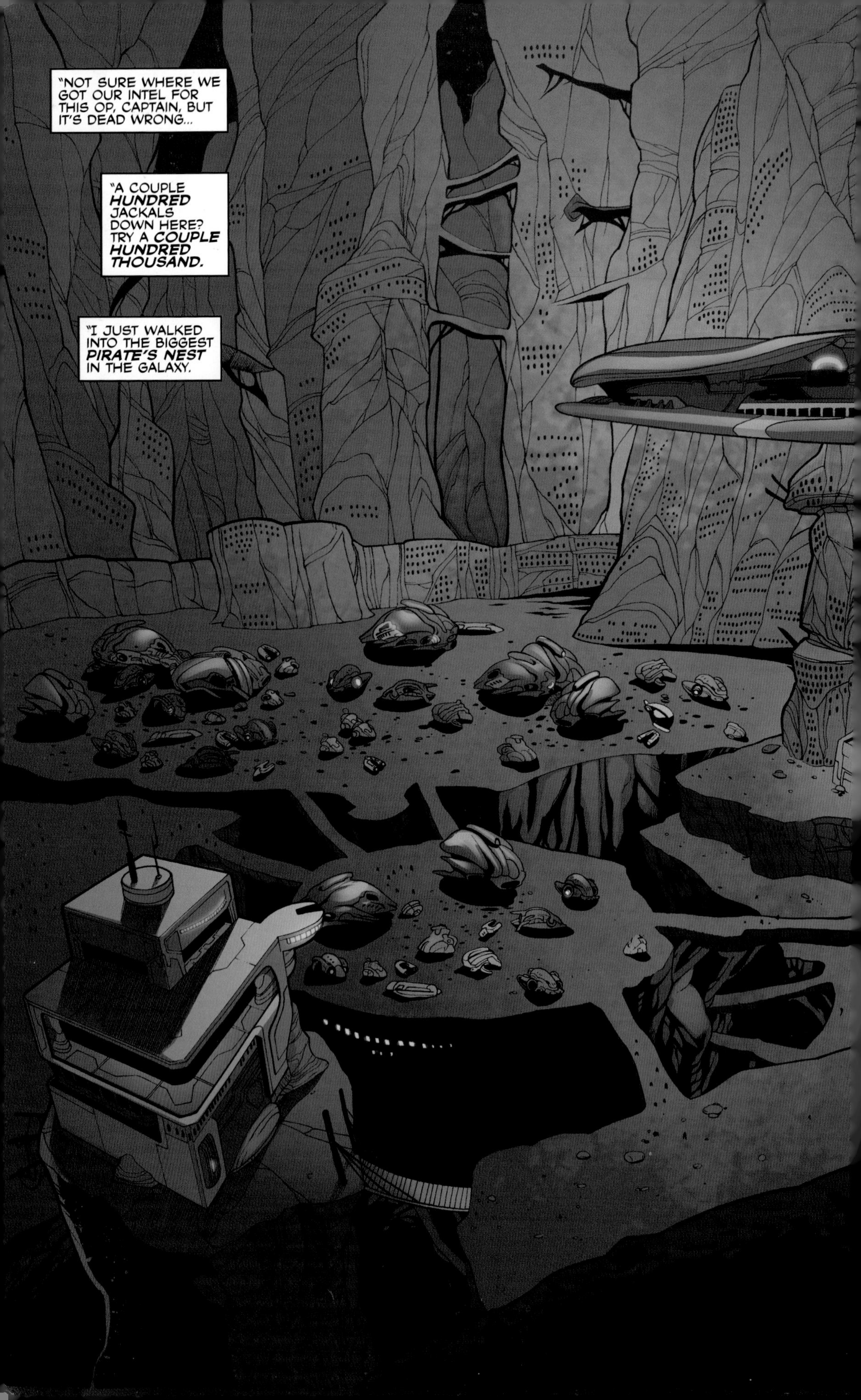
"NOT SURE WHERE WE GOT OUR INTEL FOR THIS OP, CAPTAIN, BUT IT'S DEAD WRONG...
"A COUPLE **HUNDRED** JACKALS DOWN HERE? TRY A **COUPLE HUNDRED THOUSAND.**
"I JUST WALKED INTO THE BIGGEST **PIRATE'S NEST** IN THE GALAXY.

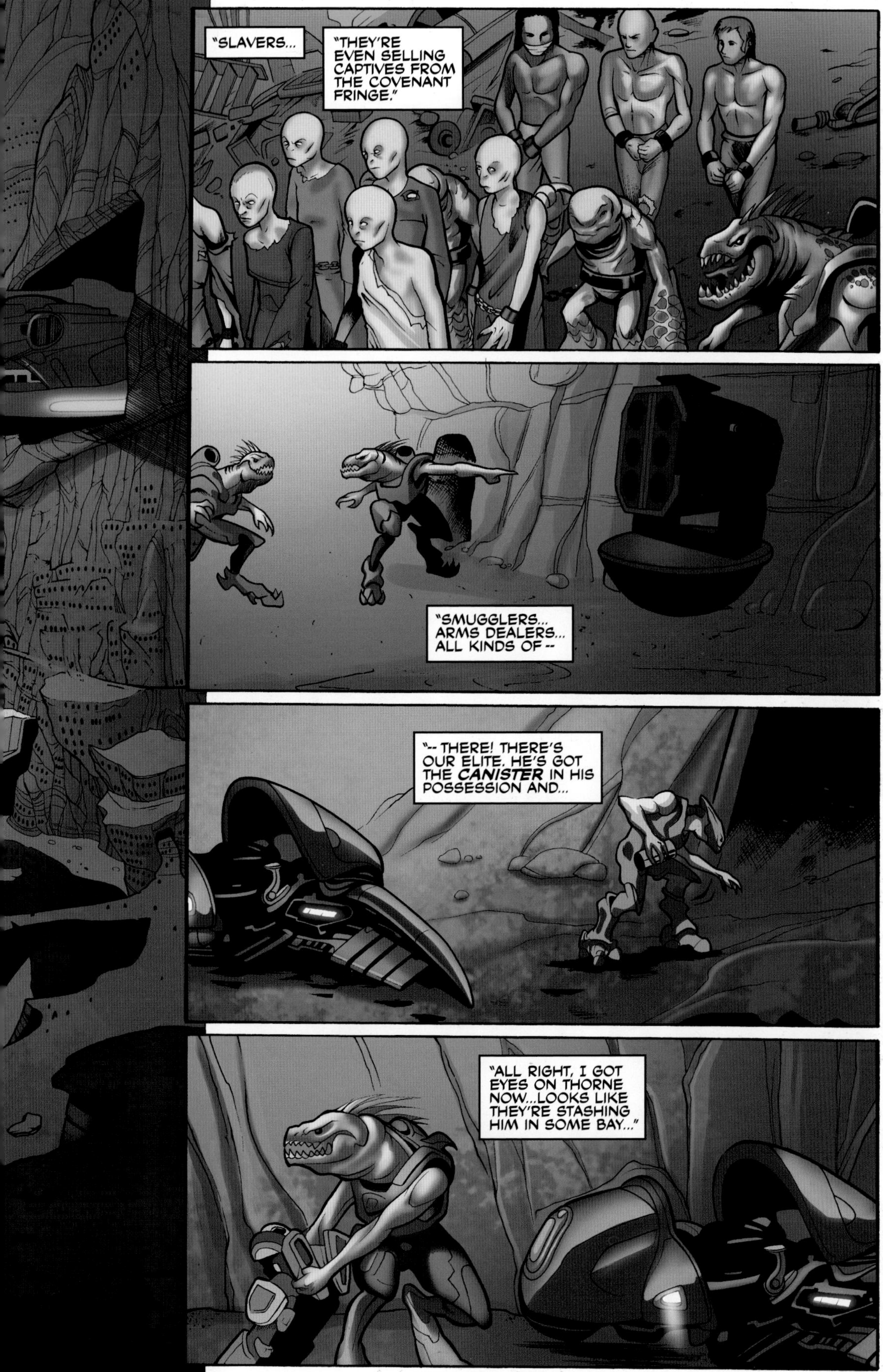
"SLAVERS...
"THEY'RE EVEN SELLING CAPTIVES FROM THE COVENANT FRINGE."
"SMUGGLERS... ARMS DEALERS... ALL KINDS OF --
"-- THERE! THERE'S OUR ELITE. HE'S GOT THE *CANISTER* IN HIS POSSESSION AND...
"ALL RIGHT, I GOT EYES ON THORNE NOW...LOOKS LIKE THEY'RE STASHING HIM IN SOME BAY..."

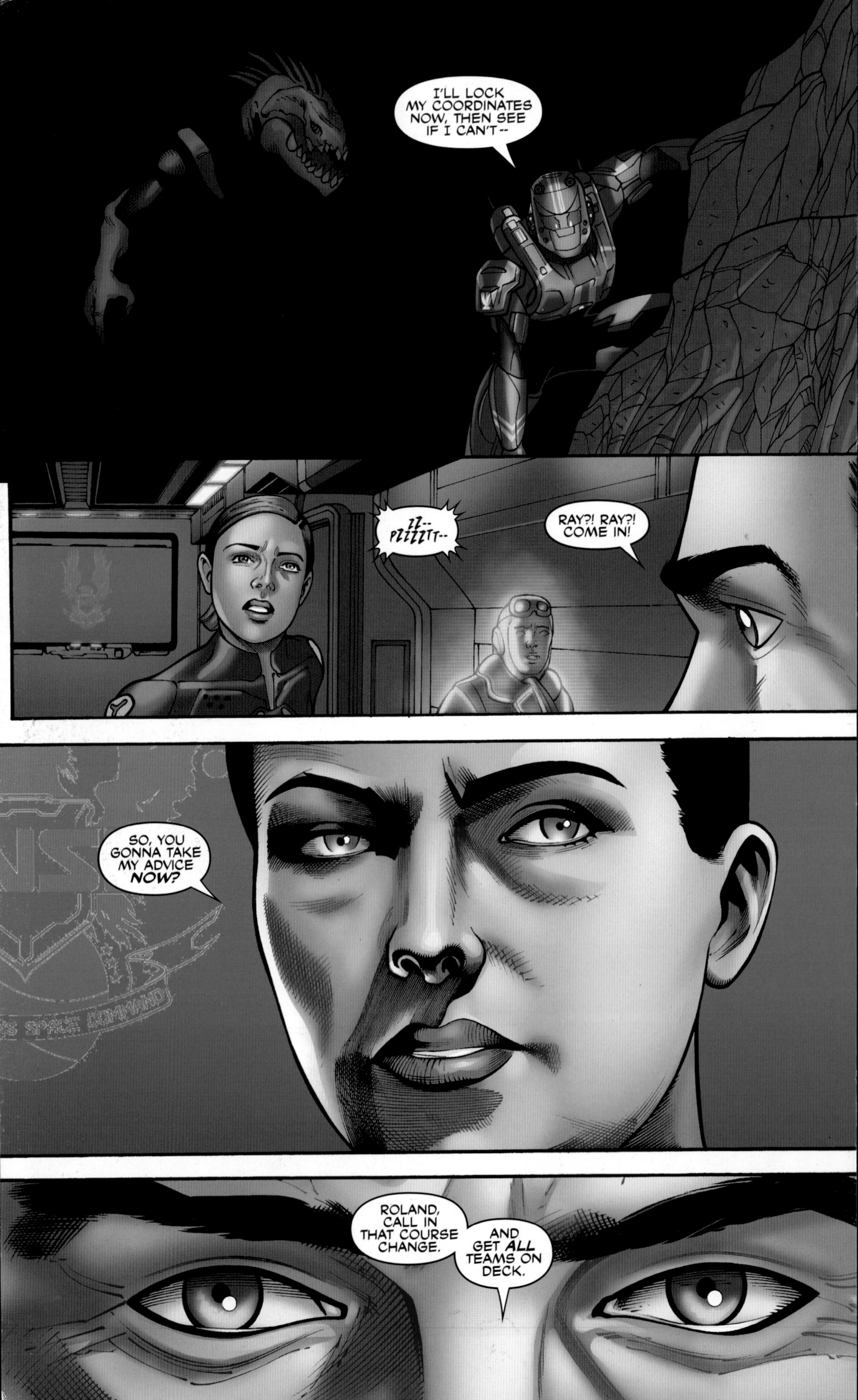
I'LL LOCK MY COORDINATES NOW, THEN SEE IF I CAN'T--
ZZ-- PZZZZTT--
RAY?! RAY?! COME IN!
SO, YOU GONNA TAKE MY ADVICE *NOW?*
ROLAND, CALL IN THAT COURSE CHANGE.
AND GET *ALL* TEAMS ON DECK.

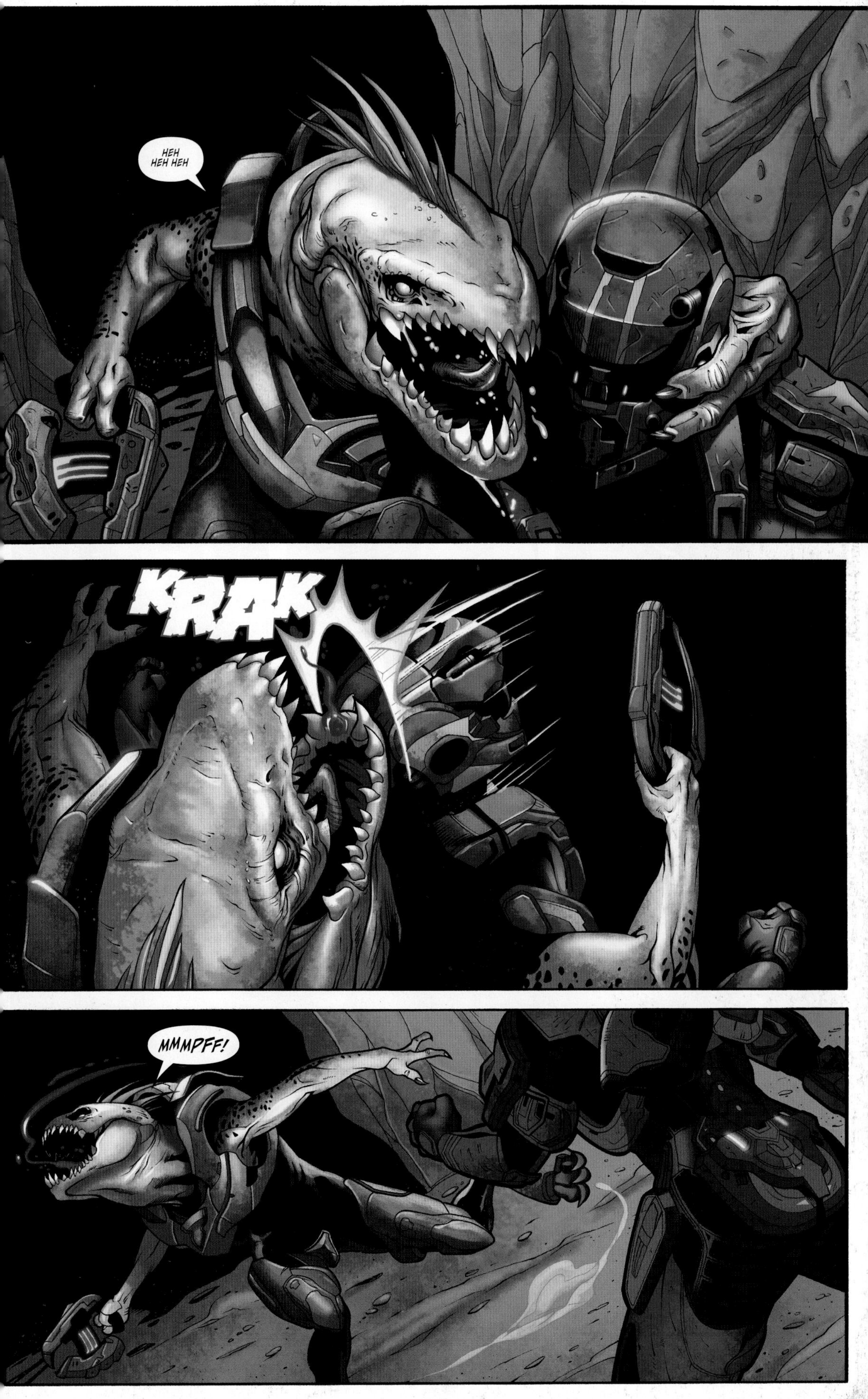
HEH
HEH HEH
KRAK
MMMPFF!

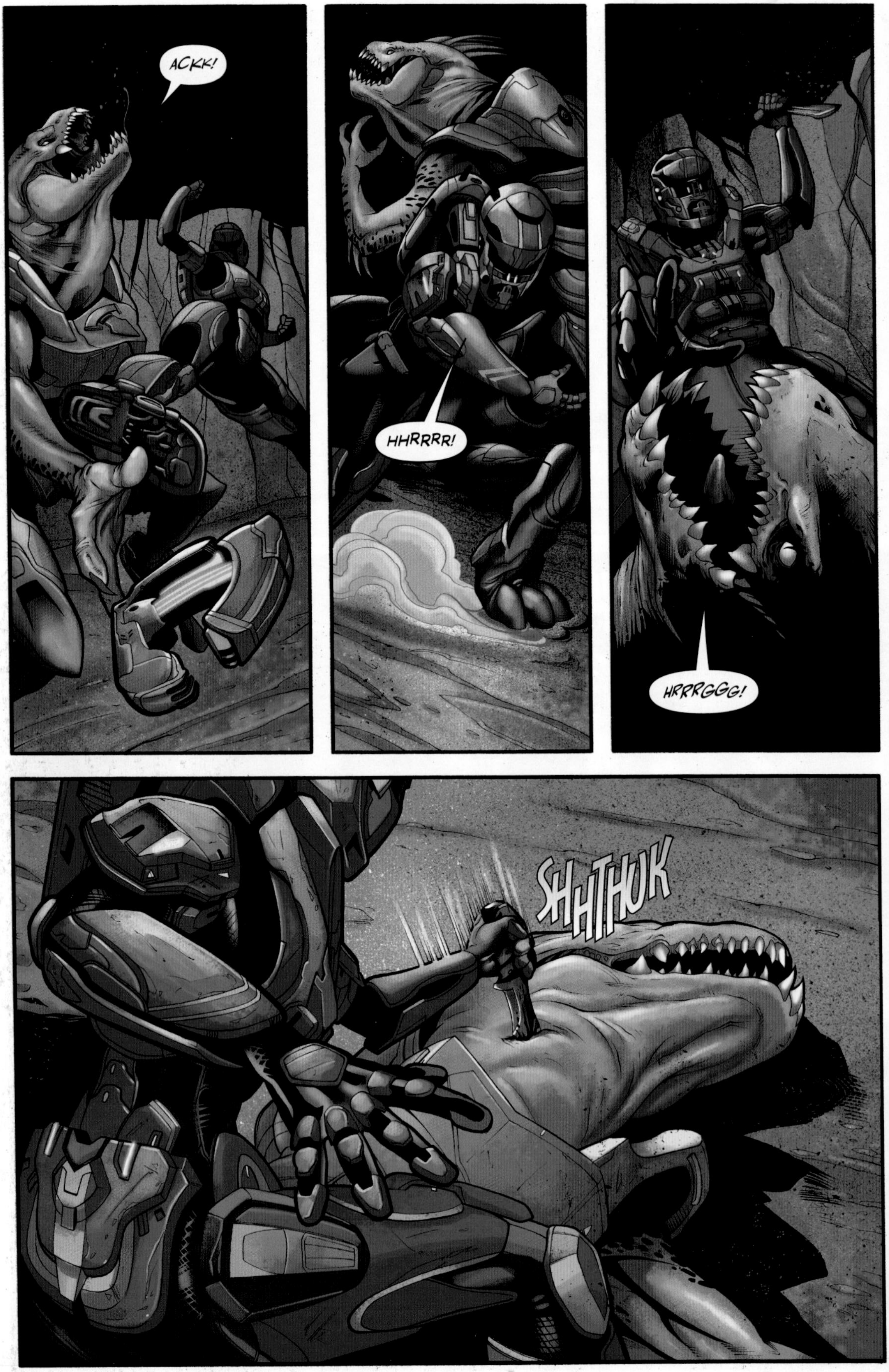
ACKK!
HHRRRR!
HRRRGGG!
SHHTHUK

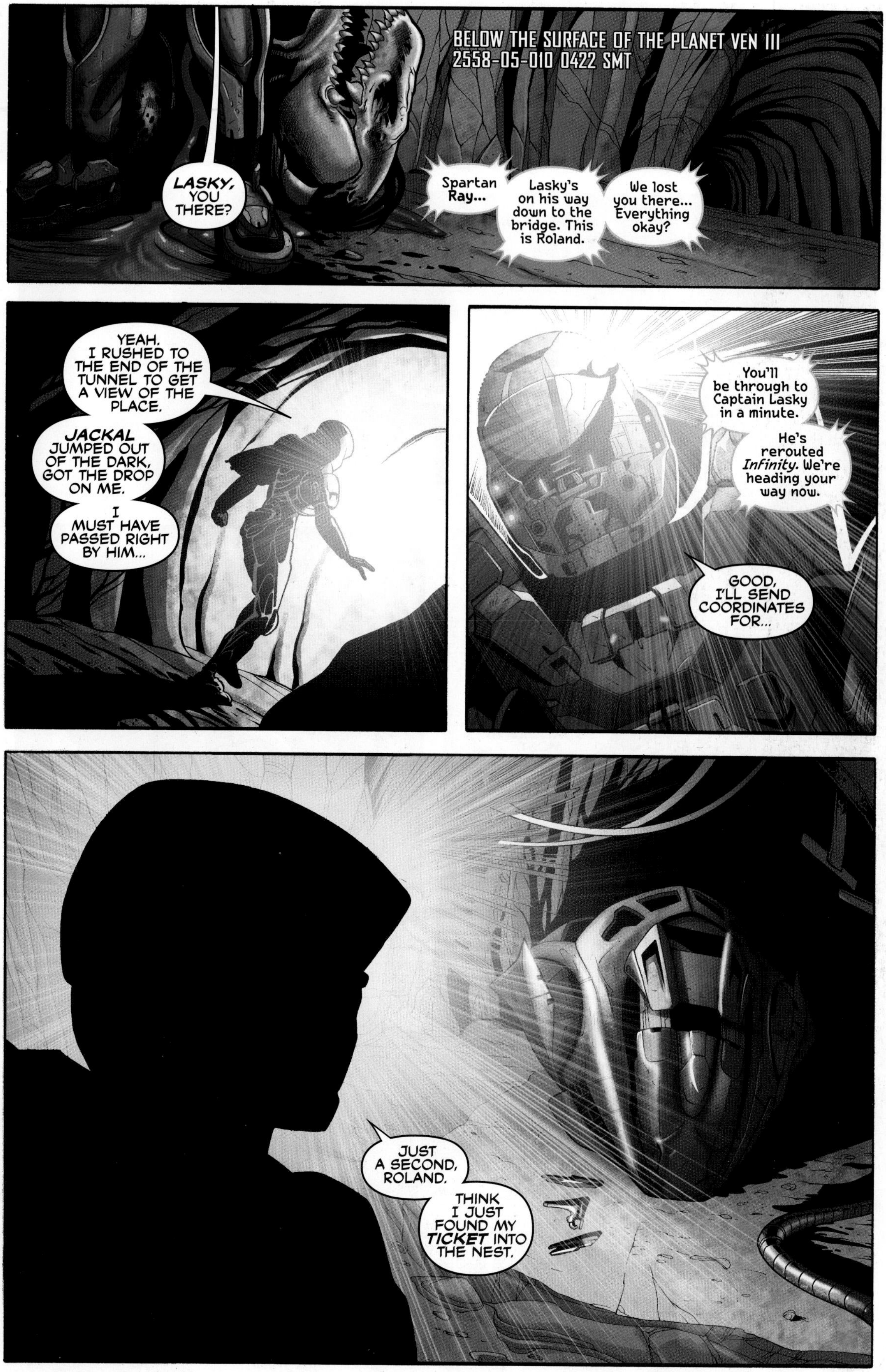

BELOW THE SURFACE OF THE PLANET VEN III
2558-05-010 0422 SMT
LASKY, YOU THERE?
Spartan Ray...
Lasky's on his way down to the bridge. This is Roland.
We lost you there... Everything okay?
YEAH. I RUSHED TO THE END OF THE TUNNEL TO GET A VIEW OF THE PLACE.
JACKAL JUMPED OUT OF THE DARK, GOT THE DROP ON ME.
I MUST HAVE PASSED RIGHT BY HIM...
You'll be through to Captain Lasky in a minute.
He's rerouted Infinity. We're heading your way now.
GOOD, I'LL SEND COORDINATES FOR...
JUST A SECOND, ROLAND.
THINK I JUST FOUND MY TICKET INTO THE NEST.

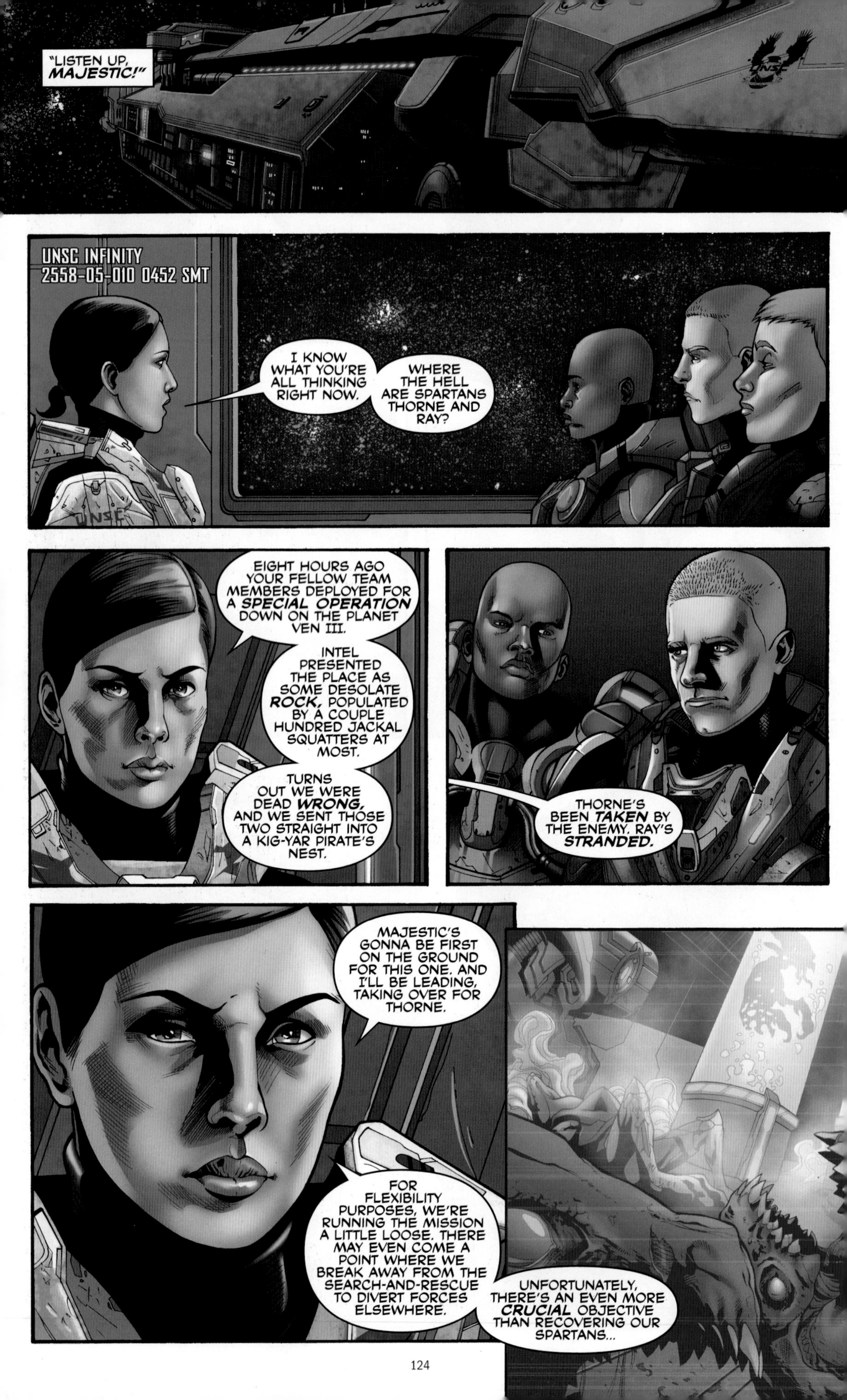
"LISTEN UP, MAJESTIC!"
UNSC INFINITY
2558-05-010 0452 SMT
I KNOW WHAT YOU'RE ALL THINKING RIGHT NOW.
WHERE THE HELL ARE SPARTANS THORNE AND RAY?
EIGHT HOURS AGO YOUR FELLOW TEAM MEMBERS DEPLOYED FOR A SPECIAL OPERATION DOWN ON THE PLANET VEN III.
INTEL PRESENTED THE PLACE AS SOME DESOLATE ROCK, POPULATED BY A COUPLE HUNDRED JACKAL SQUATTERS AT MOST.
TURNS OUT WE WERE DEAD WRONG, AND WE SENT THOSE TWO STRAIGHT INTO A KIG-YAR PIRATE'S NEST.
THORNE'S BEEN TAKEN BY THE ENEMY. RAY'S STRANDED.
MAJESTIC'S GONNA BE FIRST ON THE GROUND FOR THIS ONE. AND I'LL BE LEADING, TAKING OVER FOR THORNE.
FOR FLEXIBILITY PURPOSES, WE'RE RUNNING THE MISSION A LITTLE LOOSE. THERE MAY EVEN COME A POINT WHERE WE BREAK AWAY FROM THE SEARCH-AND-RESCUE TO DIVERT FORCES ELSEWHERE.
UNFORTUNATELY, THERE'S AN EVEN MORE CRUCIAL OBJECTIVE THAN RECOVERING OUR SPARTANS...

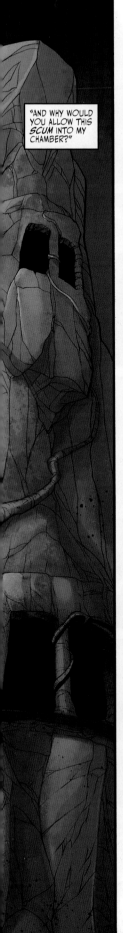

"AND WHY WOULD YOU ALLOW THIS *SCUM* INTO MY CHAMBER?"

VEN III
UNDERGROUND KIG-YAR SETTLEMENT
2558-05-010 0500 SMT

HE WOULDN'T SPEAK TO ANY OF YOUR LIEUTENANTS, MY QUEEN. HE DEMANDED A DIRECT AUDIENCE.

DID HE?

AND, BY CHANCE, DID HE PROVIDE HIS *NAME?*

MY NAME'S NOT IMPORTANT.

WHAT'S IMPORTANT IS THAT I HAVE SOMETHING YOU *WANT.*

A *SPARTAN.* STILL ALIVE. HE'S SOMEWHERE IN THIS CITY NOW.

I'LL DELIVER HIM TO YOU ONCE WE HAVE A DEAL.

THAT WOULD BE QUITE A TROPHY TO ADD TO MY COLLECTION.

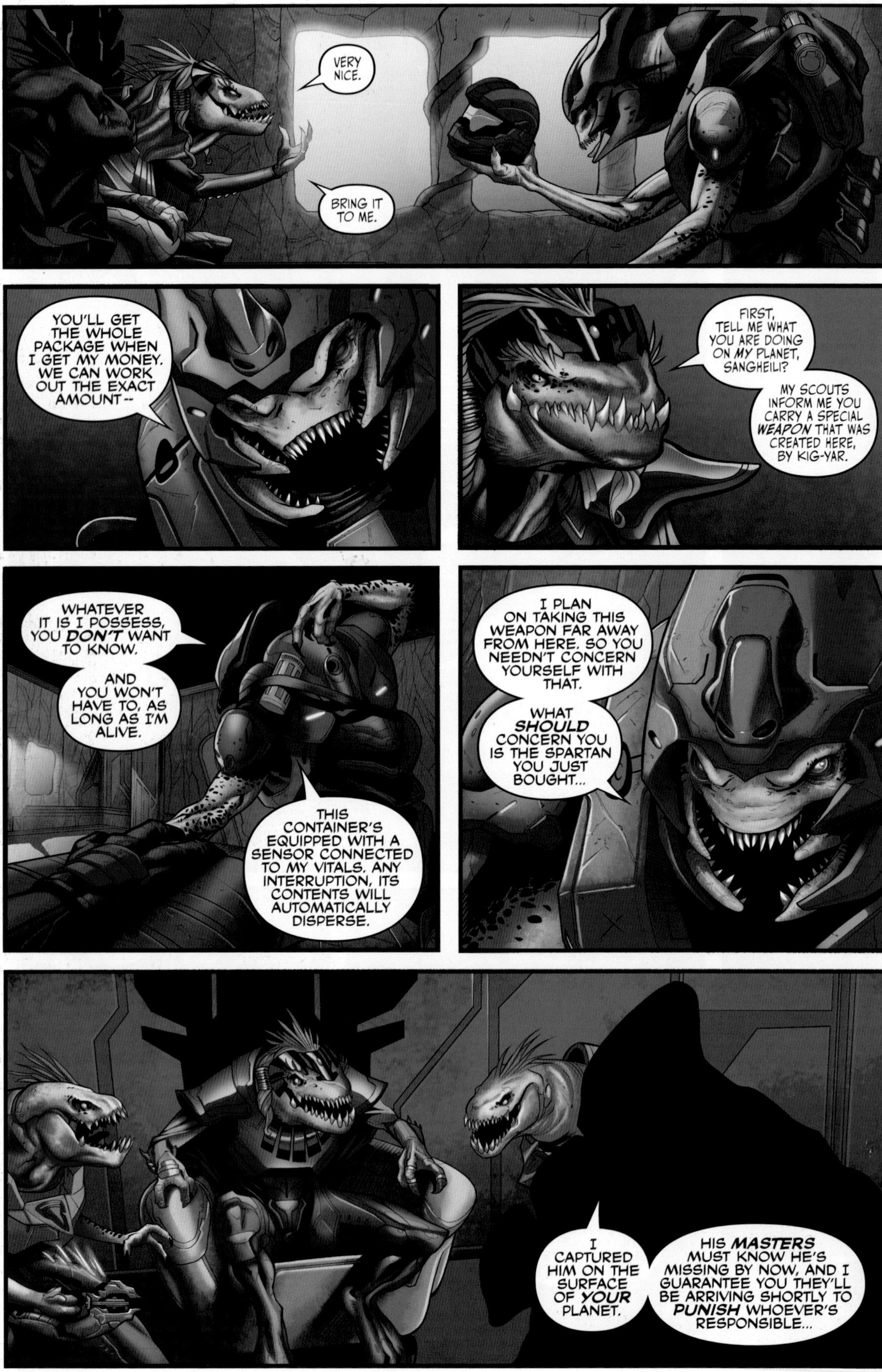
VERY NICE.
BRING IT TO ME.
YOU'LL GET THE WHOLE PACKAGE WHEN I GET MY MONEY. WE CAN WORK OUT THE EXACT AMOUNT--
FIRST, TELL ME WHAT YOU ARE DOING ON MY PLANET, SANGHEILI?
MY SCOUTS INFORM ME YOU CARRY A SPECIAL WEAPON THAT WAS CREATED HERE, BY KIG-YAR.
WHATEVER IT IS I POSSESS, YOU DON'T WANT TO KNOW.
AND YOU WON'T HAVE TO, AS LONG AS I'M ALIVE.
THIS CONTAINER'S EQUIPPED WITH A SENSOR CONNECTED TO MY VITALS. ANY INTERRUPTION, ITS CONTENTS WILL AUTOMATICALLY DISPERSE.
I PLAN ON TAKING THIS WEAPON FAR AWAY FROM HERE. SO YOU NEEDN'T CONCERN YOURSELF WITH THAT.
WHAT SHOULD CONCERN YOU IS THE SPARTAN YOU JUST BOUGHT...
I CAPTURED HIM ON THE SURFACE OF YOUR PLANET.
HIS MASTERS MUST KNOW HE'S MISSING BY NOW, AND I GUARANTEE YOU THEY'LL BE ARRIVING SHORTLY TO PUNISH WHOEVER'S RESPONSIBLE...

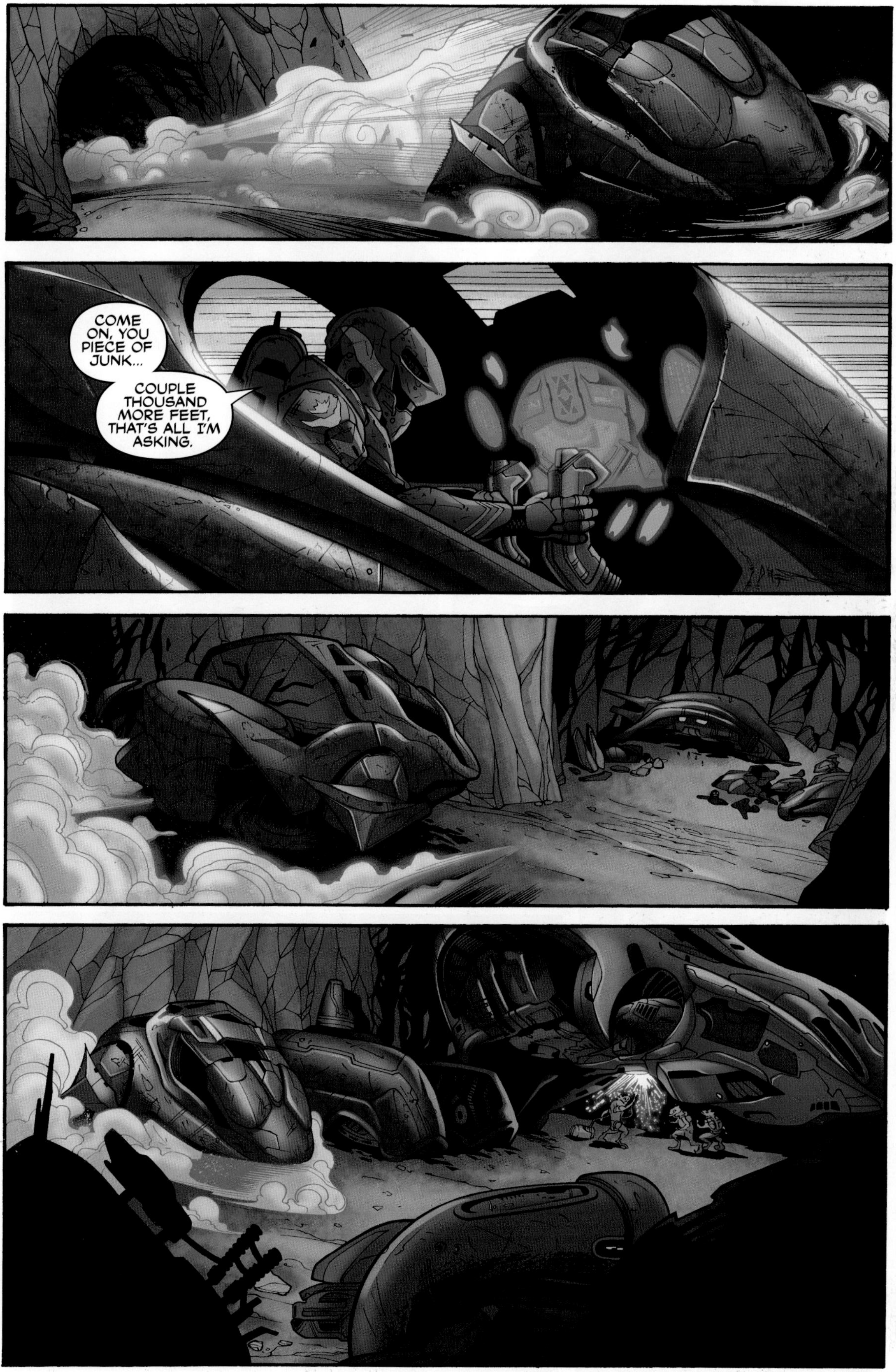
COME ON, YOU PIECE OF JUNK...
COUPLE THOUSAND MORE FEET, THAT'S ALL I'M ASKING.

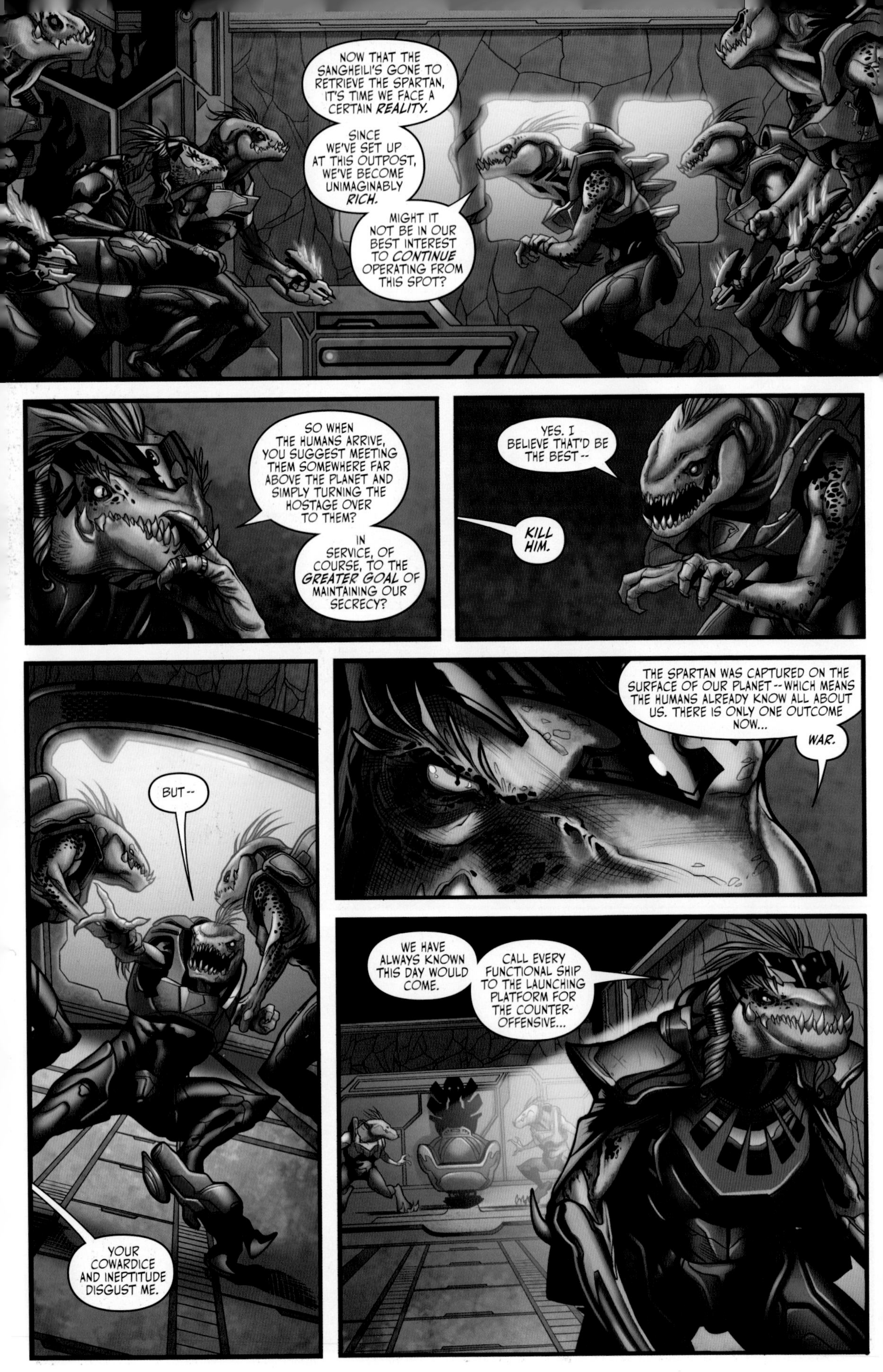
NOW THAT THE SANGHEILI'S GONE TO RETRIEVE THE SPARTAN, IT'S TIME WE FACE A CERTAIN REALITY.
SINCE WE'VE SET UP AT THIS OUTPOST, WE'VE BECOME UNIMAGINABLY RICH.
MIGHT IT NOT BE IN OUR BEST INTEREST TO CONTINUE OPERATING FROM THIS SPOT?
SO WHEN THE HUMANS ARRIVE, YOU SUGGEST MEETING THEM SOMEWHERE FAR ABOVE THE PLANET AND SIMPLY TURNING THE HOSTAGE OVER TO THEM?
IN SERVICE, OF COURSE, TO THE GREATER GOAL OF MAINTAINING OUR SECRECY?
YES. I BELIEVE THAT'D BE THE BEST--
KILL HIM.
BUT--
YOUR COWARDICE AND INEPTITUDE DISGUST ME.
THE SPARTAN WAS CAPTURED ON THE SURFACE OF OUR PLANET--WHICH MEANS THE HUMANS ALREADY KNOW ALL ABOUT US. THERE IS ONLY ONE OUTCOME NOW...
WAR.
WE HAVE ALWAYS KNOWN THIS DAY WOULD COME.
CALL EVERY FUNCTIONAL SHIP TO THE LAUNCHING PLATFORM FOR THE COUNTER-OFFENSIVE...

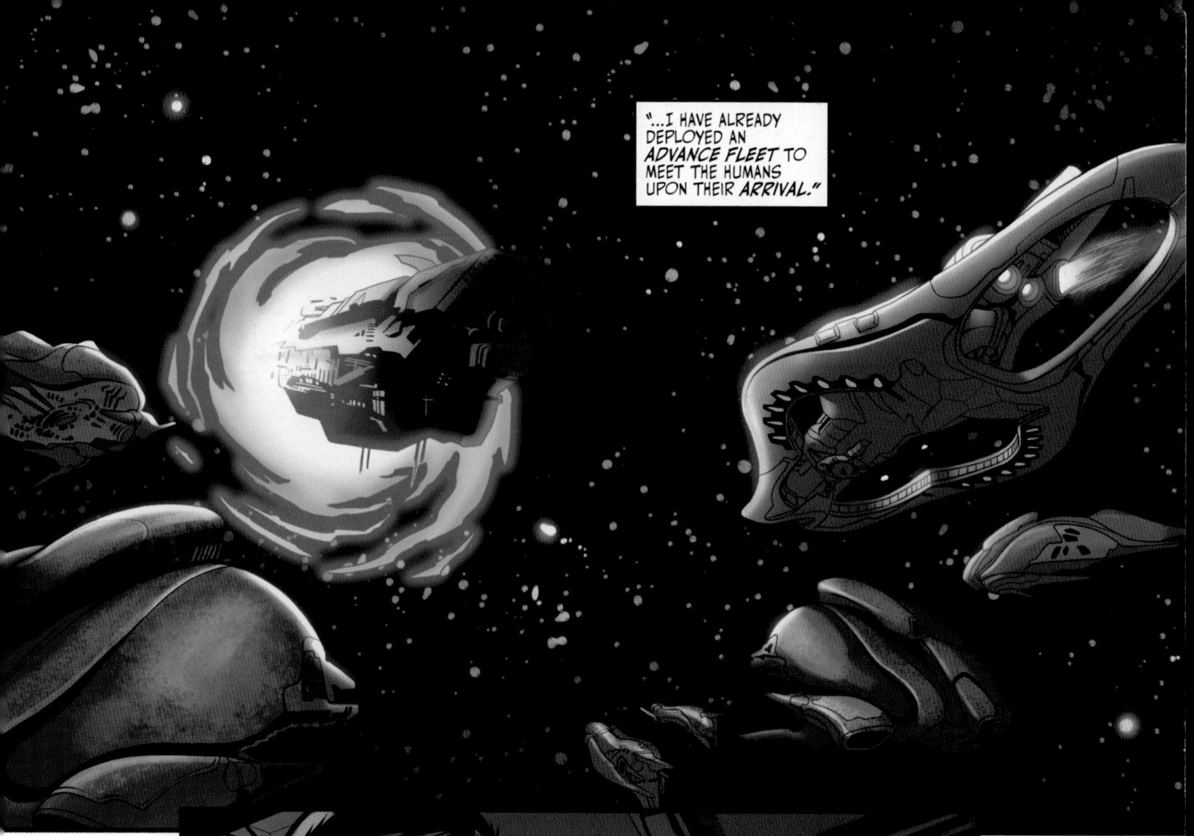
"...I HAVE ALREADY DEPLOYED AN ADVANCE FLEET TO MEET THE HUMANS UPON THEIR ARRIVAL."

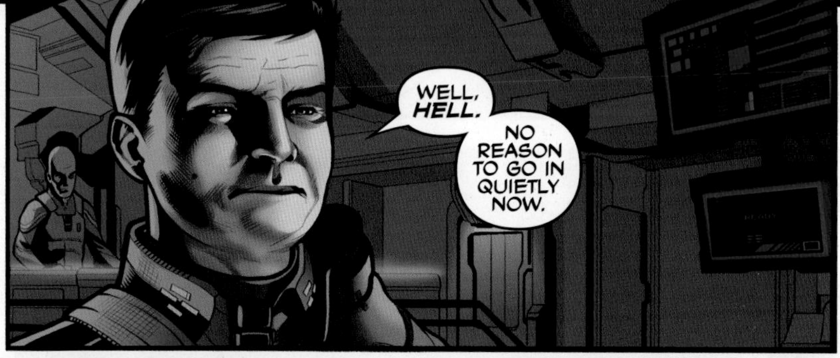
WELL, HELL.
NO REASON TO GO IN QUIETLY NOW.

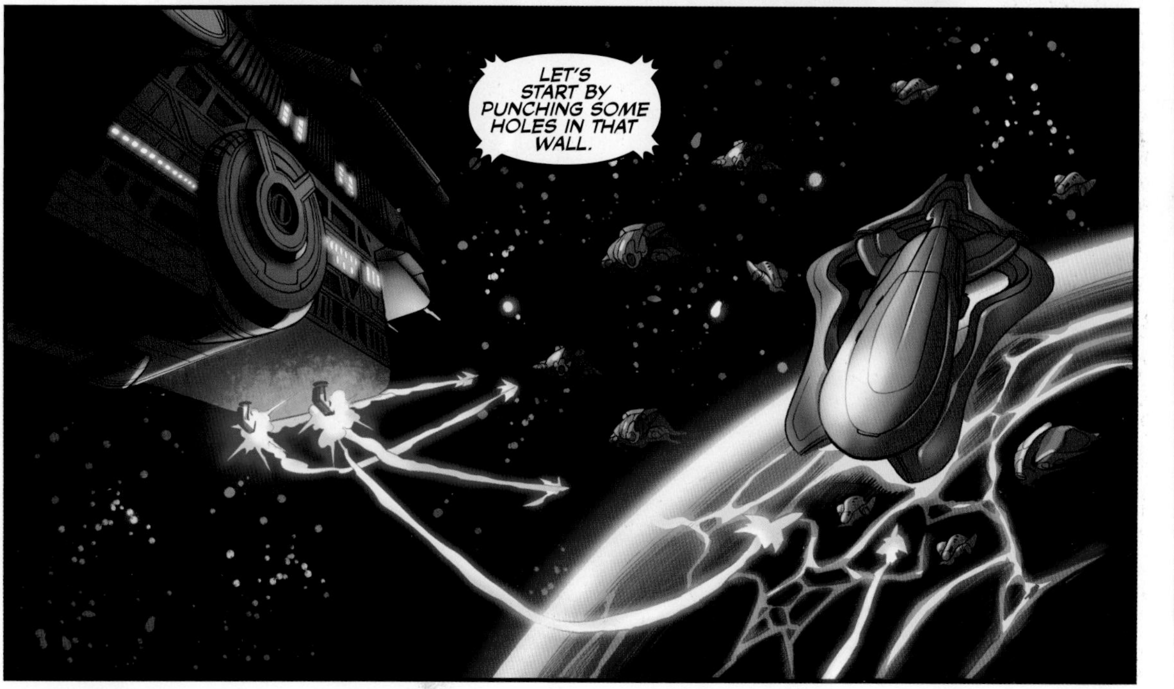
LET'S START BY PUNCHING SOME HOLES IN THAT WALL.

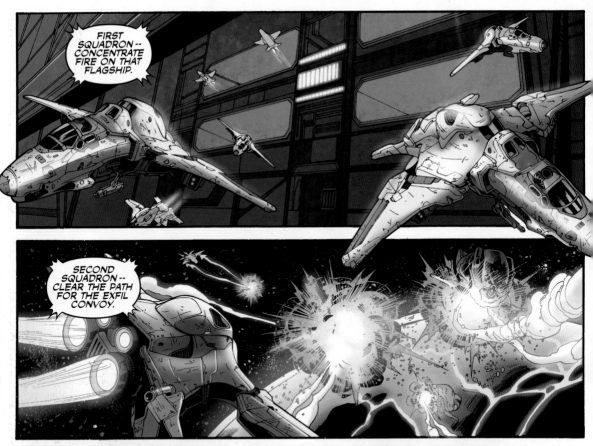

FIRST SQUADRON -- CONCENTRATE FIRE ON THAT FLAGSHIP.

SECOND SQUADRON -- CLEAR THE PATH FOR THE EXFIL CONVOY.

STAY TIGHT! KEEP THE SHAPE!

WE'RE THROUGH, CAPTAIN! APPROACHING VEN III'S ATMOSPHERE NOW...

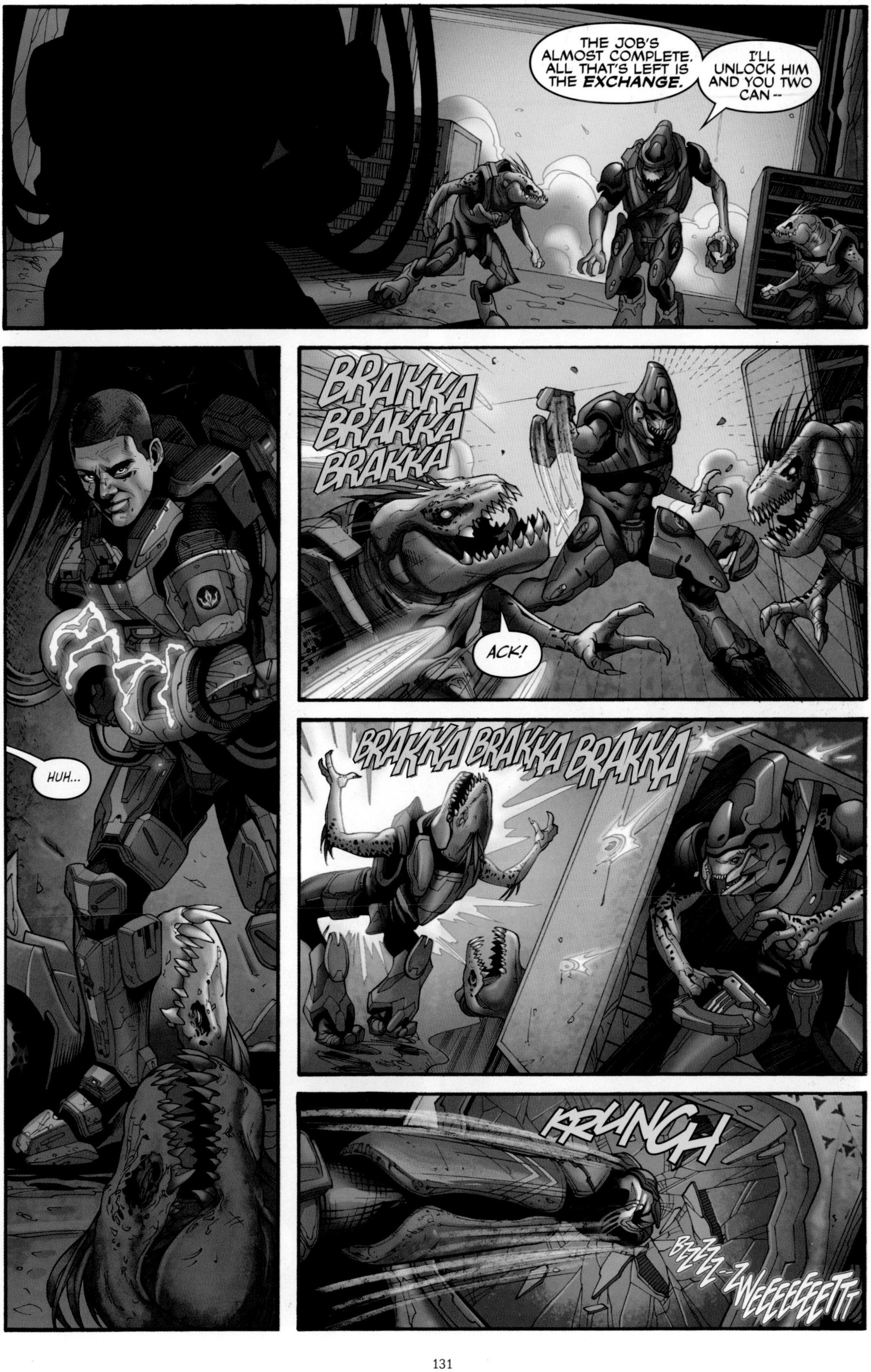
THE JOB'S ALMOST COMPLETE. ALL THAT'S LEFT IS THE EXCHANGE.
I'LL UNLOCK HIM AND YOU TWO CAN --
BRAKKA BRAKKA BRAKKA
ACK!
HUH...
BRAKKA BRAKKA BRAKKA
KRUNCH
BZZZZ--ZWEEEEEEEETTT

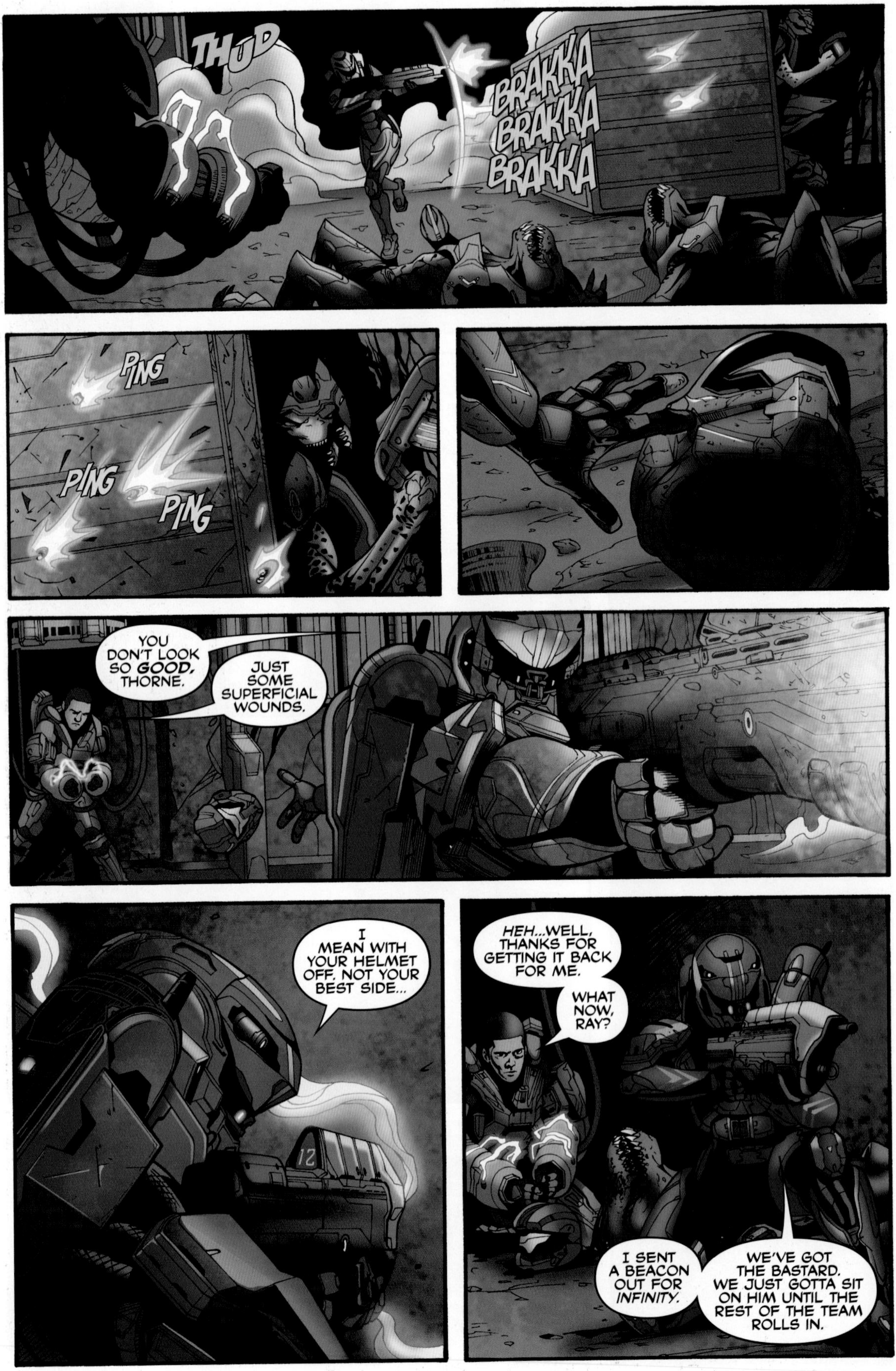
THUD
BRAKKA
BRAKKA
BRAKKA
PING
PING
PING
YOU DON'T LOOK SO GOOD, THORNE.
JUST SOME SUPERFICIAL WOUNDS.
I MEAN WITH YOUR HELMET OFF. NOT YOUR BEST SIDE...
HEH...WELL, THANKS FOR GETTING IT BACK FOR ME.
WHAT NOW, RAY?
WE'VE GOT THE BASTARD. WE JUST GOTTA SIT ON HIM UNTIL THE REST OF THE TEAM ROLLS IN.
I SENT A BEACON OUT FOR INFINITY.

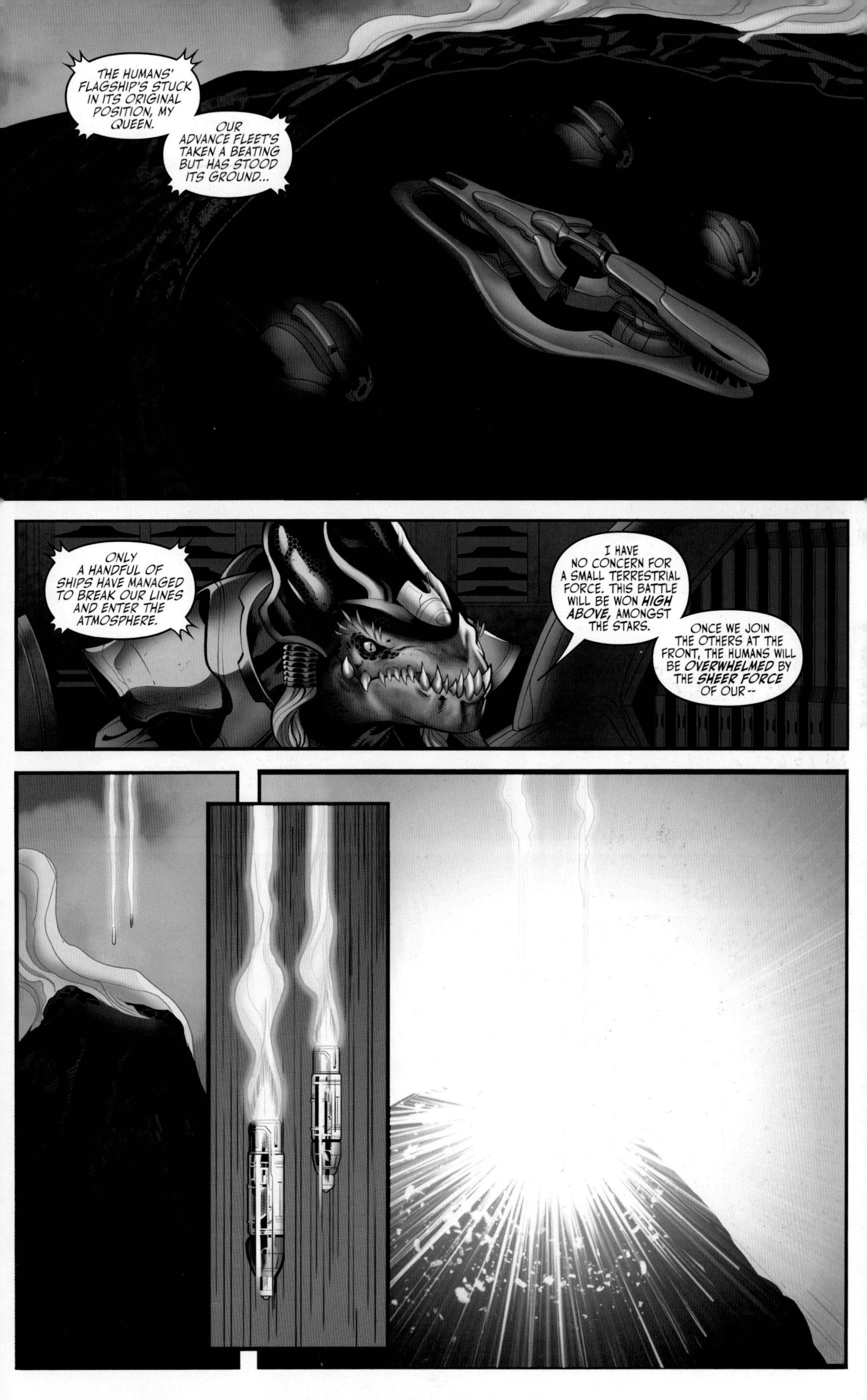
THE HUMANS' FLAGSHIP'S STUCK IN ITS ORIGINAL POSITION, MY QUEEN.
OUR ADVANCE FLEET'S TAKEN A BEATING BUT HAS STOOD ITS GROUND...
ONLY A HANDFUL OF SHIPS HAVE MANAGED TO BREAK OUR LINES AND ENTER THE ATMOSPHERE.
I HAVE NO CONCERN FOR A SMALL TERRESTRIAL FORCE. THIS BATTLE WILL BE WON HIGH ABOVE, AMONGST THE STARS.
ONCE WE JOIN THE OTHERS AT THE FRONT, THE HUMANS WILL BE OVERWHELMED BY THE SHEER FORCE OF OUR --

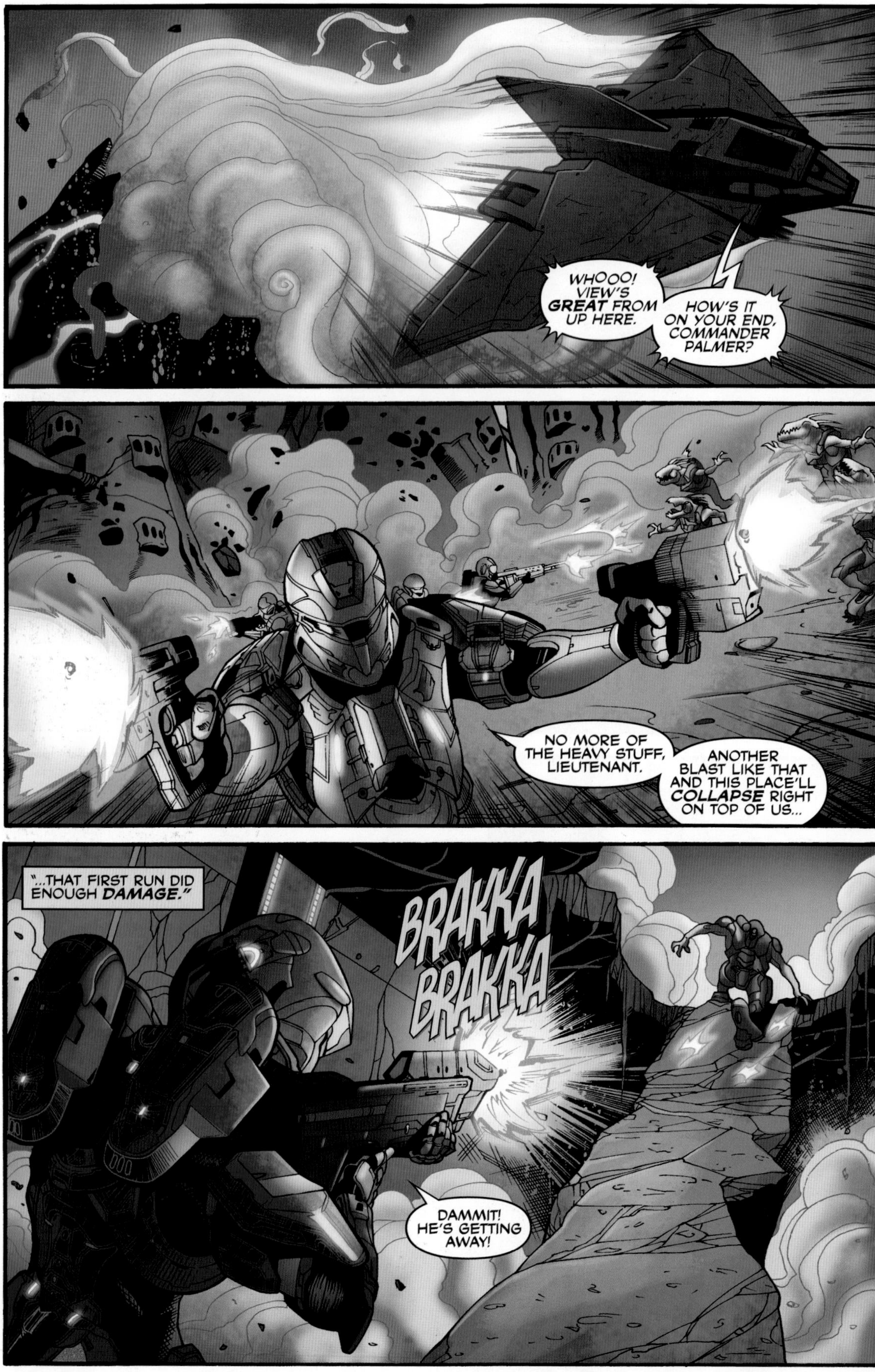
WHOOO! VIEW'S GREAT FROM UP HERE.
HOW'S IT ON YOUR END, COMMANDER PALMER?
NO MORE OF THE HEAVY STUFF, LIEUTENANT.
ANOTHER BLAST LIKE THAT AND THIS PLACE'LL COLLAPSE RIGHT ON TOP OF US...
"...THAT FIRST RUN DID ENOUGH DAMAGE."
BRAKKA BRAKKA
DAMMIT! HE'S GETTING AWAY!

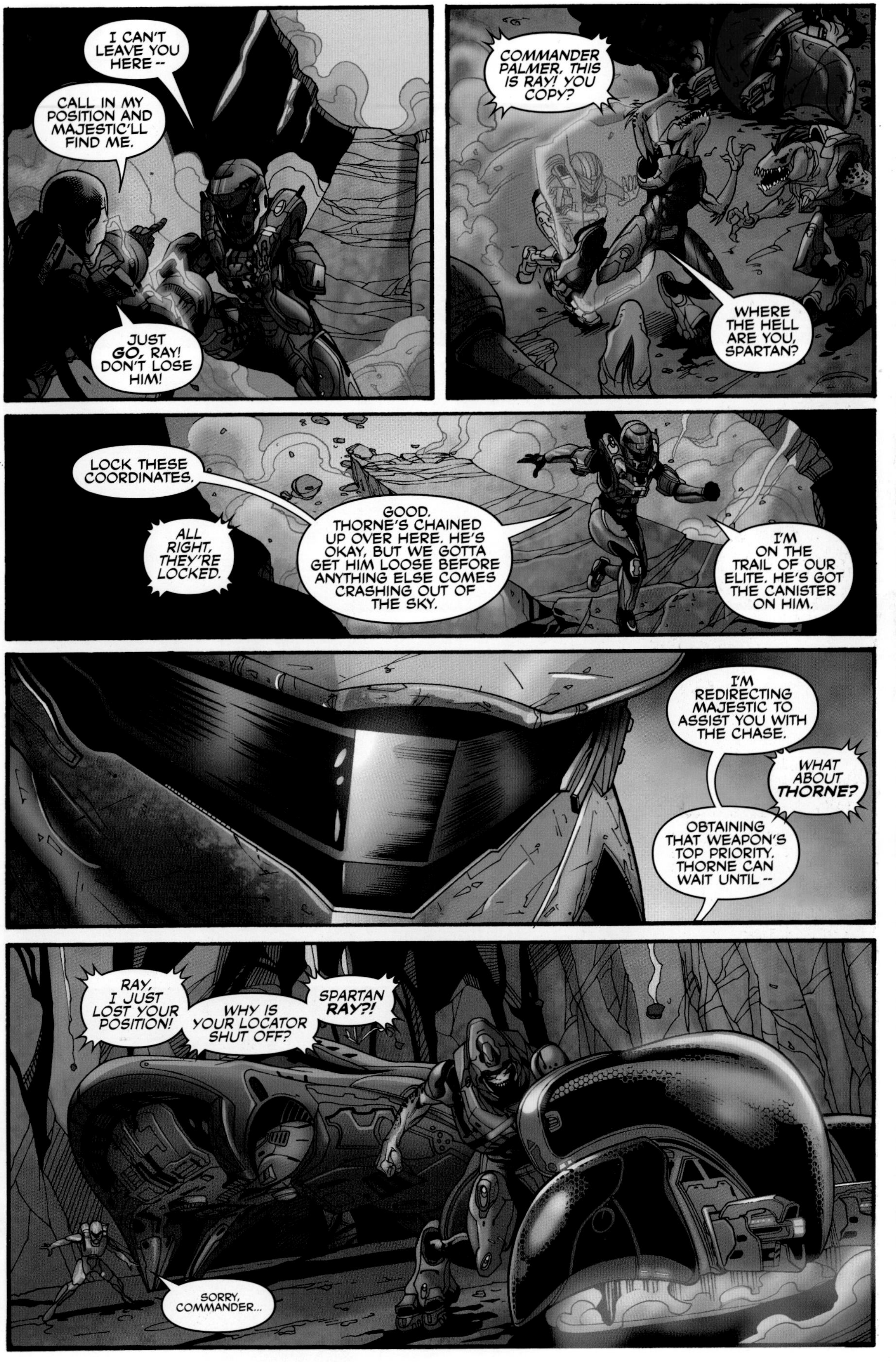
I CAN'T LEAVE YOU HERE --
CALL IN MY POSITION AND MAJESTIC'LL FIND ME.
JUST GO, RAY! DON'T LOSE HIM!
COMMANDER PALMER, THIS IS RAY! YOU COPY?
WHERE THE HELL ARE YOU, SPARTAN?
LOCK THESE COORDINATES.
ALL RIGHT, THEY'RE LOCKED.
GOOD. THORNE'S CHAINED UP OVER HERE. HE'S OKAY, BUT WE GOTTA GET HIM LOOSE BEFORE ANYTHING ELSE COMES CRASHING OUT OF THE SKY.
I'M ON THE TRAIL OF OUR ELITE. HE'S GOT THE CANISTER ON HIM.
I'M REDIRECTING MAJESTIC TO ASSIST YOU WITH THE CHASE.
WHAT ABOUT THORNE?
OBTAINING THAT WEAPON'S TOP PRIORITY. THORNE CAN WAIT UNTIL --
RAY, I JUST LOST YOUR POSITION!
WHY IS YOUR LOCATOR SHUT OFF?
SPARTAN RAY?!
SORRY, COMMANDER...

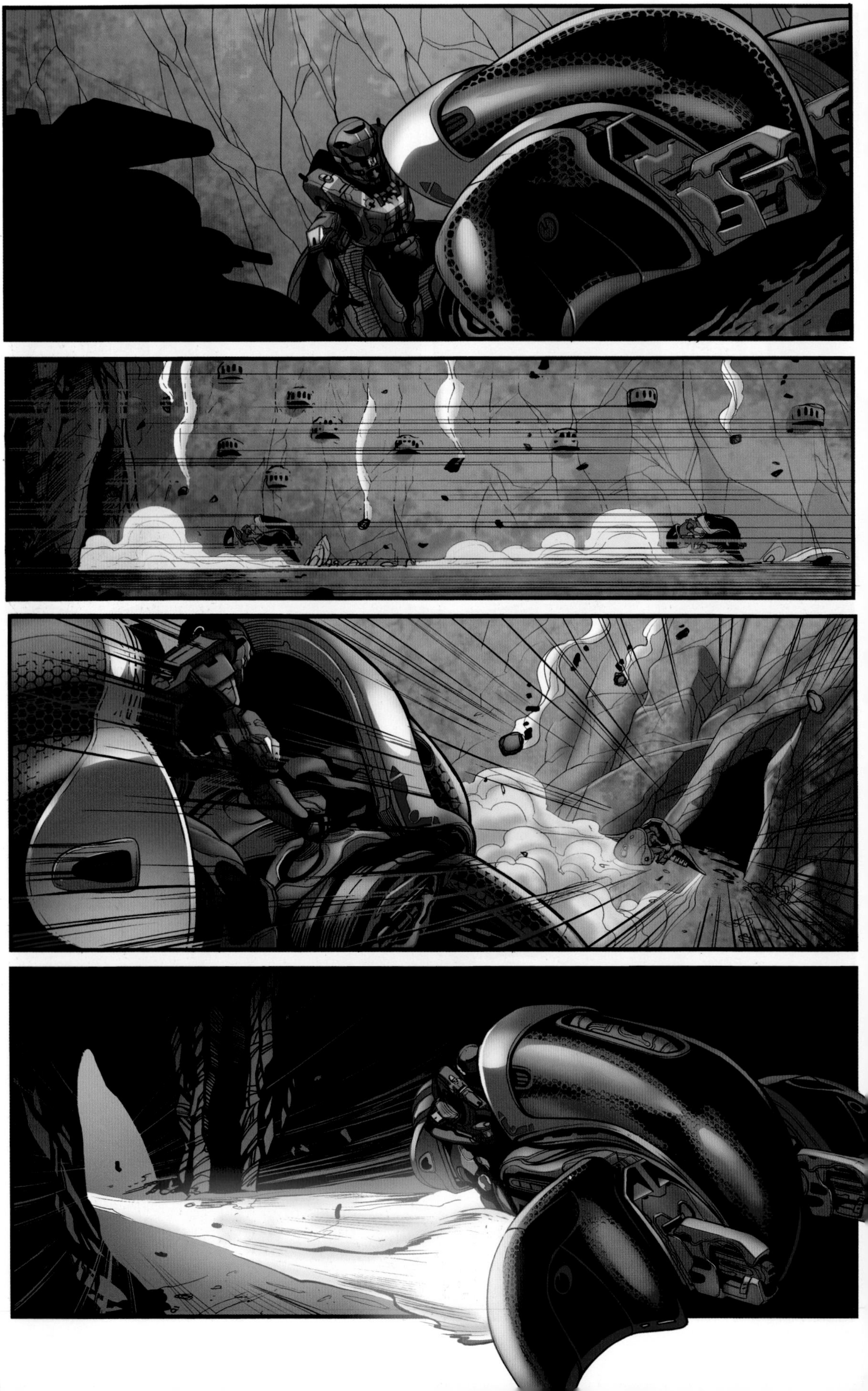

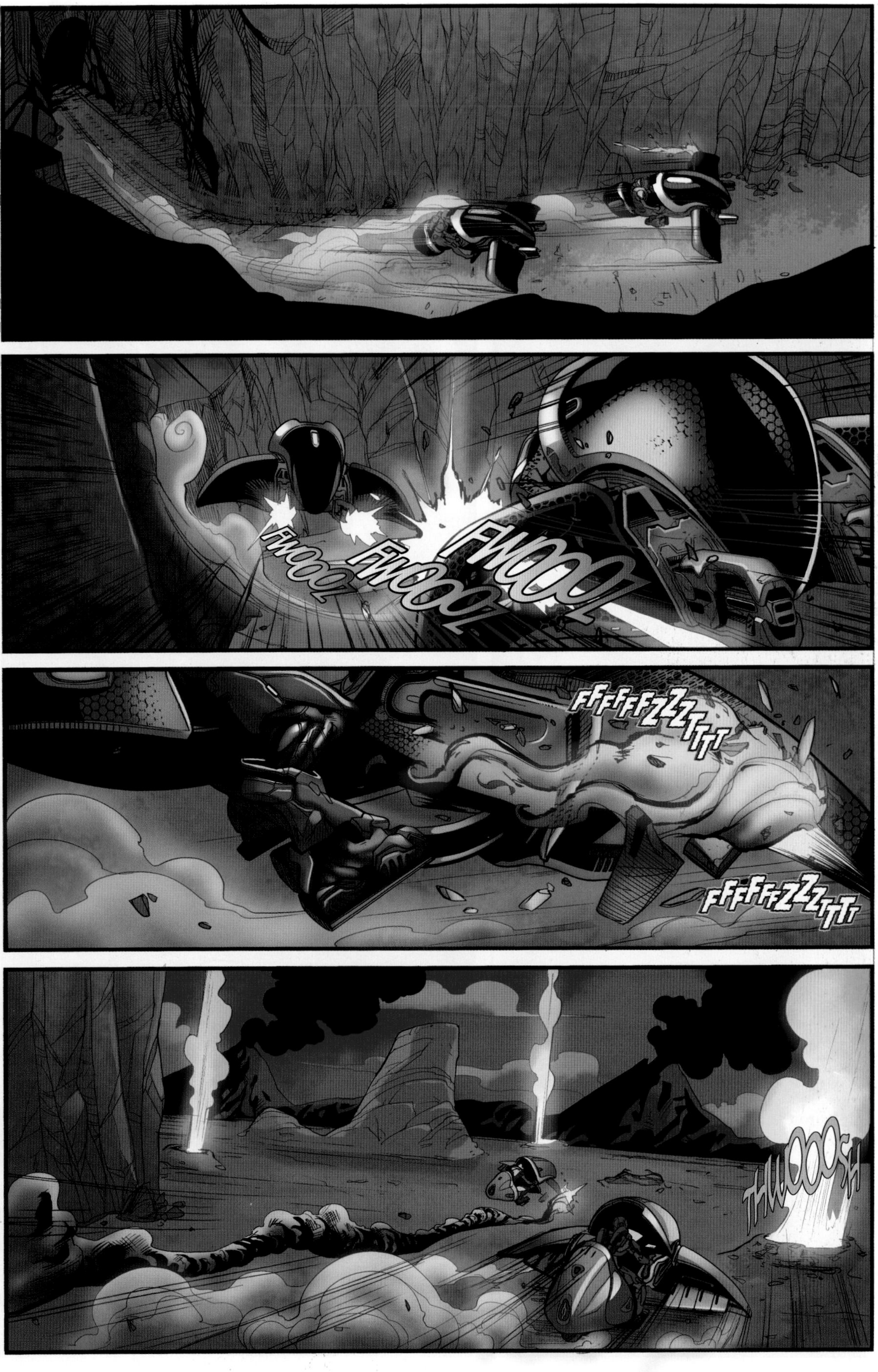
FWOOOZ
FWOOOZ
FWOOOZ
FFFFFFZZZTTTT
FFFFFFZZZTTTT
THWOOOSH

THWOOOSH
THOOOOM
UF!
THWOOOSH
SKREEE...

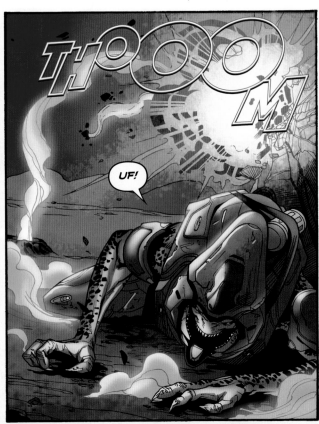

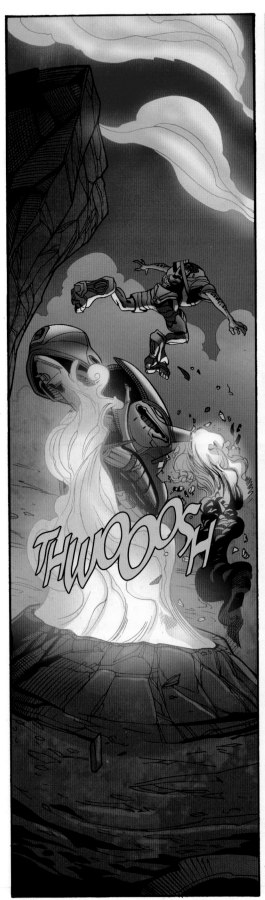

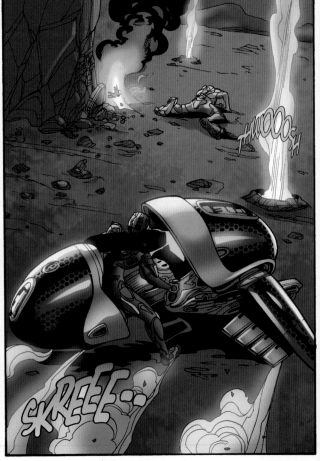

UUGGHH...

YOU WANT TO LIVE, HAND OVER THE CANISTER.

HEH.

AFRAID I CAN'T DO THAT.

IT'S NOT REALLY MINE TO GIVE AWAY...

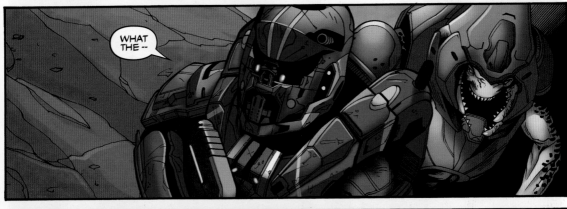

WHAT THE --

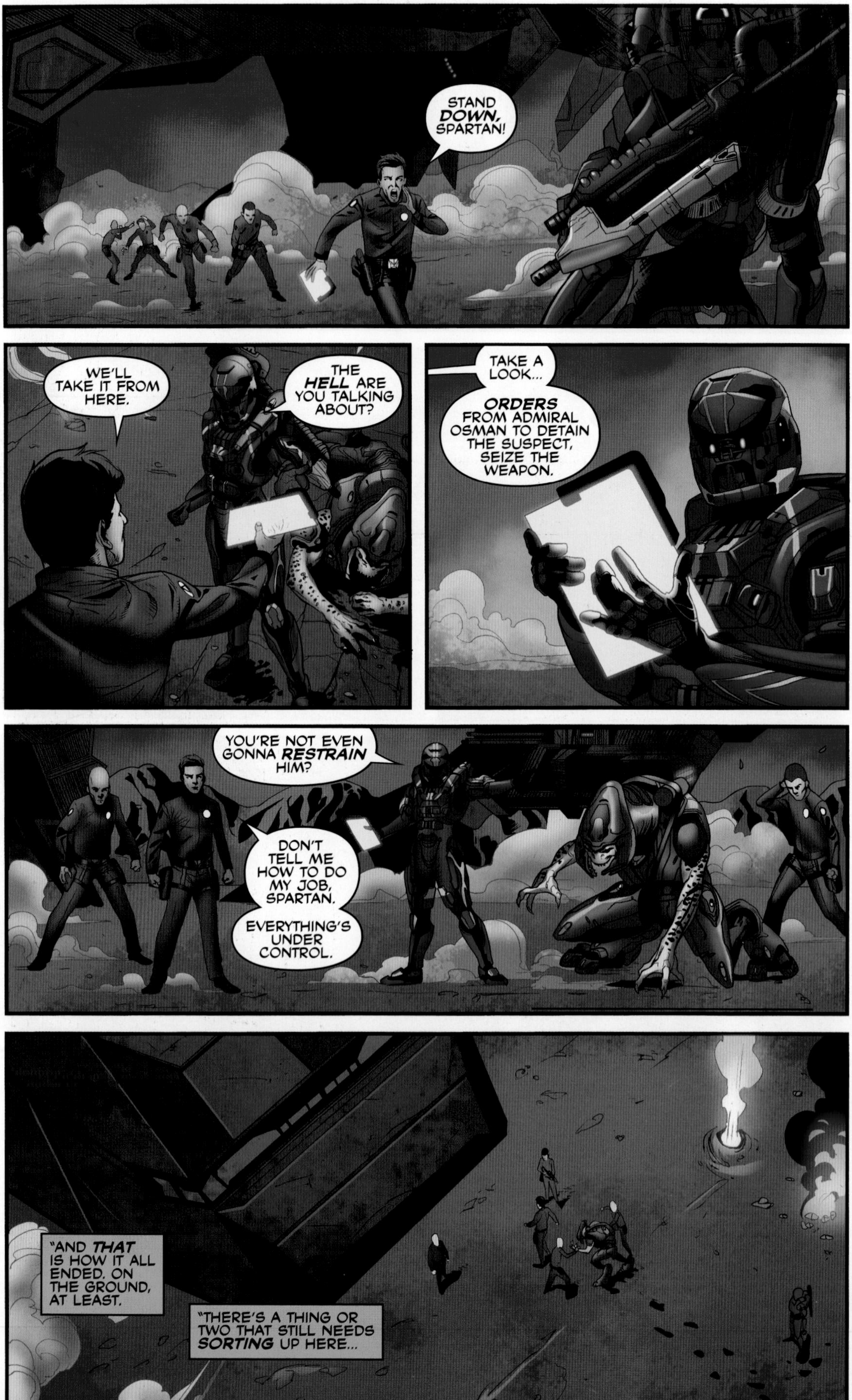

STAND DOWN, SPARTAN!
WE'LL TAKE IT FROM HERE.
THE HELL ARE YOU TALKING ABOUT?
TAKE A LOOK...
ORDERS FROM ADMIRAL OSMAN TO DETAIN THE SUSPECT, SEIZE THE WEAPON.
YOU'RE NOT EVEN GONNA RESTRAIN HIM?
DON'T TELL ME HOW TO DO MY JOB, SPARTAN.
EVERYTHING'S UNDER CONTROL.
"AND THAT IS HOW IT ALL ENDED. ON THE GROUND, AT LEAST.
"THERE'S A THING OR TWO THAT STILL NEEDS SORTING UP HERE...

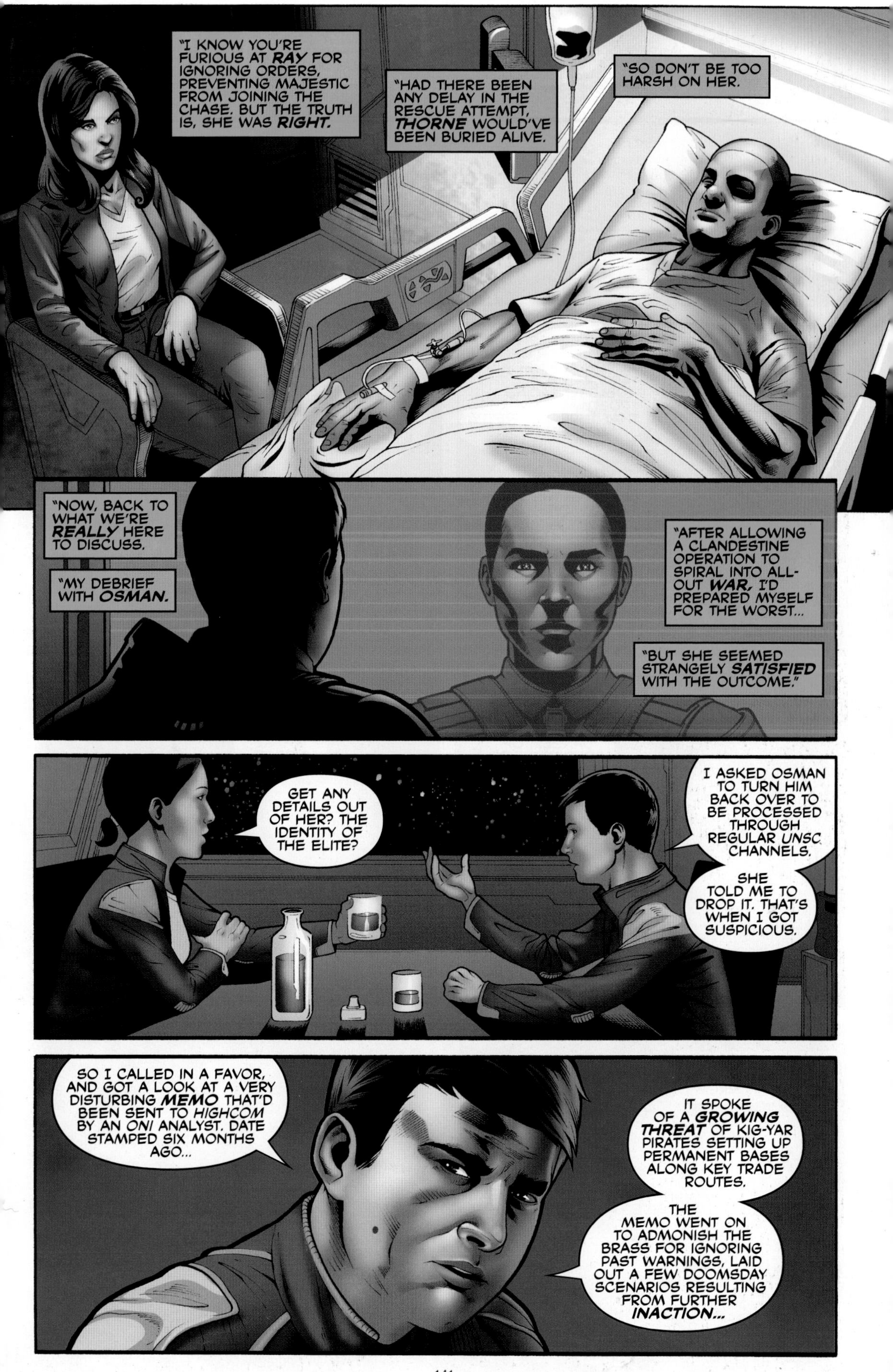
"I KNOW YOU'RE FURIOUS AT RAY FOR IGNORING ORDERS, PREVENTING MAJESTIC FROM JOINING THE CHASE. BUT THE TRUTH IS, SHE WAS RIGHT.
"HAD THERE BEEN ANY DELAY IN THE RESCUE ATTEMPT, THORNE WOULD'VE BEEN BURIED ALIVE.
"SO DON'T BE TOO HARSH ON HER.
"NOW, BACK TO WHAT WE'RE REALLY HERE TO DISCUSS.
"MY DEBRIEF WITH OSMAN.
"AFTER ALLOWING A CLANDESTINE OPERATION TO SPIRAL INTO ALL-OUT WAR, I'D PREPARED MYSELF FOR THE WORST...
"BUT SHE SEEMED STRANGELY SATISFIED WITH THE OUTCOME."
GET ANY DETAILS OUT OF HER? THE IDENTITY OF THE ELITE?
I ASKED OSMAN TO TURN HIM BACK OVER TO BE PROCESSED THROUGH REGULAR UNSC CHANNELS.
SHE TOLD ME TO DROP IT. THAT'S WHEN I GOT SUSPICIOUS.
SO I CALLED IN A FAVOR, AND GOT A LOOK AT A VERY DISTURBING MEMO THAT'D BEEN SENT TO HIGHCOM BY AN ONI ANALYST. DATE STAMPED SIX MONTHS AGO...
IT SPOKE OF A GROWING THREAT OF KIG-YAR PIRATES SETTING UP PERMANENT BASES ALONG KEY TRADE ROUTES.
THE MEMO WENT ON TO ADMONISH THE BRASS FOR IGNORING PAST WARNINGS, LAID OUT A FEW DOOMSDAY SCENARIOS RESULTING FROM FURTHER INACTION...

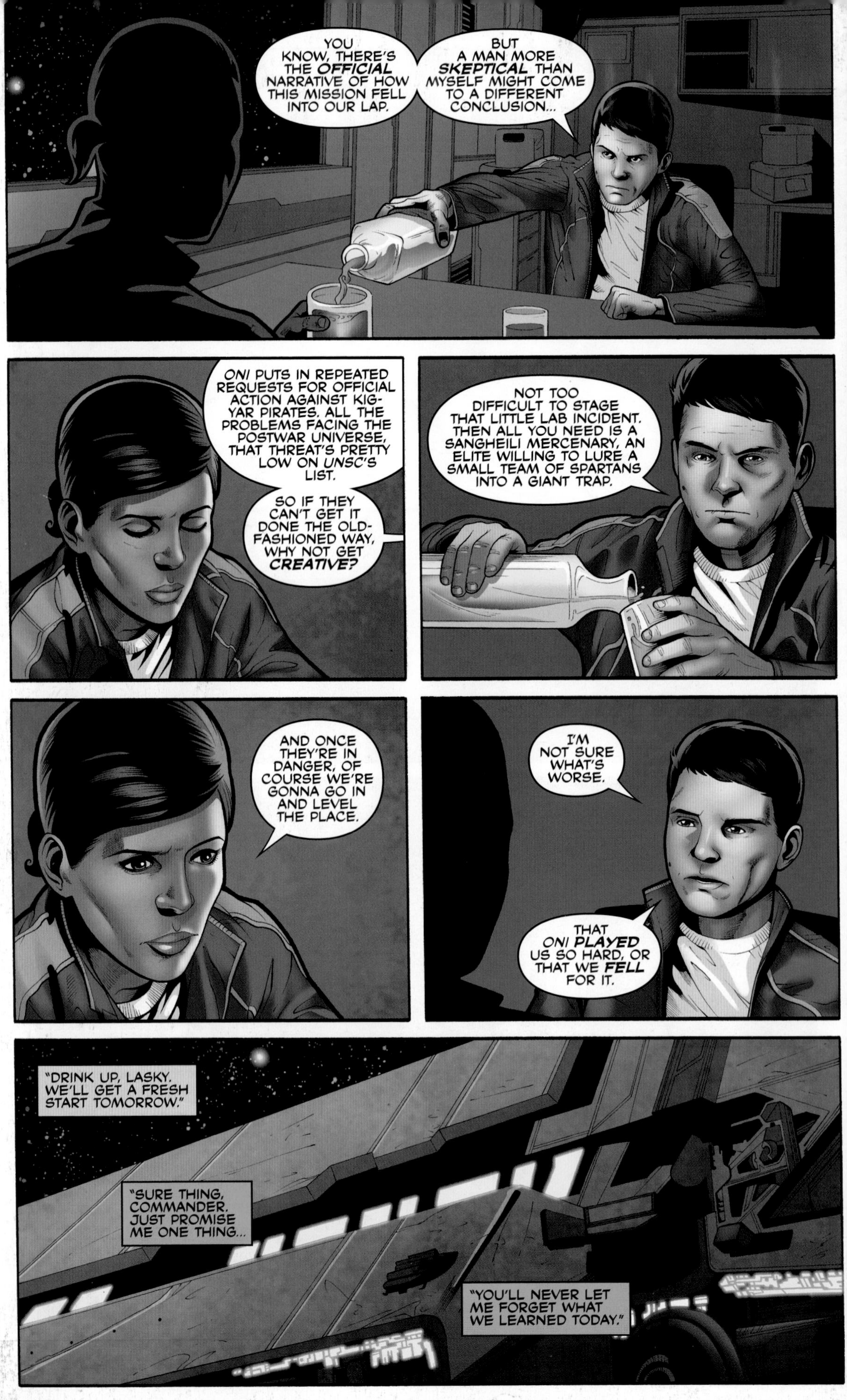
YOU KNOW, THERE'S THE OFFICIAL NARRATIVE OF HOW THIS MISSION FELL INTO OUR LAP.
BUT A MAN MORE SKEPTICAL THAN MYSELF MIGHT COME TO A DIFFERENT CONCLUSION...
ONI PUTS IN REPEATED REQUESTS FOR OFFICIAL ACTION AGAINST KIG-YAR PIRATES. ALL THE PROBLEMS FACING THE POSTWAR UNIVERSE, THAT THREAT'S PRETTY LOW ON UNSC'S LIST.
SO IF THEY CAN'T GET IT DONE THE OLD-FASHIONED WAY, WHY NOT GET CREATIVE?
NOT TOO DIFFICULT TO STAGE THAT LITTLE LAB INCIDENT. THEN ALL YOU NEED IS A SANGHEILI MERCENARY, AN ELITE WILLING TO LURE A SMALL TEAM OF SPARTANS INTO A GIANT TRAP.
AND ONCE THEY'RE IN DANGER, OF COURSE WE'RE GONNA GO IN AND LEVEL THE PLACE.
I'M NOT SURE WHAT'S WORSE.
THAT ONI PLAYED US SO HARD, OR THAT WE FELL FOR IT.
"DRINK UP, LASKY. WE'LL GET A FRESH START TOMORROW."
"SURE THING, COMMANDER. JUST PROMISE ME ONE THING...
"YOU'LL NEVER LET ME FORGET WHAT WE LEARNED TODAY."

Illustration by Anthony Palumbo

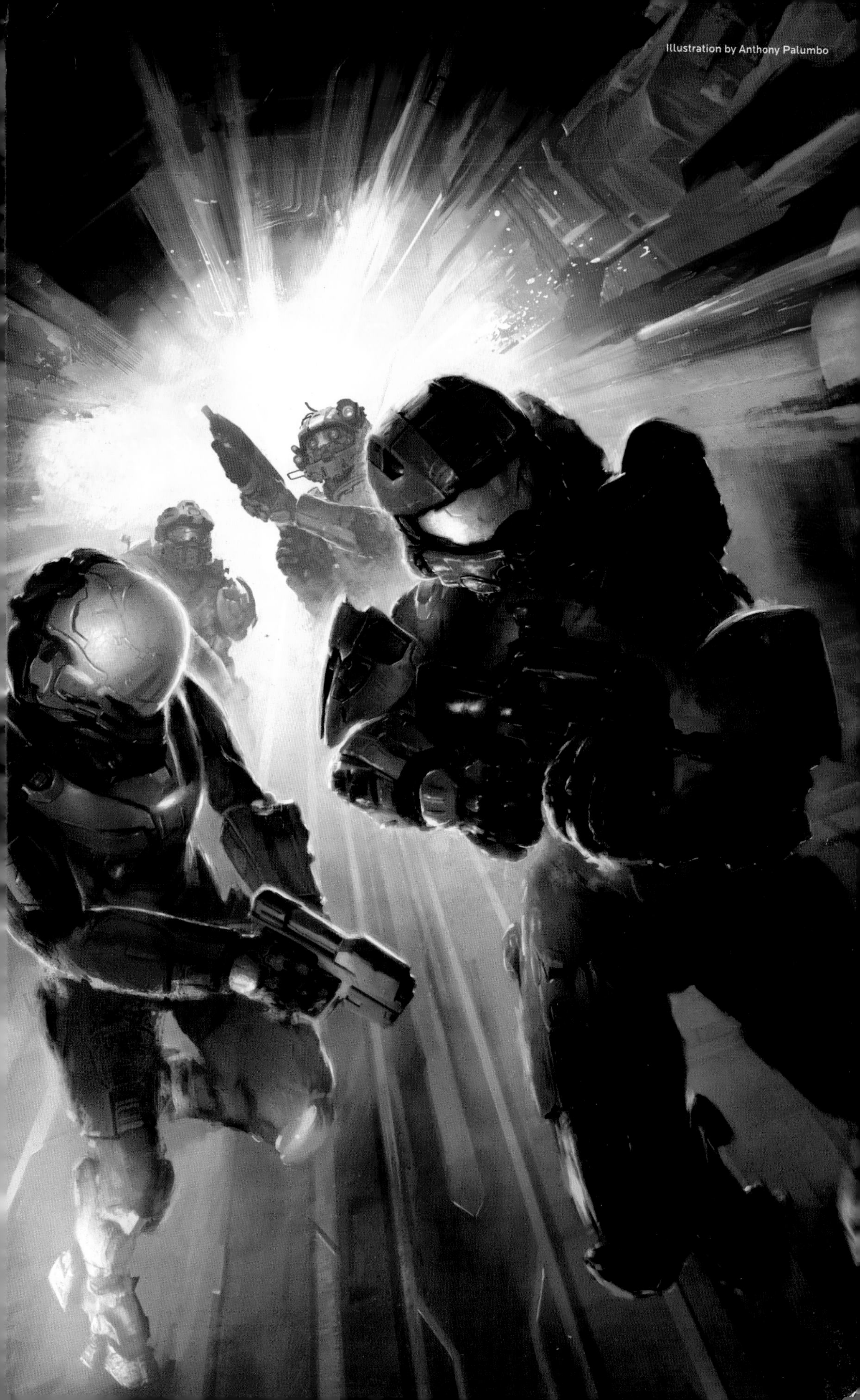

HALO®

MORE DARK HORSE BOOKS FROM THE HALO UNIVERSE!

HALO
INITIATION
BRIAN REED
MARCO CASTIELLO
The exciting lead-in to HALO: SPARTAN ASSAULT!

HALO: INITIATION
BRIAN REED // MARCO CASTIELLO // MICHAEL ATIYEH

Before she was a super-soldier defending humanity as part of the Spartan-IV program, Sarah Palmer was an ODST—Orbital Drop Shock Trooper—carrying out the most dangerous missions behind enemy lines! Join her for the dramatic journey from the ranks of humanity's toughest leathernecks to the highest echelon of elite warriors in the galaxy.

$14.99
ISBN 978-1-61655-325-8

HALO
CHRIS SCHLERF
SERGIO ARIÑO
RICARDO SÁNCHEZ
VOLUME 1
ESCALATION

HALO: ESCALATION VOLUME 1
CHRIS SCHLERF // SERGIO ARIÑO // RICARDO SÁNCHEZ
JUAN CASTRO // ROB LEAN // JASON GORDER

Following the events of *Halo*® *4*, the UNSC *Infinity* is deployed to security detail for a peace summit between the Elites and Brutes. When the negotiations are ambushed by a mercenary fleet, the *Infinity* is drawn into a plot which leads to the discovery of a long-lost UNSC asset trapped behind enemy lines. This volume collects *Halo: Escalation* #1–#6.

$19.99
ISBN 978-1-61655-456-9

DARKHORSE.COM | HALOWAYPOINT.COM

AVAILABLE AT YOUR LOCAL COMICS SHOP OR BOOKSTORE!
To find a comics shop in your area, call 1-888-266-4226. For more information or to order direct visit DarkHorse.com or call 1-800-862-0052 Mon.–Fri. 9 am to 5 pm Pacific Time. Prices and availability subject to change without notice.